THE WAY OF GO

*8 Ancient Strategy Secrets for Success
in Business and Life*

———•———

Troy Anderson

FREE PRESS

New York   London   Toronto   Sydney

FREE PRESS
A Division of Simon & Schuster, Inc.
1230 Avenue of the Americas
New York, NY 10020

FREE PRESS and colophon are trademarks of Simon & Schuster, Inc.

For information about special discounts for bulk purchases,
please contact Simon & Schuster Special Sales:
1-800-456-6798 or business@simonandschuster.com

Manufactured in the United States of America

1   3   5   7   9   10   8   6   4   2

Library of Congress Control Number:
2004046939

ISBN 0-7432-5814-2

CONTENTS

———•———

PART I

———•———

THE WAY OF GO

MASTER PIECES

Across a board hewn from an eight-hundred-year-old kaya tree of finest yellow wood and even grain, two gladiators of mind and strategy—one armed with lens-shaped white stones carved from thick, white, evenly lined clamshells, the other armed with like-shaped black stones carved from a famed black mountain of slate—meditate and sweat over the formations before them.

Before this game ever started, the two competitors had trained for decades in the various known forms and patterns of the game. Each had experimented and tried out the latest fads and research, but each had now come to fashion a style unique unto himself. Surpassing their former contemporaries who did not give themselves to the mystery, structure, and nature of the game—a prerequisite to achieving the status of master—the two are equally matched and equally determined to win.

With Black's next play, the direction of the fight will be decided. Along the lines of the board, etched centuries before by an artisan who specialized in lining boards with a samurai sword dipped in black ink, the next move will either split White's position in two or defend against White's last move, an assault on Black's massive territory now encompassing almost a quarter of the claimable territory of the board. The scenarios branching even ten moves out from this next choice number in the millions of possibilities, each aiming at the singular goal of the game—to control just one more intersection than the opponent does of this 19 × 19-line cosmos of 361 intersections. These masters compute, partly by analysis and partly by intuition, magnitudes better than even the best computer program in the world.

Armed with the human perception of shape and patterns and an ability to apply analogy and metaphor to experiences forged through thousands of games and years of expert tutelage, the players find that a move appears, a path shows, a way can be envisioned. While weaker players profess their control and mastery, these masters know that only when they've quieted these naïve thoughts will they be able to hear the faint truth that the juxtaposition of stone, line, and wood reveals.

The players compete to enforce their will on each other, but the board is the only provider. If they could see beyond the pat forms, the years of experience, and the rhythm of their competition, the secret might be revealed—*kami no itte,* the hand of God, the one true move out of more than a trillion possible ways the game could go.

Reaching into a cherrywood bowl, Black takes one of the remaining stones and strikes it down on an unoccupied intersection, a move of a master who realizes that mastery is a path, not a destination.

In this single strike, Black counterattacks White's onslaught. From here on out, the course will be violent and chaotic, and with each move the two stone sages will exchange the lead multiple times as each move keeps a tight finger on the ebb and flow of this game's natural order. With each move, a masterpiece of Black advantage and then White advantage dances across the board, leaving fractals of White and Black territory spotted with empty intersections unplayed.

While onlookers gawk at the reversal of fortune, an entire sea change coming after each seemingly impossible creative outburst, they say, "How could Black possibly come back after that?" "How can White survive that assault?" "It's all over for Black." "White's defeat is assured now." For the players, balance, tantamount to proper play, dictates that if their prior moves were sound, then there will be a way out. Without mistake, you need not fear the darkest situation; you can trust the nature of the game, there will be a way through.

A SHARED NATURE

This is Go at its ultimate—two players fighting, struggling, yet respecting that the game comes from the moves and opportunities before them. Games like these truly are works of art to those who can appreciate their depth, soundness, and rhythm. But what does this art, this competition, have to do with you? Everything.

Go is the simplest of games, but it can be terribly complex. It is a most beautiful game, but I cannot train your eyes quickly enough to see this beauty, unless you're already well in the know. Indeed, if you are looking to learn how to play because you want to see this beautiful art form etched through competition, skip the next eight chapters, read the primer in the Appendix, get yourself a Go board and stones, or get your fill virtually at thewayofgo.com. But for everything I cannot tell you about the mechanics of the game of Go, there's a trove of information about strategy, decision-making, and reality that stronger Go players have been drawing on for millennia that is applicable to about anything one might do.

The parallels between Go and other fields—business, politics, war, sports, relationships, or life in general—are uncanny and, until now, largely unwritten. Yet, whether used by an emperor instructing his child how to rule an empire, by Mao planning to take over China, or by CEOs thinking of their businesses, Go has proven to be a worthwhile metaphor. While I cannot make you fluent in Go, I can share rules of thumb that will apply to whatever endeavor you pursue and can show how these rules' underlying structure can be invoked to give you a leg up on those who just know the rule without knowing the structure.[1]

Exploring this branch of reality called Go, and what I'll refer to as the universal rules of thumb—the shared underpinnings of Go and most any field where rules of thumb are in use—you will see

---

1. A rule of thumb is a general principle, strategy, or heuristic that offers direction, advice, or warning on picking a particular path. For instance, "a stitch in time saves nine" is a rule of thumb for tailoring that applies generally, and advocates applying preventative maintenance (a stitch in time) instead of not (not doing one stitch now, you'll need to do nine later, when things have gotten worse).

when and how to best use a rule of thumb and that there are two sides to most every maxim. No matter your art or practice, no matter your level, the physics, nature, and rhythm of what you do is similar, at its roots, to the game of Go. While there are areas of strategy, decision-making, and competition that are better described outside Go (for example, game theory), the lion's share of what top Go players use to solve their problems in Go can be, has been, and is applied elsewhere, and with great success.

THE PARALLELS

Many of the issues a Go player faces on the Go board parallel challenges experts across fields face regularly. In Go, you are constantly struggling to know:

- How to make use of limited resources and time to achieve your goals
- Which initiatives to continue and which to pull the plug on
- How to maximize flexibility but keep focus
- How to weigh competing interests, tradeoffs, or options
- When to attack and when to wait to attack
- When to lead and when to follow

Face-to-face across the Go board, without chance or other intrinsic advantages common to most strategic duels, there's no way to hide poor resource allocation decisions or poorly timed attacks; you either commit to win or give the opponent an opportunity to do so. While it is possible to recover from mistakes, should the opponent make some, at all times you are on the razor's edge of strategic decision-making. One hair's-breadth off strategically and the game can turn. This is the battleground on which Go's strategic understanding is forged and what makes Go such a natural metaphor for other realms.

Most strategic resource allocation decisions are—at their roots—classic Go strategy problems:

- How do we enter a situation where an opponent is well established?
- If a competitor enters our area, what should we do?
- If we have six weak areas and two strong areas, how do we allocate resources appropriately?
- When do we sacrifice and when do we build?
- When should we do preventative maintenance and when should we go after the bigger fish?
- How do we create a strategic plan of operations when things change so quickly?

These are classic Go questions that many leaders have addressed with their understanding of Go. But instead of keeping the applicable bits the exclusive province of strong Go players who can see the parallels, you will get the boiled-down essence of their knowledge so that you can just add your experience and expertise and perhaps think of things in a new way.

AN INDIRECT MAP

Note that you cannot just transfer the rules of Go directly to whatever you do. You cannot say that because the Go board has four quadrants, you should think of your situation as having four quadrants. This is paying attention to surface structures that have no meaning beyond the medium. A better concept to take away is that Go has many potential battlefronts that often need to be addressed despite limited resources, just as your particular situation has many potential battlefronts where you will be forced to decide what resources get allocated where.

This higher-level mapping requires that you be somewhat of an expert in your field. Because you are human, you're very good at distilling the general from the specific. This is key to applying rules and strategies metaphorically. The more expertise you have in a field, the more you will get out of the metaphor of Go. That said, neither Go, nor this book, nor anything else, for that matter, will substitute for experience.

Experience is gained only through blood and guts. The experience needed to learn Go's strategies, rules, patterns, tactics, shapes, rhythms, and philosophy and to formulate this book was the result of blood and guts spent over the Go board and in thinking about the rules system. Experience in other realms is gained the same way. There are no shortcuts to gaining experience. This system of rules and ways may appear natural, but without experience from somewhere, it's an empty system, perhaps a dangerous system. But, once you have achieved a certain level of expertise, and if you can drag yourself out of your expertise's superficial context, Go can show you new ways to wield your craft.

WHAT'S SPECIAL ABOUT GO

Part of why Go is such a useful parallel is that Go brings to the table thousands of years, billions and billions of games, and eons of trial and error, all homing in on how to win when you don't have any advantage aside from the strategic allocation of resources. This is strategy and decision-making naked. Without chance, without advantage, without hidden information, Go players must win without any of the customary benefits of life's usual victors. Sure, Go players will make use of another player's faults, predilections, and style, but the bulk of the work in Go is pure strategy.

The other advantage Go has over other fields is that each game is a complete story. The major difference between Go and war, or Go and most any other field, is that you can play thousands of games of Go in a year, but you cannot marshal the type of simple resources Go uses (361 stones, 181 black, 180 white, over a 19 × 19 line grid) in war, or in other fields, that you need to get at the strategic lessons.

That said, the majority of the rules of thumb that come out of Go were probably discovered long before Go existed. Likewise, much of what you read today about strategy from business, sports, politics, and elsewhere is not some new wonder candy. The universal rules of thumb of Go, philosophy, art, science, religion, or business have always been there for those who look for them. To benefit, you need to get out of your field-specific, surface-level understanding.

Moreover, if everything you know is embedded in the context in which you learned it, your skill is not transferable, even though it could be. To derive the rules of what you do, to get at the very nature of what you do now, you have to move from specifics to generalities.

If you can make this leap, you will receive something even many stronger Go players do not get—a host of rules and ways that are portable from branch to branch, a passport to use (or abuse) knowledge from one field and apply it to another. What can be seen in the game you play are the things that transcend the particulars, a system of organization and categorization that works in Go and that will work elsewhere.

GO AND CHESS

But what about chess? Certainly, chess, the game of kings, is Go's equal. Why not just boil down the rules of chess and do the Way of Chess? There are important differences between the two games (aside from the author's not being sufficiently strong at chess):

- Chess has 64 squares and 32 are occupied at the beginning of the game; Go has 361 intersections and none are occupied at the beginning of the game. Chess pieces move in interesting ways; a Go stone does not move around.
- Chess is largely a tactical game that requires stringent analysis and a focused analytical brain. Go can be just as tactical as chess, but is more strategic, and those relying purely on intuition, shape, and aesthetics can play at the higher levels. A famous chess grandmaster once said that chess is 99 percent tactical. No top Go player will ever say that.
- If you were to add up all the possible chess games two people could play, you'd have about 10^{120} possible chess games; the number of possible Go games is somewhere between 10^{170} and infinite, depending on nuances of the rules. (Note: The

number of atoms in the universe is approximately 10^{88}.) Indeed, if every atom in the universe housed the entire Earth's computer computing capacity, you still would not be able to calculate all the possible Go games without letting those computers run for years on end. The effect is that Go will not succumb to a brute-force approach.

- In chess, the battlefield is the chessboard, and if one side gains an advantage it is very difficult to make it up; Go can support more than five chessboards' worth of battlefields, and even if you lose multiple battles, you can still win the game.
- The best chess-playing computer program can challenge the best human player and win; the best Go-playing computer programs can barely beat middle-level amateurs, and many artificial intelligence programmers equate the challenge of programming Go with that of programming human intelligence.
- Chess has six different kinds of pieces, each with special moves, and there are a variety of rules; Go has one kind of piece and the simplest of rules.
- Many chess masters have become Go converts, claiming that Go is the superior game; no Go masters have become chess converts, claiming chess to be the superior game. Noted Emanuel Lasker, world chess champion, "If there are sentient beings on other planets, they play Go."
- Chess is often a game of attrition, with each side trying to thwart the other's defenses and chip away at the opponent until only a single piece remains. In Go, while you can annihilate a much weaker opponent, most closely matched games testify to the give and take needed to win. The resulting picture at the end of a game of Go is a testament to a battle for share, not assassination, with each side corralling a sizable share of the board.

While chess is a wonderful, brilliant game, Go is the simpler, deeper, more strategically complex game, and more of a challenge for the computer programmer looking to program software to play at the top levels.

Why is Go so difficult to program? Aside from the astronomical number of possible scenarios that a computer would need to compute, the traits in which humans still dominate computers—pattern recognition, analogy, and aesthetics, to name a few—are the types of traits programmers would need to replicate in order for computers to compete effectively with humans. Computers are still far from doing this.

Despite numerous advances in science, analysis, data mining, and computer dating, it's important to remember that even the lowly board game Go is not an area where people programming computers can compete with a five-year-old human's intelligence. While science has really picked up the pace the last five centuries, there's still a long way to go until you can manage well without a human providing the wetware input. Yes, science's tools and applications can be fantastic, monstrous, efficient, or helpful, and do things humans cannot even come close to doing, but there's still an art, an intuition, a homunculus in the machine that exposes their limitations. Go is particularly good at exposing this weakness in computers.

AN ANCIENT CHINESE MICROCOSM

While Go today serves as a souped-up back-of-a-cocktail-napkin tool for strategic planning and other decision-making, the ancient Chinese found the Go board more than a mere analogue for life. It truly was a microcosm of their worldview. The board itself is composed of a 19 × 19 grid, with 72 edge points, a total of 361 intersections, and is split-able into four equal quadrants around one center point. The ancient Chinese lunar calendar was based on 72 five-day weeks for a total of 360 days revolving around a center, with four seasons breaking up the year. Coincidence?

The ancient Chinese philosophy of yin-yang, expanded more extensively in Taoism, is still prevalent today in various arts (tai chi and feng shui, among others). The color black, yin, represents the onset of an increase in shadow length, but also femininity, the moon, youth, and passivity. Yang, the color white, represents the onset of a decrease in shadow length, and also masculinity, the sun, old age, and aggressiveness. Core to their intertwining is the idea that one is a necessary part of the other.

The yin-yang symbol represents an entire year's lengthening and shortening of shadows, from their longest during the winter solstice (the southernmost point), to a middling level during the vernal equinox (the westernmost point), to their absence during the summer solstice (the northernmost point), back to a middling level during the autumnal equinox (easternmost point). But this is just one calendrical aspect.

There is no birth without both woman and man. There is no day without light and night. The whole is split in two, but balanced. The arts of acupuncture, chikung, feng shui, judo, karate, tae kwon do, tai chi, the tea ceremony, and wushu all take root in this understanding and perspective. Restore the balance between the elements and you restore health, subdue attacks, and fend off evils of all sorts. Go likewise draws on this duality.

A DUALISTIC STRUCTURE

The rules of thumb of Go take root in this duality, as does what's at play in modern physics' understanding of the nature of light. Without the concept of duality, you are left with a one-sided view of a two-sided reality. With just one perspective, you'll miss at least half the situation and, more important, something about its nature.

In physics, you'd be remiss to describe light with only one view. If you describe light only as a particle, it would explain why there are shadows, but it won't explain the wavelike diffraction light exhibits. Under the larger idea of quantum electrodynamics, you'd best be ready to think of light as two different animals depending on what you're trying to do or measure.

Go is immersed in duality. On the surface, Go is a contest between black and white stones. It is one move for you and then one move for me, opponent, proponent, opponent, proponent, until game's end. Underlying this surface duality is a duality of strategy that sings from the same page as yin and yang. Want to attack the opponent? Defend. Want to build territory? Take none. Want to control the rhythm of the game? Don't control anything. Want to gain an advantage? Sacrifice. These answers seem like the kind of Taoist or zen riddle that kept monks up at night, but in fact, these rules are sometimes true, sometimes not. Like a beam of light, the duality of the answer is a part of the game that you either learn or never progress beyond.

DUALING IN THE WEST

In the West, there is a tremendous bias toward using "yang" strategies (aggression, leading, quick victories, or attacking) rather than "yin" strategies (passivity, following, long-term wins, or defending). Go shows how the other side of the coin, yin strategies, can be equally severe in competition, and how they can also lead to victory. Vince Lombardi once said, "There's only one way to succeed in anything, and that is to give it everything." Go's universal rules show how to put all available strategies to use, how the other side of strategy can complement the strategic arsenal of many Western strategists, and how favoring only one side of strategy's intrinsic dualism unnecessarily limits options, flexibility, and potential.

The Way of Go shows you the power of using both sides of the strategic coin, in the context of business, sports, politics, and life, and illustrates how to put rules derived from Go to use, while fully cognizant of their ties to this duality. The duality is part of the rules' superstructure. With a fuller perspective on the rules, from their dualistic underpinnings, you can get into the structure of rules that apply to you and get out of that structure new ways of dealing with problems in your field. Not doing so dooms you to the narrow-sided perspective of someone who thinks only about there being "no holes on my side of the boat."

RULES AND RULES

The rules governing strategy and decision-making, however, are not the kind of rules that govern play in Go—the descriptive rules. Instead, this is a book about rules of thumb, not mechanics of the game itself, and is therefore about best practices, maxims, proverbs, parables, and axioms that are the normative rules, or for the sake of brevity, the rules of Go. These are the kind of rules that apply across fields, subject matter, and life. The rules that are the mechanics of the game, the descriptive rules, are covered briefly in the Appendix.

As with most fields, in Go, you are not introduced to the rules in any sort of systematized way. You learn them when you break them and someone wants to give you the general principle. The reminder is often the pithy catch phrase that comes with or after the blunder.

Oftentimes, Go players use colloquial non-Go rules to describe a situation, using common, everyday expressions. For instance, "a stitch in time saves nine," "an ounce of prevention is worth a pound of cure," or "safety first" are things you might hear one Go player coach another player on. These aren't rules exclusive to Go or life, but are rules that express an underlying principle that is pervasive throughout every field.

These aforementioned Go/non-Go rules have a common parent. Most people, however, have never thought through the connections between these rules under a single topic heading. What

The Way of Go illustrates is how Go's classification system for rules is a good systemization of rules from life you already know, but you probably haven't organized. Even without learning the mechanics of Go, you can get the benefit of eons of Go play: You need not learn Go to benefit from its wisdom.

You'll see that having a checklist, and more important, a depth of understanding of these rules and their opposites will enable you to start synthesizing your understanding of duality in your own areas of expertise and experience. You can then step back and look at your understanding of rules for strategy in your own field and discover their similarity to something as foreign to you as Go, and learn how to take your own expertise and apply it where you want.

Note, *The Way of Go* will not cover the many pointless rules that persist in management, sports, politics, and life in general—"Play to win," "Do the project with the highest return," or "Do what makes you happiest." These aren't rules; they're truisms, tautologies, or pithy slogans used to pummel the naïve into thinking the speaker some sort of mystic or sage—basically filler. Unfortunately and fortunately, such rules are inane. Unfortunately because there are no shortcuts or rules that apply all the time, fortunately because there are no shortcuts or rules that apply all the time.

STRATEGY

Before jumping into the rules, we should talk about the word "strategy." Most decisions seem ripe for the label "strategic." It's permissible English to use strategy to describe everything from the tactical (small-scale actions like "a bottle-opening strategy") to the truly strategic ("strategy for resolving the Israel-Palestine crisis"). When referring to strategy in this book, the distinction between tactics and the truly strategic is important.

Strategic choices in most fields have two key elements: once made, they are not easily reversed, and they have significant implications financially, politically, positionally, or militarily. Tactics are those small-scale devices, techniques, and patterns that are considered in light of the bigger picture, direction, competition, or strategy. True strategic choices are also commitments to a direction, way, or goal; tactics are how they are carried out.

In Go, you have both strategic commitments and their tactical finery. All moves in Go are irreversible. Once played, a stone remains on the board and does not move. Each move you make is such a tactical investment in your strategy or not. Your strategy in Go, should you employ one, dictates how your pieces coordinate around a shared goal and what direction your tactical moves should aim for (for example, lose locally here, but win globally across the entire board). A sound strategy can dictate many tactical losses. Unsound strategy can be fraught with tactical wins only to lose in the larger scheme of things.

The rules of thumb in this book apply to strategy more than tactics. While there are many Go books covering Go's tactical rules of thumb, there are none that attempt to structure all the various strategic rules of thumb, until now. Strategy requires abstraction, removing oneself from the tactical, to see the larger picture. By looking at the rules of Go in abstract, you can then move them from Go to whatever you do. While in abstract, these rules can move from field to field, their structure and types are largely fixed. These types are encoded by the mnemonic acronym GO'S RULES.

GO'S RULES

GO'S RULES are the root concepts behind the way strong Go players make decisions and are root proverbs from which most other proverbs and rules spring. Catalysts for success in almost every field imaginable, they are apropos metaphors for applying Go to real-world situations. Each rule, with its related axioms, corollaries, and antitheses, shows how to find advantage in a balanced and principled way.

Getting the balance right between the two sides of these root concepts makes a strong chain toward your goal. If either is a weak link, you can go only so far with a one-sided expertise and perspective. You must have both to excel, and the dual nature requiring both is not prone to the one-sided trickery you might be able to pull off with weaker opponents. To solve any problem, to master any art, to create any strategy, you must find the balance between the two polar opposites for each of these rules. You have to master the spectrum and the distinctive natures of its polar opposites.

There are eight parent sets of strategic rules in Go. These eight parent sets cover all the strategic rules of Go and the lion's share of the strategic rules of other fields (war, politics, business, sports, and so forth). Each parent rule set, except the final set, is a dualistic pairing of competing ideas on a spectrum. Under each parent are dozens of child rules and child rule sets that correspond to the parent rules. For most of the child sets, there are grandchildren and so on. This setup is important for two reasons: It gives you a good way of remembering the broad scope of strategic rules one should consider when making strategic decisions, and it helps to group common rules under one roof.

It is important to note that this treelike structure is more bushy than branchy. That a rule falls under one parent doesn't mean that it doesn't relate to a different parent. Indeed, the rules cross-pollinate. There are aspects of some in others. Nonetheless, the broad spectrum of rules, their theses and antitheses, all thrive within this simple acronym and learning this structure will help you understand strategy at its roots.

GO'S RULES

1. Global Local—From What Perspective Are You Looking?
2. Owe Save—Are You Taking Risks or Playing Safe?
3. Slack Taut—Are You Playing Loose or Tight?
4. Reverse Forward—Are You Looking Backward or Forward?
5. Us Them—Who Is Friend and Who Is Foe?
6. Lead Follow—Should You Seize or Wait?
7. Expand Focus—Do You Diversify or Unify?
8. Sorry, There Are No Rules

SO WHAT

The reason this book is entitled *The Way of Go* and not *GO'S RULES* is that the way is the point, not the anecdotes, tricks, or bag of handy rules. While you can just walk away from reading this book with more rules of thumb under your belt, and they will no doubt serve you well, you'd be missing part of the picture. Instead, know up front that this Way of Go is like every other traditional Japanese Way (Way of Tea, Way of Martial Arts, Way of Flower Arranging, and so forth) except for the religiosity. As such, the discoveries with their parallels to war, business, politics, biology, or whatever are not unique to Go. It's all just the same old underlying stuff. The Way of Go, or any other true way, is the progress toward the underlying—the true grit.

In Go, this Way is also known as seeking "kami no itte" (pronounced "Commie No Eat-tay") or the "Hand of God"; playing living Go. It's a quest for dropping all artifice and uncovering the one best, the one right, the quintessential move. Indeed, the goal of the struggle determines the quality of the seeking. The top Go players in the world, for the most part, are done seeking fame, fortune, or more notches on the long-standing trophies. The top Go players seek to become better at their art and would rather leave one game, nay, one move, worthy of the history of the game than amass more dollars. While Go is still a profession, its true masters are on a never-ending quest for true Go. The Way of Go is such that there is no new way of play, just the continual reaching and striving to get closer to the truth. The closer the strongest Go players get to the truth about the game, the stronger they get, the stronger we all can become in Go through their sharing, their games with us. What this Way of Go book shows, however, is that Go in abstract is revealing about more than just Go.

Will you read something new here and see that it sheds light on things in a new way? Yes. Is it possible to find these truths elsewhere? Yes. Will you find a nice system aside from this book that exposes the underlying principles of strategy, decision-making, and competition that have guided hundreds of CEOs, generals, and politicians across Asia based on the game of Go? No. Will you see familiar strategies that appeared in Go long before they were popular and thought to be discovered? Yes.

In business, in politics, in many other fields, there are always gurus of the new. The new will supposedly do away with the old thinking (for example, the Internet Economy or New Economy). But, when you boil down the strategists, the gurus, the hype, you see that it's a repackaging of the ancient. While the technology now is significantly better than the technology of Aristotle's day, the root issues with which we deal have changed little.

While, to us, much of what Aristotle and others of his time thought seems really stupid and ignorant, many ideas of our time will also appear stupid to people of the future. But, in ten thousand years will we still have a dichotomy between Global and Local? Yes. Will GO'S RULES still be dictating the play of humans? If we last that long. The Way of Go looks to expose the rules that will last, expose the failure of one-sided perspectives and strategies, and provide you with a trajectory to find your own Way in whatever you do.

BECOMING A PROFESSIONAL GO PLAYER AND UNDERSTANDING THE WAY

While Go is indeed zen, the embodiment of yin-yang, and a Way on a par with any of the Ways of those seeking enlightenment (zen, Way of Tea, Way of Archery, Way of Flower Arranging), I believe it necessary to dispel some of the awe and mystery associated with such things, especially as concerns my admission and entry into the Japanese Professional Go Academy as an "insei" (Japanese for a student on the path to becoming a professional Go player).

I first heard of Go in my dorm at Stanford. I was a habitual war game/strategy junkie and a Korean dormmate of mine approached me with this game called "baduk," the Korean word for Go. He took out the board and asked me to try a few moves. I had no idea how to play and put a few pieces here and there, and he said I had a remarkable intuition for the game. "Uh, OK." I didn't think much about the game for another nine months.

As offensive tackles for the Stanford football team, my room-mate and I would often have down time between practices before the school year. Instead of cards or Ping-Pong again, I remembered baduk and bought my first Go game to while away the hours. My roommate trounced me more times than not and I wondered about my Korean dormmate's ability to read Go players. Simple game, but apparently I was not so good at it.

It wasn't until the start of the school year, when I was going to live among non-football-playing students, that I thought about re-ally trying to get better at this game and beating my now former roommate (at this point, my Go world was just three people). I got a few books and was on my way back to my dorm when I saw a bunch of people playing Go in the student union. I stopped by and one of the top players, Reid Augustin, offered to play a game with me. Well, the board I used with my former roommate was a 9 × 9 board and this was a 19 × 19 board, a whole world of difference. Not only that, but he gave me a nine-stone handicap to make the play more competitive. After playing about a hundred moves, I had one small area in the center of the board and he had killed everything else. A number of onlookers remarked at my talent and the savvy required to have any pieces still alive against this 5-dan.[2] Again, I was finding myself thinking, "Uh, OK . . . I just lost big-time. What am I missing." Turns out, quite a bit.

As I got back to my dorm room and met many of my new

2. Go has a wonderful ranking system. You start as a 35-kyu, which is on a negative scale, and you progress up to 1-kyu. For each difference in level between you and the opponent, you can place a stone on the board before play begins, and unlike other games with a handicap, the nature and challenge of the game remains, up until nine stones are placed. At the time, I was probably 30-kyu, so I should have received more than nine stones, because once you get to 1-kyu, you switch to dan rankings, which are on a positive scale. So, I should have received a thirty-five-stone handicap. Karate and some other martial arts use this same type of scale; all belts up to black are kyu rankings, and thereafter the levels are just degrees of black belt. A 5-dan in Go then is like a fifth-degree black belt in karate.

dormmates, I found that one, Barney Pell, was a 5-kyu Go player. A chess master who had lived in Japan, he was also a strategy-game addict, and for the next few months my studies took a backseat.[3] I was engrossed. I then started to gather and absorb everything and anything I could on Go. Even while going to the training room to get my shoulder, knee, ankle, wrists, neck, feet, or back worked on before practice, I would read about Go. When Japanese exchange students from Keio University showed up in our dorm that spring quarter, I was dismayed to learn that none of them played Go (this was before the cartoon Hikaru came out in Japan and catapulted Go's prominence to the level of pop sensation). As a consolation, one did say that a friend of theirs, Kiyoshi Sakamoto, a 4-dan, would be visiting soon.

Sakamoto looked at Go as a metaphor and deep reflection of life. Even as some of the finer elements needed translation, I could see through his eyes the depth, the draw of the game. Although I am sure I asked rudely and quickly to play, he was happy to feed my Go frenzy. I became even more entranced with this remarkable game through the eyes of someone who saw it as something more than a game.

My progress in the game was good, but aside from the student union players and my dormmate, my Go world still seemed a bit small (this was before there were Internet Go servers), so I started going to my "neighborhood" Go club, the Silicon Valley Go Club in Cupertino, some twenty miles away. It was there that I was introduced to the man who would become my Go teacher, Paul Hu.

Paul was one of six children and was one of the top amateur players from Taiwan. He did not come to the United States to play Go, but "to live the American Dream." A waiter at one of the Chinese restaurants in Palo Alto, Paul was discovered by two of the benefactors of the Silicon Valley Go Club, who assured him that he could make as much or more as a Go teacher. Indeed, Paul made significantly more once I became his student.

---

3. OK, they also took a backseat my freshman year, but then I was playing war games, such as Empire and Strategic Conquest, on the computer.

Up to this point, my understanding of Go was rather bookish. I had learned most of the fundamentals, but I was not getting at the deeper essence. Paul's teaching style was metaphorical and this was exceedingly well aligned with my learning style. Paul would describe positions on the board using excerpts from his date the night before, guitar playing, or any life event that had a direct parallel to the game at hand. With Paul, life and Go were not two, and the variety of metaphors spanned home, politics, the economy, and his rampant dating style. I started to see the potential Go had for explaining life.

Paul was also big on rules. In pretty good but still a bit busted English, he'd say things like, "Don't do the 'dame' (pointless) thing," "Three cuts means bad," or "Play to the virgin territory" at various times while reviewing my games. These were the big take-aways for me. I learned that if I could play in such a way that I made only mistakes that generated new rule admonishments, I was making progress. And indeed, I was.

My family lived in Seattle, and not too far away was an adjunct professional of the Nihon Ki-In, Sen Suzuki-sensei. A chain-smoking, whisky-guzzling, Nichiren Buddhist priest/Go professional, Suzuki-sensei immediately fell in love with me because I was a linguistics major writing a dictionary on the language of my great-great-grandmother, the Native American language Miluk. Suzuki-sensei had all sorts of theories about how Japanese and Native Americans were brothers and how place names throughout Washington state were Japanese in origin (for example, "Yakima" would mean "Fire-Horse" in Japanese). When I shared a Miluk story about Miluk people who went to Japan to live, we really hit it off. Aside from our mutual interest in transpacific anthropology and linguistics, however, we also got in a game of Go.

At the time of my first visit with Suzuki-sensei, my Go progress was really hitting a stride. It was like the beginning of an exponential curve for me that had started just before my leaving for Seattle, thereby coinciding with my game with Suzuki-sensei. After the game, he remarked how wonderful my positions were and how he detected "a little genius" in my game. I took that feedback back to Paul, and he was a bit jealous that I was seeing another teacher.[4] He had no reason to be, for in the course of the next four months my rank jumped from about 8-kyu to about 5-dan, which was inversely commensurate with my bank account and was, as far as anyone I know knows, the U.S. record for growth in Go strength between these ranks.[5]

At the tail end of this exponential curve, on my second visit with Suzuki-sensei, he experienced a completely different player and was floored. Most times, someone's strength in Go does not move much—a grade or two, max—and for some people that can take years. In this second visit and game, Suzuki-sensei encountered a wholly different Go strength. At the end of the match, we went through a number of moves as he commented, "Genius," "Genius," "Genius." Suzuki-sensei was happy I had taken his pointers seriously from our last match. "Uh, OK." He quickly said that I should consider entry into the Nihon Ki-In as an insei. Now, I was floored.

For the small subculture of Go players in the United States, the Nihon Ki-In is like Mecca, the holy of holies, Nirvana. To suggest that I go play in Japan was like a dream. I said, "Sure," and he began to make the arrangements. He asked when I could go to Japan and I figured after I graduated. "Fine," he said.

Paul was going to be upset. Upon my return to California, Paul was indeed upset, but he understood. Going to Japan would be the best opportunity for my Go and, although there still was plenty for me to learn from Paul, going to Japan was the opportunity of a lifetime.

Thinking about going to Japan, I started to read up on things like zen, Buddhism, Japan, and Shinto and started to take classes

4. Paul, despite being an amateur, was as strong as most professional Go players, but he really excelled at teaching Go. Suzuki-sensei was a professional, but Paul would most likely have had no trouble beating him.

5. Indeed, I ultimately had to sell my car to continue paying for lessons with Paul.

in Japanese. I had already had some experience with aikido, but started digging more into the philosophies of Japan. Reading books on zen and Buddhism, I found the remarkable similarity again with Go, so I looked forward to seeing how zen and Go would mesh in my training there.

Upon graduation, I booked a trip to Japan and left. I did not contact anyone before leaving. I had no note or anything from Suzuki-sensei, I just left. Moreover, I left knowing only about half a year's worth of college Japanese. When I arrived, I remember standing in the Ueno train station, the first stop in Tokyo from the airport, and looking up at the billboard with all the hotels in the area with about six suitcases in hand.

A Japanese woman came up to me and asked me in English if I needed help. I said I was trying to find accommodation here in Tokyo. She was flabbergasted. Did I just come into Japan with no plan or arrangements for my stay? She asked what I was doing in Japan. I told her I was here to play Go. She asked if I had made any arrangements to do that. I said no. At that point in my life, I was not into making plans. While I had discussed my entry into the academy with Suzuki-sensei, I did not have an itinerary or even a phone number so as to make my next move. Obviously a friend to lost souls, this woman helped me find accommodations in a room about as long as I was tall and about as tall as my shoulders for the bargain-basement rate of about a car payment. She then asked if I had any friends in Japan. I gave her a few phone numbers and she started dialing.

I could hear the shock on the other end of the line as she called friends of mine who had visited Stanford from Japan. What was I doing in Japan? they'd ask her. She tried to explain that I was here to play Go, but it must have come across as if I was looking for a game . . . a long way to go for a Go game. I spent the night in my "luxury" room and the next morning I checked out and went to visit Kiyoshi Sakamoto.

Sakamoto's English is pretty good because he runs one of the top English cram schools in Japan, but still he was rather speechless. Since it was the weekend, I stayed at his house and we played any number of games. Obviously, I had spent the in-between time since our last visit studying Go. The next Monday, I went to visit the Nihon Ki-In headquarters. I went up to the foreign office and after finding some people who could speak English, I explained what I wanted to do and they asked me to sit in the middle of an entire office floor a couple of floors down.

Now this was what I had been expecting. I had read all the stories about zen students going to the monastery and having to sit out in the cold for days on end before entry, so I sat as if I were going to be there for days. I am not sure if they had forgotten about me or not, but I knew the waiting-for-entry game from the books I had read and so kept my cool. Of course, this was a bit different. The chair I was sitting in was rather small, and instead of being outside, I was in the midst of a rather busy office floor, now populated with one giant former offensive tackle sitting as quietly and patiently as possible while people rushed around him scratching their heads.

After a couple of hours, I was whisked downstairs to the restaurant on the first floor. An agent for Mr. Oeda introduced himself and asked me a bunch of procedural questions. He was filling out a form. After another hour, Mr. Oeda came and we were introduced. They had an exchange in Japanese that was too fast for me to understand, and then Mr. Oeda's agent asked me if I was ready to go. "Go where?" I asked. *"Anno . . . za Kenshu Sentaa."* Hmmm. Oh! This was supposed to be in English. "The what?" I said. "The Kenshu Center . . . the house for inseis." "Sure, but I don't have my bags here." "Well, we can go and see and the next day you can stay."[6]

I remember vividly my shock upon first visiting the Go academy. After all I had read about the Ways of Japan and zen Buddhism, I figured I would need to shave my head, wear a robe, and

---

6. To become part of the Nihon Ki-In is no simple process. An insei had to be sponsored by someone in Japan. But because of Suzuki's affiliation with Oeda and Oeda's leadership position within the Nihon Ki-In, I think I was helped along and I suppose in those waiting hours, Mr. Oeda, a professional 9-dan and a sizable football fan, adopted me.

take a vow of silence before entry. I had visions of sitting and thinking about mud or rice or something. Inside the academy, I expected to see something off the set of the TV show *Kung Fu*: lines of shaven-headed kids all studying intently with the repose of sages while blind masters went around thwacking them on the head for not seeing the inner beauty. Many of the pictures of some of the famous Go players show them in their traditional robes, heads shaved, in the dojo—the place of enlightenment—studying intently. Quotations from my readings and movies filled my head on the long train ride to the academy: "Don't look at the finger or you'll miss all that heavenly glory," from *Enter the Dragon*, was one. I was ready to shave my head, endure the walks on rice paper, and contemplate a grain of rice as the sound of one hand clapping played in the distance. After forty-five minutes we arrived in Makuhari, and I was ushered inside.

Instead of a monastery, it was a free-for-all. Instead of a hall filled with smallish monks, it was a dormitory of Nintendo addicts, comic book junkies, and love-crazed teenagers who were running around the hallways laughing, joking, and dressed in either softened punk or prep-school tartan. There were no stern zen priests with horsehair whisks. There were no kids with shaved heads, though some were sporting interesting mullets. While there was a dojo, it wasn't a sacred antechamber; it was where we would play, every weekend for nearly an entire year, thousands of matches.

Here I was, this Stanford graduate and former offensive tackle entering this dorm for five- to eighteen-year-old Go prodigies from around Asia whose average age was probably ten and whose average size was probably a little smaller than one of my legs. Not quite what I expected, but certainly no one was prepared for me either. Fortunately for me, there were not only people who spoke English there (some of the older kids and the housefather), but there was another Westerner—Hans Pietsch from Germany—who spoke excellent English.

The schedule at the academy was simple. Study Go from Monday to Friday, play tournament matches Saturday and Sunday, and after a while Cho Chikun-sensei, the only player to win the Japanese Triple Crown of Go and one of the true masters of the game, started teaching us on Tuesdays and Thursdays weekly.

The next weekend was my first tournament match. My first opponent was a nine- or ten-year-old kid named Onodera. He and his friend Yagi were annoying brats, just like any nine- or ten-year-old might be. The match started off in my favor. As I had a decent opening, I dominated, but as the middle part of the game reared, my positions collapsed.

While I was losing my match, Onodera would mock my mannerisms, make faces, and giggle while his friend Yagi watched and stared at my face as my positions on the board crumbled. Obviously, he did not know he was at this Westerner's Go Nirvana. Indeed, Yagi was probably better suited to play Dennis the Menace than Kwai Chang Cain. And no, I did not pummel him into the tatami, despite the comforting imagery such thoughts provided.

After a number of months of study and losing to just about every child at the academy, I found new levels of humility that I did not know I had. As a child, you can learn Go like you learn language, effortlessly. Put a bunch of kids in with a bunch of very strong Go players and they pick things up via osmosis. Unfortunately, this talent to soak dries up by the time you are eighteen, so I had to continue plugging away as I always had, all the while losing again and again to the likes of Onodera and Yagi.

Never mind the losing, something was still amiss. OK, so I was not in a monastic setting. OK, so I was surrounded by prodigies who seemed more interested in DragonBall Z (which was a hit while I was there) than in serious Go study. But what about the Way? What about Go as a path of zen? After my Japanese got a little better, I started inquiring about this. When I started asking if anyone thought of Go as something more than a profession, all said yes, but no one was doing anything about it. The investigation and spirit required to succeed in professional matches was certainly arduous, and at the highest level transcended delusive thinking, but still, where was the Way? I had read about there being sages and masters for every other art, every other pursuit with any modicum of depth, and here was this most profound, deep, and wise art with no Way per se. Absurd. About nine months in, it hit me. It's the zen Buddhist notion of the Genjo koan.

The Genjo koan is the zen challenge of everyday life. It is being fully aware in the moment. It is the understanding that at any moment you could be dead and, therefore, you should live accordingly. That doesn't mean to stop and go through the four stages of denial, anger, sadness, and acceptance, but to live in the existential now. To live. You don't need to invent a Way, when the Way is already in action. That there was no exegesis, no religiousness, and no priests didn't mean there was no Way and that people weren't following it.

With this realization, I no longer needed to be a professional Go player. I could play Go anywhere, and the Way, deeply embedded within it, would be available. As soon as I arranged (this time I actually made arrangements) to leave, my Go strength grew. There's something to be said for detachment. By the time I left, I finally was able to beat my nemeses, including the smug Yagi and the taunting Onodera, and even a match against Hans, who was now wavering between A and B class. I left with a bit of a Go player's pride. I could beat up on nine-year-olds, many of whom are now professional Go players.

Back in the world off the Go board, I have seen just how pervasive and insightful a metaphor Go is. Whether in business, sports, politics, or relationships, Go continues to show me my faults, my successes, and my errors that became successful and my successes that became failures. While there certainly are areas for which Go is not the best metaphor, or even relevant, it is relevant for most of life, and this book is an exposé of the structured duality Go exposes for all decision-makers.

SECRETS

But Ancient Strategy Secrets?! Secrets for Success in Business and Life?! How is it possible? Here's a three-part supplement to the subtitle referring to GO'S RULES.

SECRET 1

How secret is a game played by more than 27 million throughout the world? How can there be four international professional associations with some six hundred professional players competing for millions of dollars annually and it still be a secret? Despite being the number-one TV show in Korea for men between forty and fifty years old; despite being the subject matter of one of the top cartoons of Japan, supplanting Yu-gi-oh and DragonBall Z in popularity; despite being the metaphor Mao Ze-dong would use to describe his battlefield and revolutionary movements; despite John Reed, acting chairman of the New York Stock Exchange and former CEO of Citigroup, describing Go as a metaphor for Citigroup's global competition; despite Bill Gates's being a champ of Go at his high school and wanting to be a world master of Go; and despite one of the top pros of the Japanese Professional Go Association's being an American, Go is a virtual secret throughout the West.

Despite four thousand years of trial and error, despite its elevation as one of the Four Accomplishments of distinguished aristocrats of Confucius's time; despite its use in Buddhist teachings; despite reference to it in Steven Wolfgram's *A New Science*; despite John Nash's affinity for it, prompting the movie *A Beautiful Mind* to depict it as the game of geniuses at Princeton; despite John Conway's inspiration from it to create an entirely new branch of mathematics and numbers; despite its reportedly being Paul Erdos's sole recreation; despite its being the predominant game of strategy among many Japanese, Korean, Chinese, and Taiwanese CEOs; despite companies such as Toyota, Nintendo, Acer, and Samsung, with leaders who have been very strong at the game, Go is a secret still kept from Western view.

Somehow, Go has remained a relative unknown in the West. Despite the West's adopting tai chi, tea ceremonies, zen, Buddhism, feng shui, kung fu, and a variety of other arts from ancient China and transmogrifications from Japan, Go (or weiqi as it is called in China, or baduk or paduk as it is called in Korea) is a well-kept secret.

SECRET 2

Many of the anecdotes in this book, while based in reality, have had certain facts changed or are composites. In all instances, however, the gist of each situation is true, and serves to illustrate and form a foundational basis for the discussion of Go.

SECRET 3

Finally, this book keeps secret the how of the game and gives you the why and some of the what. If you want to learn more about this wonderful game, you can look through the Appendix or you can browse through the website (www.wayofgo.com), but this book is not about Go, it is an explanation of Go's ties to other realms. That said, should you ever find yourself missing the metaphor or analog, please go to the Appendix and learn a bit of the game, and the parallel to Go will likely become clearer.

PART II

———•———

GO'S RULES

•———————•

CHAPTER ONE

GLOBAL LOCAL

It is easy to get lost in local battles and not focus on the global position. The winner in Go is not the player who wins the most spectacular battle somewhere, but the player who wins the war. Having a global focus in Go gives you an edge on locally minded competitors, because there can be almost a dozen different battles going on at any one time, and you get only one move at a time. The more you put each battle into a global context, the more likely you will play the right move aligned with the overall objective—winning the game. It's the same sort of thing you learn as a child. Would I rather have the piece of candy in front of me or get a whole pitcher of candy later? When you are a child, you always want that local, immediate win, no matter the bigger picture. As you get older, you realize that this local, immediate loss pales in comparison to the bigger win—except when you forget that there is a bigger picture, which happens to everyone no matter the age.

At the same time, without an understanding of things on a local level, you really don't have a good grasp of which positions are strong and which are weak. Really understanding things at a local level can lead to wonderful opportunities that are not apparent from a global twenty-thousand-foot view. Getting down in the trenches and really understanding the inner workings of your positions not only gives you a better assessment of things but also can pay dividends when situations change and a different purpose is called for locally. The founding executives of Hewlett-Packard were big fans of managing by "walking around." Instead of being cooped up in an office, away from the people actually doing the work, at HP, executives were encouraged to walk around and see things locally. Getting the worker's perspective and seeing the problems at their root level was a local, instead of global, technique that was a large part of the "HP Way" and was a foundation for understanding their business.

GLOBAL LOCAL RULES AND STRUCTURE

The principles of Global Local are that you must change lenses as appropriate to the circumstances. Your perspective, your framing of the goal, and the stage of your work all matter in considering what side of the spectrum of the Global Local duality you need to be pulling from. Without the local understanding, you cannot have a right global understanding. Without knowing where you're going globally, a lot of work locally can have you going the wrong way. Appreciate the danger of applying a rule from the wrong side of the duality.

It is a good momentum-inspiring practice to celebrate small wins, the joys of doing something right as a person or an organization. However, when these small-win celebrations cloud global issues pertaining to strategy or direction in the bigger board or picture—the one goal that has to define and measure the benefit of the small win—you obscure the bigger-picture problems. Despite the euphoria they provide, small wins can't bandage what needs a tourniquet. Small wins can be evil successes when not in the context of the global perspective.

The other side of the coin is equally nefarious. Everyone knows you should not be obsessed with quarterly results at the expense of the longer-term view. It's a poor global business attitude that is not aligned with customers' best interests. If you work for such a company, you're bound to be in for a world of hurt. You ought to quit and find another job. However, if this is your only job prospect and you have to meet your quarterly goals to stay employed, you'd better care less about the global view until the quarter's up. If you care about your global prospects, you'd best try to remain employed while you look for other work and forget all about the global till then. You may be desperate to get the sales you need this quarter, but imagine the desperation you'll experience should you be un-cushioning the couch looking for that last quarter that will get the rent paid if you're unemployed.

Keep the Global in the back of your head, but don't let it kill whatever enthusiasm you can muster to keep yourself employed and sold through the end of the quarter. As you'll discover in Chapter 2, Owe Save, you often have to pay for your mistakes. The rule in Go is "take your medicine." No matter how terrible, if you owe (like having a job with a company that thinks only quarter to quarter), you gotta pay (make your quarterly numbers or perish).

Different environments and stages of the game demand differ-ent perspectives on global and local, and we'll get to these soon, but there are also idiosyncratic pairings of global and local in other human endeavors that necessitate managing your Global Local lenses.

Short-term is the wrong time frame for a diet. If you want to be on a restrictive diet but have an unrestricted appetite and lack the discipline to see beyond the joy of eating that thing you crave, you must develop the long-term perspective first, or why start? In Go, the rule is "don't play *chutto hampa*," or don't play the lukewarm move. If you're just going to eat the way you want to eat, eat that way. Eating restrictively and then bingeing is the epitome of chutto hampa, suffering no-dressing McDonald's salads and later getting sick from eating éclairs like French fries. If you're going to start a diet, figure out how the long-term dominates the short-term, then proceed. Until the long-term diet view is bigger than the local view of the doughnut, your goal is full of holes.

Likewise, the long term is the wrong time frame for fighting fires and emergencies. A deeply religious man and his wife were at home while the kids were out and he was going about his usual thanking of the Lord for all his bounty as a fire started in another room. As the fire grew, the man prayed for direction and guidance. His wife, truly his polar complement, kicked him in the rear and told him, "Pray outside!" While the man clearly had a good sense for the big-ger picture in his eternal goal time frame, he was a bit lacking in thinking about the short-term local needs of his wife, kids, and those who depended on him. His wife, ever the down-to-earth person, would later say, "He's not getting any express trip to heaven while I'm still alive." The rule in Go is "never hurt your own stones." While sacrifice is part of the game, you never do it without exhanging for something else. Fortunately, this man's wife was calling the shots.

Managing these two lenses is part of every strong Go player's repertoire. If you cannot change the lens to go macro *and* micro, you'll miss out on opportunities from the perspective you're missing. Moreover, if the two perspectives are not balanced, you likewise suffer. You can go only so far with an expert's view of global issues without the local view necessary to enforce your global vision. Likewise, you can fight and scratch locally better than anyone, but if what you're fighting for is not clear, if you just fight to fight and don't look at what you're gaining and losing as a result of each battle, you're bound to lose the war.

But how do you know when to be local and when to be global? What kind of rules are ascribed to the two polar opposites? How to reconcile? In Go, I learned these rules in the comfort and safety of thousands of Go matches; in life, I took my learning out of the Go context and experienced it without a safety net in the real world.

My first time serving as acting president of the Coquille Economic Development Corporation, a company of the Coquille Indian tribe of which I am a member, I certainly gained a new appreciation for Global Local rules, as I had only really thought through the concept Global Local in terms of Go before this time. This changed dramatically one cloudy day.

COQUILLE ECONOMIC
DEVELOPMENT CORPORATION

The Coquille Indian tribe had been "terminated" in 1954 through an act of Congress. This act was to be the final salvo from the U.S. government against the Coquille. The Coquille had already lost most of their treaty and promised rights, and most of their ancestry to tuberculosis, smallpox, and other introduced diseases and to massacres. Its languages (including Miluk), antiquities, cultures, and lands were already for the most part gone, assimilated or disseminated. If ever you wanted to kick a tribe when it was down, you could take away its shadow of sovereignty and think you'd be done with it. But, after decades of struggle by the terminated Coquilles to unterminate ourselves, Congress was compelled to right one wrong and asked the tribe as part of its restoration act of 1989 to become economically self-sufficient. Thus was granted a restoration of rights to operate as a sovereign nation and the license to set up and initiate work as the Coquille Economic Development Corporation (CEDCO).

Ask anyone how to encourage economic development for an Indian tribe and most will respond "casino." Unfortunately, when the largest metropolitan area is Eugene, Oregon, and even that's a two-hour drive on winding roads that would make even the most seaworthy nauseated, you'd better come up with more than that. Yeah, you could fly, but at the time, the planes flying into the North Bend International Airport sat only eighteen hunchbacks whose only in-flight meal would be their knees. Not to mention that when CEDCO started it had a scant three acres to work with, three employees, nominal dollars, and the various bureaucracies of a tribe, a local county commission, a pro no-change congressman, and the largest, most inefficiently run shop in the U.S. government, the Bureau of Indian Affairs, to help "guide" it.

Despite significant political battles internally with the tribal council and membership, the external battles with the local cities, counties, and state and congressional representatives, CEDCO's overall economic development effort propelled us to one of the most remarkable growth spurts in Native American community and economic development without the advantage of being able to locate a casino next to a major metropolis. Whether walking things through the U.S. government or tussling over sovereignty and other issues, CEDCO created five different businesses that would allow us to meet Congress's mandate to become economically self-sufficient. Yes, there was a casino, but in the long-term uncertainty of regulations and law changes, we had a diversified portfolio of businesses that would sustain us through almost any sea change in perception of tribes and their casinos.

Aside from starting a housing authority, managing our grant writing, and shepherding our agricultural initiatives, I knew little of how our day-to-day business worked. We had grown from three to five hundred plus employees, went from three acres to fifty-eight hundred plus, started with practically zero dollars and now were approaching a $25 million annual run rate in revenue, all between 1992 and 1996, but still I was more of a witness to the bigger picture than the instigator. While I had certainly been responsible for a large part of this development, I was not the president. As a vice-president, you are rather sheltered from bearing the brunt of responsibility, as the buck does not stop with you.

This ended one day when the big boss left the fog-laden Oregon coast for a vacation in sunny Hawaii. Now I would wear the mantle. As the acting prez, my perspective on global and local decision-making as a businessperson would forever change. Not only was the president gone, but everything tried to go awry that day.

A BANNER DAY

As a Go player, I saw the game of business we were playing in analogue. I had a good sense for what needed to be done at the ground and localized level on the variety of initiatives on which we'd embarked. Since I knew of our overall mission, I knew from the global sense of things where things should be moving. This would be just like playing Go, I thought. Unfortunately, when you are watching a game, you can be at least three levels stronger than players caught up in the midst of the game. In Go, the number of handicap stones you place on the board for a weaker player before play begins signifies the difference in your levels. The applicable rule of Go in this situation was "kibitzers gain three stones." As kibitzer turned player, I remained oblivious to the rule, despite the rule's enforcing its truth on me throughout the day, and the rule was off by about three or four stones, unfortunately in the wrong direction.

In serious Japanese Go tournaments, the two competitors square off typically in a traditional tatami room with all the accoutrements and pageantry a simple traditional game like Go can muster. But high above the board is the reminder that the game has come into the modern era. A camera mounted above displays the moves of the two focused competitors on a viewing screen in an adjoining room for other professional Go players to watch as the events unfold. Usually, the gallery in the other room tries variations on plays, as the two players competing sweat and toil oblivious to their deliberations.[1] What always struck me as interesting was that despite all the horsepower of brains and experience and detachment from the game in the viewing room, there'd still be the occasional surprise move from one of the competitors.

While you can put things on the board in these offshoot galleries and talk and research variations on the board—a big advantage over being forced to do this work in your head as the two players in the midst of the competition are doing—the players in the match are able to come up with a deeper play, something unexpected that gets the gallery chatting up a frenzy and actually proves out, through the throng's research, to be a bit of genius. I asked one day what this was. When you are the one in the game and the meaning of the game becomes your whole world, someone on the outside, even with the benefit of detachment, cannot feel every nuance, cadence, or tickle that you, in the element, can see. On the one side I was damned by my kibitzer's cockiness; on the other, I was damned for never being the person in the hot seat, the player.

My first day on the hot seat started off just rosy. Two of our contractors were in a heated battle over tearing down a shed at our old mill site. Knowing one of the contractors was the one more important to us politically, I intended to side with that contractor. Certainly, in the overall scheme of things, I had learned the value of politics. That's global thinking, I thought. Nonetheless, as I started to side with him, I found that the conversation was going in a di-

1. In serious professional tournament matches, a player can lose between five to eight pounds just due to severe concentration.

rection we didn't want to go as a company. Where I was making good global moves with regard to politics, the pressing situation was a local one that, if not stopped, would have even more devastating ramifications than siding with the wrong contractor. I was botching my way through trying to fix the situation, pissing off the political ally whose support now certainly had a good chance to flag by making the numbskull contractor look like he'd convinced me, when the next situation broadsided me.

The EPA was investigating our housing development and cranberry farming sites about five miles down the road. Apparently, they were investigating claims, from one of our disgruntled former employees, that asbestos was buried on the reservation. Leaving the two contractors to work things out with my new, shoddily supplied fix, I raced a bit above the speed limit to go greet the EPA's investigators.

They were looking for our company president. I let them know that the president would be out on vacation for another week, but that they could discuss whatever they wanted with me. They let me know that they were starting an investigation on the basis of the claims from the former employee and wanted to know if they had our full and complete cooperation for conducting a search. Well, the badge and cards seemed real enough, but what were our rights in this regard? The employee's alleged claim was that asbestos from the building I had just left was deposited underground in this new development.

I assured them that the former building owners had found the building clean of asbestos, per an environmental review from a company I respected, but I started to wonder. What the heck is asbestos anyway? We weren't the ones to commission the environmental study—the company from which we acquired the building did. Were they dumping this site because of the asbestos? Was this all some sort of setup? Investigators enforcing EPA laws pick up on such flags and start probing. Fortunately, I was still ruminating and not as tuned in to their grilling—a good thing, in retrospect—but then finally, the cobwebs lifting, I let them know that we had nothing to hide, but that we'd still need to contact our attorneys before I could help them further.

Just as I grew comfortable with this response, I got a call that the rains from the night before were flooding the basement of our new assisted-living facility and library another twenty miles south. Still reeling from the experience of getting the EPA officers to back off a bit, I told the EPA officers they could use the housing development office onsite to make phone calls, but that I needed to go deal with another situation elsewhere. In a bout of time-flying fun, I had not resolved the brouhaha between the contractors, nor was I terribly effectual on the start of a lengthy investigation—ultimately favorably resolved—by the EPA. The twenty-minute drive south had my mind, as well as my car, racing.

While this had all the elements of a game of Go—deciding how to act in local situations, with each decision having bearing on the global goal—I found that I was a much stronger Go player than executive at this stage of my business life. While experience in one thing can never stand in for experience in another thing, the rules from Go applied, but my experience was lacking and my ability to see into the local situations was far from perfect. Calming myself a bit, I arrived at the assisted-living facility and library more ready to be mindful of what strategy would be best to follow.

The library was indeed ankle deep in water. Yes, this would be a problem. And, yes, there was an opportunity to kick the contractor's butt over the mistakes, but instead, I asked our future GM of the building to help get someone to pump it out and did not speak with the contractor. I left soon after arriving, knowing full well that I was not dealing with this problem to the best of my abilities. And this was the start of better play on my part.

From the Global Local perspective, this was not where I needed to spend time. Yes, I could have spent hours finding and then beating up the contractor, I could have ensured that the water was removed and that evidence of cause and effect were fully documented, but in the global scheme of things, this local win would have been a loss globally.

ONE MOVE, ONE OPPORTUNITY,
TOWARD ONE GOAL

In Go and in life, you have limited resources with which to get things done. In Go, it's a move. You get one opportunity per turn to affect as much of the board as you can in your favor. The more the board fills up, the less opportunity there is to affect things. Initial decisions and moves leave their legacy. You cannot read out all the possible situations on the board, or for that matter, what will happen in life. You can only do your best to follow rules that apply across Go or life and try to make the best decisions you can. By changing your lens, global or local, you can get either detailed or holistic, deep or shallow, short term or long term. Without the ability to move the perspective from global to local and vice-versa, if you are only good at looking at things from one perspective, you will lose out to the opponent who can do both. Not looking to lose to this day—so far a most vigorous and staunch opponent—I knew the most pressing problem was the EPA situation, then the bickering contractors, and then the flood.

The EPA had already convinced themselves that we were a worthy investigative target; no matter reality. Whatever discussions we had now would steer the investigation. Since I was not clear on anything, given my own suspicions, doubts, and ignorance, the best move from the long-term global perspective would be not to shape a direction for them or a foreseeable trajectory for us. This is the kind of global thinking that parallels well with the beginning stage of a game of Go.

THE BEGINNING STAGE

At the beginning of a game of Go, the board is completely empty. It's as if a new state in the United States were to materialize suddenly with a population completely oblivious to soft drinks, and Coke and Pepsi were granted the coexclusive opportunity, in turn, to start making investments that would tie up stadiums, movie theaters, restaurants, and street corners to start vending their wares.

Let's say for the sake of argument that the two companies are the same in the eyes of the consumers; that the consumers targeted will be convinced by and then loyal to whoever approaches them first; and, since this state government wants an even race, all aspects of operational excellence, prices, and so forth between the two companies are to be exactly the same (how doesn't matter, just play along). The winner of this new state race will be determined by who controls a larger share of the fixed number of venues, as opposed to the greatest sales, profits, and so forth. Whoever controls a larger share of the state venues, after all the venues have been accounted for, will be granted a monopoly for this state's entire soft drink needs. This is how a cola war would look if it were Go.

As you might imagine, at the outset of this cola war things are so wide-open that it's important not to fixate on any one area. Nonetheless, for every move you make, you are making a claim on whatever area you move on. While this early scaffolding does not the final areas make, it does assert rights and influence for whatever player enters an area first.

For example, let's say Coke's first investment in this fresh Go-board-like state was to go after movie theater companies, and for each investment in a movie theater, you gain insight, influence, and experience into the movie theater mindset and more probability of landing future deals there. Pepsi, coming in later and trying to bargain with these theaters, would be at a disadvantage, because Coke was there first. Likewise, if Pepsi first went after stadiums, Coke would be at a disadvantage if Coke went after stadiums later. In Go and life, there are first-mover advantages. Just as neither cola company can go after everything all at once in this fictional state cola war, you have to make choices at the beginning that are like listening posts on the future—you cannot expect every initial investment to pan out, nor should you disregard your initial plays as unimportant. Look globally, act locally, but don't set anchor locally when things are just starting out.

In my situation with the EPA, the EPA made the first move in areas where it was at an advantage—the former employee's claim, their superior information about what asbestos is and how much of it would make its presence illegal, and so forth. If I started down the path of questioning things and, quid pro quo, answering things, I would be at a disadvantage in this regard, because I was behind in the local understanding of that area.

EFFICIENT DISTRIBUTION

At the beginning stage of a game of Go, the first moves on the virgin board are typically scattered in unplayed areas. The point is that you don't want to overconcentrate in just one area. Because each stone does have influence on adjacent unplayed areas and less so on already occupied areas, a stone can be a more effective influencer in a new open area.

In the cola war, if Coke really did not want Pepsi to enter its movie theater market, it could play all its initial moves to shore up contracts with the theaters and exert influence on the other theater owners due to its power of investing in movie theaters earlier. While Pepsi would not be able to take over those contracts from Coke, because Coke moved there first and because Coke continued to invest in that quadrant, for each of Coke's moves in theaters, Pepsi would be able to make initial investments elsewhere.

If Coke used its first twenty investments in movie theaters, it could really lock up the theater market. But, if Pepsi were to take its first twenty investments and make initial investments in stadiums, restaurants, grocery stores, vending machine placements, and airlines, among other opportunities, it would have a first-mover advantage in many markets. While none of them would be locked up the way Coke had locked up the theaters, Coke would have to respond to Pepsi's initial plays across all the other markets. In Go, if you were to do the same thing, you'd be far ahead in theaters, but far behind everywhere else.

As with most things, in Go initial investments or moves have more influence than later investments or moves. Why? It's like eating the first chip from the bag. Your first chip resonates like no subsequent chip. As you continue to munch, each subsequent chip, if uniform, has less and less effect on your taste buds, hunger, and desire to eat more chips. For parents teaching their kids, it's called getting full. For economists, it's the law of diminishing utilities. For Go, it means that your initial moves, while no particular one eternally damns you to recommit to that particular local area, your initial moves in one area need to be considered with respect to the global perspective of the entire board, because they do have influence, and therefore represent a bargainable value. Just as a sketch is a precursor to a drawing, and the plan needn't be the execution, one's initial moves can only be effective if they are seen for what they are—options or probes of a potential future, which one can trade, use, or sacrifice later for something more strongly tied to a win.

With each move Coke makes in the movie theater market, its influence on that area has less effect. Because Pepsi is making moves in virgin territories, Pepsi's moves are having the biggest bang for the investment in each separate and unplayed venue. If Coke is smart, it will do as Pepsi does and will not focus exclusively on one area at the beginning, but instead scatter investments around. This is exactly the kind of thing good Go players do in the initial stages of the game. Neither committing too fully nor giving the opponent a disproportionate opportunity to go after unplayed areas, each side sketches investments around the board. The idea is not to ultimately own those areas, but to have their investments make the biggest possible impact on the goal. These are appropriate local moves toward a global goal—set stones not set in stone.

For the EPA situation, I would want to do the same thing. Could I get into a local battle, which in this case would be going through the details of a particular site, what I knew of it, who's to blame? Sure. But what impact would my words have on the global situation? What if what they were really interested in was something else, but they wanted to start here? In Go, you never want to do this. You never want to hurt your other stones or opportunities. The rules in Go are "don't hurt your own stones" and "don't help your opponent play perfectly."

Talking with the EPA about any sort of general process that was instituted to prevent us from doing something stupid, as they claimed in the first place, might stimulate asking why there were even general processes like that in the first place. Admitting that we don't even know what asbestos is hurts our credibility as managers. Talking about how the former owners might be culpable, but we certainly wouldn't be, is sure to raise all sorts of issues that would not be wise at this stage of the game. These were all initial areas where the EPA agents already had plenty of moves. The beginning stage should not be devoted to addressing things locally. At the beginning stage, you have to stay global. The rules in Go are "play to the stage of the game you're in." "Don't play end game before middle game." "Don't play middle game before the beginning stage." "Don't play beginning stage moves in the middle game."

No One Decides

The other important thing to realize is that no matter the stage of the game, no matter the game you play, you don't decide what will happen. Neither you (singular) nor you (plural, your company, yourself, your kids, your investments, your government) decides. Oh sure, you can plan as if the environment won't change, the opponent won't change, all the little bits of chaos embedded in butterfly wings flapping won't affect you, but ignorance is not an excuse. You'll suffer thinking you can decide what will happen, so why do it? You can make informed, smart choices, but you have no right to the expectation that those choices will work out. Chance pervades.

In Go, one typically learns this rather late. You try to surround this area or that area, but in the end, something goes awry and you don't get either. As you improve, you find that some of your best plans never come to fruition. You never find the primrose path to an assured victory, because the opponent never walks into your well-laid trap. As you get stronger, you find you have less and less control over what the outcome of the game will be. Strange, but nonetheless, true.

With each game, you are making a unique imprint on the historical record of all games since Go's inception some four millennia ago, a unique expression of art, personality, desire, weakness, and strength between you and the opponent, between the two of you and the board itself. Sure, you can replay old games, but in the heat of real play, no two games will be alike. Of course you can ignore the heat of the real game you are playing and just wrangle a particular area to your own liking; manifest a local win.

In Go, in writing, in loving, in business, this kind of mistake assumes one's own power is greater than it is. True, you can do exactly what you'd like. You can follow the Coca-Cola example described above and just surround movie theaters, but that won't win you the game. To win, in a real game, fought by both sides, whether it's love, war, sports, business, or Go, you have to respect that you don't decide what happens when you can't know all the possibilities. Call it God, call it fate, call it unearthing a fossil, call it physics, but you don't decide what the winning way is, what the right way is. The winning way flows with and respects the uncertainty of the right path, and the winner is the one who best aligns with it. Every other way is a contrivance and not optimal play.

In the beginning stage of Go, you must respect that you do not know where the ultimate territory will be. Period. Any deviation in your mind from this understanding about territory will be a mistake. As a result, your initial plays must respect this uncertainty. You can try to influence as much of the board as you can, you can coordinate your moves to the greatest extent possible, but no matter what you do, you must not play as if the local areas where you play your stones will become your territory. Your opening moves should put you in position for whatever the board will call for, not vice-versa. There is a metaphorical hand that guides things and you'd best be prepared to go where it draws you.

It's an important lesson beginners need to hear. Oftentimes, I hear rank beginners say things like, "This is going to be my area." Such ideas are dispensed with early in a budding Go player's career. You don't know where your territory will come from ultimately. Yes, you can take a particular area, but then you're playing I-can-be-a-baby-about-this-and-do-what-I-want instead of Go. Throughout the entire beginning of the game, you should be putting yourself in position to win, not saying where you will be. Saying you know where you will be even forty moves out is practically heresy.

In our cola war, one side might hold the theater contract and the other an airline contract, but because of tussling over stadiums, the two sides, if playing optimally, may relinquish their initial holdings elsewhere to gain the appropriate advantage over stadiums. If stadiums are where the key battle will be that wins the war, each side had best exchange ownership over the now-inconsequential to affect as greatly as possible what needs to be fought to win the game.

For the EPA, the real question might not be asbestos on the reservation, but the cleanup of the old mill. Likewise, the real question might not be the old mill or the reservation, but whether their disgruntled informant might be perjuring himself. When the future is unknown and the game is just getting underway, don't squirm about local incursions and who has what. If there's a lot of game left to play, you have to stay focused on the ultimate goal in the beginning—putting yourself in position to go where needed when the fighting of the middle game starts.

BEGINNING STAGE COMPANIES

Smart startups do this by nature. They don't buy complex accounting systems as their first purchase. They don't make the chief administrative officer their second hire. Company logo statues, parking spaces, and mahogany placards with the founding principles don't make much sense when you don't even have a customer. Smart startups avoid all the institutional trappings until they evolve from startup to established company. At a time when a company is building and every moment is stacked against it as it tries to get to a critical mass and not run out of cash, the startup must focus on its primary mission, not the details and accoutrements of established businesses, which should come at a much later stage of the game, if at all.

Just as the trappings should not be the initial goal, you don't want your initial products to be too bogged down in your initial dreams for them. You don't need to look too far across the pantheon of world-leading companies to see the merits of not being tied to your initial moves. Intel did not start out as a microchip company. It started its game selling memory. Hewlett-Packard did not start out thinking about how to acquire Compaq or how to be a service company. Microsoft was a cool street traffic recording company before it moved into programming languages and operating systems. For these companies, great first investments were not anchors, but outposts to greater things. The rule in Go is "Don't get attached to your first moves or plans." There is a time for being attached to your moves, but the beginning stage is not that stage. This global rule isn't limited to Go and business.

ON THE REBOUND

In dating, a prevalent problem is the rebound. Even after the pain of separation has subsided and they are able to start going out again, people tend to think and behave as if there are still pieces on the Go board from the old relationship, the old game. This is not the case. If it's really over (and yes, those of you who have lost love, sorry, it's really over), you have to look at the world as a whole new Go board. Just as you finish one game and another starts, when one relationship is over, another starts. You don't have any rights to the territory of the previous game. The territory in that old relationship that you just loved and still crave is not yours anymore. You have to give it up. All the cool moves you made last time are in the past. They won't matter to anyone new.

Likewise, you haven't given away things that you lost in the last game. It's a new deal in both respects—your old benefits are gone, but so are the old detriments. It's a completely fresh opportunity to rethink, and you must rethink. Just as the game of Go never repeats itself, life will not repeat itself, even if you want it to. So, as you start afresh, you sketch, you probe, you detach from the old relationship. If you don't, you're damned to the same fate any low-level Go player would be—clinging to territory that has no record of your owning it and giving up on a whole board's worth of opportunity that's out there for the taking. While you can plan and dream, you cannot expect things to ever be the same. The rule in

Go is "Every Go game is unique." That old love, that one that got away, that sale that was this close, that game that was yours for the taking ain't ever coming back. Move on.

Spread Out Isn't Global

As a consultant to and employee for a variety of companies, I have been hit over the head more times than I'd like to mention with the three-year plan or the five-year plan. While there is certainly something to be said for thinking forward into the future, it is something entirely different to say where you will be in that future. It's akin to an NFL coach saying at the beginning of the game that in the third quarter, twenty minutes into the quarter, we'll punt. Sound ridiculous?

In my first weeks on the job at one company, I witnessed this exercise going on. "Our plan for the following years is to do the following initiatives . . . by third quarter next year, we will have made investments in a, b, and c . . . in the fourth quarter, we'll employ X employees in this division and start Operation Y, which will show our customers that we're still number one." Could this really be a thinking person's way? It's OK to dislike uncertainty, it's another thing completely to disrespect it. This was not NASA. It would not take ten years to plan a launch, build the spacecraft, and shoot it to the moon and back, while a budget and plan needed to be presented to someone today. This was a service business. The customers moved, changed preferences, lied. While it's OK to think globally, it is another thing to insert local pinpoints in a long-term flow and call that global thinking.

When you plan for the future, things will move. Customers will move. Competitors will move. The environment of Go stays fixed, but in life, even the environment moves. While you want to think through things as much as possible, you must realize that there are too many variations to try and possibilities to consider. Your global goal and the global plan, therefore, need not to be rooted in local ideas. A plan that is respectful of the future does not try to predict the future to a T. A plan that is respectful of the future reevaluates situations continually, respects investments already made, and is a set of principles and evaluative means for seeing and acting on the global goal, howsoever it needs to change. The rule in Go is "Plan to discard the plan." More on this in Chapter 4, Reverse Forward.

Whether at the beginning stage of Go or the start of strategic planning in an enterprise, you must respect the invisible hand. Can you make staged commitments? Of course. But don't try to define where your ultimate territory will be. The rule in Go is "Stones become fixtures." While your stones are part of a friendly environment, they are fixtures—dispassionate sunk costs stemming from the idea that occurred to the player at the time the move was made. While global stones played in the beginning stage of the game are like an option that can be traded, extinguished, or exercised, know that these options do not require follow-on purchases. The key is to be flexible, because the future is uncertain. In Go, if the opponent does something wacky or stupid, you will have to adjust quickly to take up the opportunity, which may not exist for long. The rule in Go, as in life is "Strike while the iron is hot."

As you'll see later in Chapter 7, Expand Focus, it's difficult to be focused on anything other than the one goal of the match you're playing; therefore, it's difficult to know what in the beginning is going to be right. You have to be ready to move, shift, be flexible. The rule in Go for this is "Don't anchor your stones." That is, while you cannot move a stone once it is played on the board, likewise, once you've done something, you cannot go back in time and change it. You don't have to treat that stone as an anchor on its local influence, power, or abilities. Looking at its global purpose, it might be best to ditch it, use it, or exchange it for something else. As the game unfolds, as the invisible hand moves, as the physics of the board melds every stone's relation to a near-infinite calculus, you must remain global, and ready for whatever is going to be right later. At the beginning of the game, far off from the ultimate implementation, you must be prepared to make changes when you can.

For the EPA, then, a better plan was for me not to make assumptions about where this game was going. I'd be better off making probes into what they were thinking if it didn't mean my committing to anything. Try not to hurt matters by making any assumptions about the future and keep as many possible scenarios unplayed locally as possible. Arriving back on the scene, they still wanted more details. "Who was doing digging here?" "What's in this area over here?" Do you know where the bodies are buried, essentially. Getting local with these guys would be a mistake at this beginning stage. There were other things to consider aside from whether we had defensible answers to all their local inquiries.

Was this part of a larger plot? While they said it was a particular former employee, was it possible there was another aim to what they were doing? Could evasive answers to these particular questions be the sort of misdirected answers that would help some other line of attack that wasn't obvious to us? Was the EPA teaming up with another group so that these answers would help their inquiry? Anything was possible, and without insight or preparation, it would be foolish to engage in answering anything. While it is true in general that you never want to answer inquiries of law enforcement officers without your attorney present, it was especially true when the tempting thing to do was to answer what seemed like harmless questions that could be answered and seemed good for the local situation.

Stonewalling worked. The investigators left. And yes, it is a simple lesson to clam up when you're under investigation and your attorney is not present. Yes, it is a simple lesson to think globally in the beginning and not make assumptions about the future. Yes, Go is a simple game that follows the same sort of commonsense rules that apply in life. But the practice and diligence of following common sense and the standard rules is something else entirely.

If they knew more of the why, if they knew more of where global strategies fit in relation to beginning stages of things, perhaps fewer people would fall under a noncommonsensical spell than if they had just heard the rule. Knowing the context of the rule, you can apply the rule more broadly by removing the surface-specific contexts. Will you still have people who read this and jump into a new relationship after a long relationship ends? Yes. Will you still have entrepreneurs who read this and fall for the ego-soothing trappings of more established businesses? Yes. You can know the rules, but knowing is not enough.

The rule has to be ingrained. To ingrain a rule, you often have to fail. Sometimes you have to fail so often, so completely, and so devastatingly that the silence at your grand failure is so complete, so wiping clean of former preconceptions, that all that is available to you is the rule crying out "Play globally in the beginning." The toll to get the rule can be pricy, but it allows you to cross over to other rules. If you've been burned at something, you're unlikely to forget. If you've succeeded without failure, nothing really gets burned in.

THE MIDDLE GAME

After the beginning stage of a game of Go—the more global stage, in which each player is jockeying for position around the board—comes war. The middle game starts as the two opponents develop differing opinions about who gets what. This stage taxes the frames and sketches developed in the opening through multiple skirmishes, all-out brawls, and chaos of the worst kind. Here, one's ability to read many moves ahead can make the difference. "Can I save areas one, two, and three and let four and five go and still win?" As if one were playing on multiple chessboards, but with only one move to play at a time, one's abilities, intuition, analysis, pattern recognition, and ingenuity are challenged for the one hundred or so moves that compose the middle game. This is the stage of the great dramas, the heart of the most famous games. This is the home to both global and local thinking.

In the opening, you typically do not butt heads with the opponent. There is a lot of open space, you can peacefully stake claims across the board. Uncertainty is so palpable that if you stick to your global guns, you really can't take yourself out of a match too much. That ends in the middle game.

When you and your opponent stop investing here and there, you start to wonder who has more. If you have more, you try to increase, defend. If the opponent has more, you try to decrease, attack. And, with potentially five or more things to look after at a time, and with only one move to do so, you have to be strategic globally and locally. Where's the most important area? What's the biggest move? Where am I strong? Where is the opponent strong? Where am I weak? Where is the opponent weak? Every move counts. The middle game is a razor-sharp tightrope. One slip to either side or just resting on the wire and you'll be either falling fast or cut in two. The middle game ends some 40 percent of all professional games.

This stage of the game is not the place for the flighty fantasy and open dreams of the beginning stage. In the middle game, you have to be honest. Is your stake there secure? Do you really have a way out if attacked? Did you make an overplay and need to fix things up? Brutal honesty wins more games than hope. "I hope my significant other doesn't abuse me." "I hope that our CEO really is the right person to run the company." "I hope my kids aren't doing drugs." "I hope that our sales are really going to be good next quarter." "I hope that our investment in the latest acronyms (CRM, ERP, Y2K) will pan out."

These sentences reek of desperation and are the kind of statements that cannot be made if you're looking to win in the middle game. By the time the middle game rolls around, the underlying path of the invisible hand is becoming clear. Things and territory that at first were mere potential may now be actually mapped to some extent. Brutal honesty. The Middle Game demands it, whether on the Go board or off.

MIDDLE GAME FLOGGING

Golf likewise oscillates from global to local. Off the tee, you can put the tee at whatever height you like, you can stand where you like with respect to the fairway beyond you. The distance to the pin is a known quantity. The fairway or the hole is the goal that drives you. That's beginning-stage golf, a lot more singular feeling than Go, but it's still how you want to put yourself in position for the next shot. It's global.

On the green, if the grass is cut relatively the same, the ball will roll as the contours of the hills and valleys dictate. It may be hard to read it all out, but this is not middle game, it is end game golf—local. The hours on the putting green will pay dividends. You can err in your judgment of the physics that will apply or you can err in the mechanics of your stroke, but if you were a machine physically and physics-ly, your putts would be like so much putty in your hands. Putting is not a global panoply of options and opportunities, it's a tactical tenacity toward a subterrestrial target.

Middle game golf is the rest of golf and is betwixt global goals and local loci. In middle game golf or Go, you cannot know every lie your opponent may present you. You cannot practice shooting from every possible sand trap lip, from the multitude of various depths of a ball's embedding, from the different coarsenesses and consistencies of sand. Hitting out from every type of tree, every type of rough along the fairway, accounting for every variable of wind, rain, grass, and humidity is not part of even the most practiced golfer's routine. It's not practical to practice for every specific circumstance, just as it's not practical to think practice conditions will prevail in real games. The rule in Go is "There are no rules for the middle game." Don't think some rule is going to help you when there are so many situations that are new, not just to you, but to Go, with each game.

Moving from the beginning-stage-like conditions of the EPA episode, let's revisit in more detail the middle game frenzy of the contractors back at the mill. Contractor A, the political ally, the savvy business team, the connected and powerful player in the local community, was up in arms against Contractor B, the cheap, get-it-done-fast laborer who now was using his Cat (the colloquial term for a bulldozer, typically manufactured by Caterpillar, although this Cat was a Kubota) to knock down parts of the old buildings that were going to get rebuilt as part of our offices.

Contractor A knew that some of the old paneling and wood from this former shed scheduled for demolition was of value to the new construction. You can't get that kind of wood anywhere these days. Also, knowing part of the larger vision, the global view of things, Contractor A did not want to waste an opportunity to get some free rare raw material.

As with most middle games, things aren't always so simple. Extracting wood in a preserved, pristine way takes time, and time was a luxury at this point. Contractor B was acting on the vacationing president's order to remove this shed in time for the roads people, who could only come in the next day to pave a street to the new casino's back entrance. If they didn't start hauling this thing down by late today, there would be no way to finish clearing it so that the pavers could pave.

Contractor A had an excellent retort. What was the use of paving the way to the back entrance of a casino that wasn't even due to be open for the next five months? So what if it wasn't paved, it would still be traversable, albeit a bit rugged. The road pavers weren't going to cost more if they couldn't come tomorrow. Indeed, the pavers would have preferred to get a reprieve and not go out of their way to move from the project they were on to do this one-off paving.

Contractor B played twenty questions, twenty fear questions. "Didn't the president say do this today?" "Are you deliberately disobeying what he said?" "Isn't he expecting upon his return to have this done?" "Aren't you just filling in for him while he is gone or are you supposed to be making your own decisions?" And so on and so forth.

I asked out loud if the president had known this valuable wood was inside the shed. I got two different answers. Contractor A saw the opportunity and responded that if the president had known of the wood, he would have forestalled the tearing down of the shed and the paving. Contractor B, not to be outdone, said that the president wasn't an idiot. He'd been inside the building plenty of times and knew his wood. He'd obviously seen this wood in there and didn't think much of it because he told us to just "rip it down."

Making matters worse, I knew that Contractor A was also involved in building a health clinic elsewhere for the tribe. They were strongly allied with the tribal council, which held plenary authority over the economic development corporation, albeit its reign had never been tested to date. Would angering Contractor A compel Contractor A to go to the tribal council and establish more control? My paranoia was building as I realized that politically I'd better side with Contractor A. "Let's let them take the wood out. The pavers won't mind," I said.

This made Contractor B furious. Continuing the Socratic mode, the questions became more colorful. "You *&#!@! punk. What the #@&#@ do you think you're *@&@! doing?" "Are you outta yer &$#@ mind?" "Ya think yer smart letting these pencil-necked &##%@ jerk you around?" Ah, relief. I got a certain joy out of watching Contractor B spew, Contractor A tallying up my brownie points, and . . . uh oh. "You &$#@ watch what happens when the #%@* electric company can't get in there!" End of Socratic mode, end of story. The rule in Go, for any local fight, is "Once you see a solution, look again." Completely disregarding any semblance of my Go tutelage, I had sided with Contractor A despite the admonition.

I'd forgotten about the building needing to be razed so that the power company could get in to remove some of the old transformer lines and other things that were part of the old mill. The shed abutted the whole works. Since the president had promised the power company people that the shed would be gone before they started work, the power company had moved up the appointment to remove it by a couple of months. This was a date fixed months ago, a far-distant memory for me, but not for Contractor B. The rule in Go is "Even the weakest opponent can play the right move." While I had sided with the stronger, more politically connected side, and certainly the less colorful, I would now need to switch sides.

"On second thought, we'd better clear it," I said. Contractor A, unaware of the power company promise, blinked hard. "What!" "I thought you just said that you agreed to postponing the shed's demolition so that we could get all this fine wood out of there?" "You gotta be kidding me . . . why are you doing this?" Before I could answer, I got the president's secretary running up to me with a very urgent phone call. Apparently, there were some federal investigators down at the reservation . . .

Since it was still early, I knew that this didn't have to be concluded right now. Contractor B could clear the shed in about five hours, after I spent some time figuring out what else was going wrong today. "Please, both of you, wait till I get back before we decide what we should do. I have to go see about some trouble down on the reservation. I'll be back soon."

STUCK? WHAT'S THE GOAL

These are typical middle game circumstances. Moving from the beginning, where you place some bets, the middle game is where you aren't just anteing in, you have to decide to throw good money after good, or after bad. Moreover, because the middle game is fraught with multiple skirmishes across the bigger board, you have to choose your battles wisely. While driving down to see the EPA, I was able to reflect a bit on the situation.

OK, so it seemed that razing the building was the best thing to do because of the power company's coming. If the president knew the power company hadn't done its job while he was away, there'd be hell to pay. But, what would the president have done if he knew the wood was still in there? Hold up the power company? Make Contractor B work through the night? Was the wood worth it and did he know about it?

What about Contractor A and the potential for convincing the tribal council to come out and help shepherd me while the president was gone? That was sure paranoid. Really, what was I thinking? But, that Contractor A didn't get the tribal council to go that far didn't mean that Contractor A couldn't cause a stink. With all this development, things were already brewing with the tribal government about who owned what and where the power was. There was no doubt about their ultimate reign, but what about public impression, the eyes of the tribal members? While things had been going well so far, there's hardly any development in Indian Country, or anywhere else for that matter, where a good deed goes unpunished. There were numerous local situations, all with global ramifications.

Comparing local situations and alternatives is not simple. There are millions of variations, and the rule in Go is "Stones don't move." That is, no matter how poorly you played before, you need to account for and respect the moves, however you played them. They've become either weaknesses or strengths, have helped toward the goal or not, but they are in the past and now are part of the environment. You cannot move them any more than you can move or alter your past. What you can do with them now depends on moves you make now. While some earlier decisions may be unalterable at this point, early on in the middle game, the game is like so much magma—hot, gooey, pliable, and ready to coagulate to the goal of your choosing. Your old plays are sunk costs.

My moves this morning had had an effect. Momentum and feelings had changed. The effects, while reversible, could still have bearing later in the game. I might be able to spend time with both contractors and get them to see the more global picture, to see that we all win by following a particular direction. Or, more likely the case, I would be seen as wishy-washy and not to be trusted with a made decision. You can't continue play as if you haven't made a mistake. The Owe part of the book is coming up.

The evaluation is, of course, still the same as in the beginning. The goal is to win the game—in Go, to control more intersections than the opponent does; in life, whatever that analogue is. For CEDCO, our goal was to make a 10 percent profit on $100 million in revenue so that the tribe could be self-sufficient. Through lengthy studies, someone came up with the tribe needing $10 million a year in order to survive without federal assistance. That was the overarching global goal.

How did knowing the goal help the middle game situation here? Well, if I had the local knowledge of the value of the wood, the detrimental cost of moving around the power company, and the probability they'd have to move the date, given that Contractor B might or might not be able to work past 6:00 p.m., the political values, the irritation of Contractor B in general, and so forth, I'd have all the background research done that would answer my question. When one is omniscient, even the most strategic considerations can become tactical. But when you don't even have the local facts straight, you cannot possibly align yourself to the global goal. In Go, detail determines the whole and the whole informs the details. The crux of Global Local analysis lies in this tension between knowing the local values between positions and how those local values pertain to the global goal. In Go, the way one does this is to ask the Four Questions.

THE FOUR QUESTIONS

In Go, you have to separate the local situations, evaluate the pieces, then tie it all back together. The Global Local combo rule in Go is to ask Four Questions—Where am I strong? Where is the opponent strong? Where am I weak? Where is the opponent weak?—and then play closer to weakness and farther from strength. In business, this is called SWOT analysis—strength, weakness, opportunity, and threat. In sports, it goes by a number of different names. It's the basic calculus of strategy and in most situations in Go and elsewhere, the answer to the Four Questions gives you the answer at least 50 percent of the time.

To do proper Four Question analysis, look at each particular battle distinctly. Am I ahead or behind in each battle? As a beginner, you cannot do this analysis well, but you can cheat to some extent by just comparing positions based on time, number, and space (for example, "I have ten pieces to the opponent's seven in this area; therefore, I am stronger here" is one simplistic analysis; see the Appendix for more examples). Whose turn is it? Do I have more resources in the area than the opponent does? Am I taking up more space than the opponent does? As you get stronger, you look at how things interconnect. You can tell at a glance their efficiencies and overall effectiveness and likewise look at the opponent the same way. The stronger you are, the finer the distinctions you can make between what is strong and what is weak.

Summing up all your positions relatively determines the positions from strongest to weakest. From this global perspective on multiple local ones, and with limited resources to commit, it's best, oftentimes, to play the move that is closer to your own weakness. Better yet, also be far from your own strength and far from the opponent's strength. In Go, the rule is "Play the multiple-meanings move." The more of the Four Questions you can address with one move, the better. This will be covered to a greater extent in Chapter 7, Expand Focus.

In my particular dilemma about what to do with the contractors at the mill, after leaving the flood to flood and after stonewalling the EPA, my initial analysis was a good read of the Four Questions. Where was I weak? Aside from all over, my particular weaknesses were, first, a coming power company visit that needed reinforcement in order to happen (namely, the razing of the shed); second, my paranoia, fear, or later-to-be-proved-correct premonition that the tribe was looking to take away the corporation's power, otherwise known as watch out for Contractor A; third, the dearth of fine woods that could complete the interior design; and fourth, not knowing what the president knew and did not know. Where were my strengths? Since I was the client, the contractors would need to bow to my direction, so I had, first, the ability to make a decision stick; second, the ability to get the contractor(s) to work extra hours or late; third, the resources to get the job done; and fourth, the mantle of the president.

My opponents' strengths were a bit more difficult to read. While in Go, you can see the whole board and know exactly what your opponent is doing at all times, outside Go you do not always know this. The equalizer is that in Go, as much as you do see, there's much that you likewise do not see. You cannot read the entire game out unless you are close to the end. Likewise, the opponent may be feinting, misplaying, ignoring, or baiting you with or without your knowing it. You are again hampered by your own strength or weakness, and whatever holes there are in your personality in your daily life will likewise blind you in Go. The rule in Go is "You cannot know the opponent's mind just by seeing the opponent's stones."

Nonetheless, in Go and in life, you make the best decision you can based on what you know. You can probe the opponent's intentions, do your best not to make your plans too obvious, monkey with the opponent so as to draw out hidden schemes, and so forth, but your information is only going to get so good. At some point, you still have to act on the basis of the information you have and the environment before you. To my knowledge, the contractors' strengths were many.

Each contractor could decide to walk; while unlikely, this was within their power. Each had information about his own projects that far exceeded my own; while I had the mantle, I did not have an extensive explicit, implicit, or tacit knowledge dump. Each contractor had ties to the rest of the community and, for Contractor A, ties to the tribal council. Each contractor had access to our plans and desires for building out the old mill site and therefore could help or hinder progress for it. These strengths and more were weighing in my mind.

The contractors' weaknesses, partially mentioned in my strengths, were that both needed the money, both were working for a sovereign government, which would be difficult to collect from in the event things really went sour, and both had been given strict direction to follow my orders by the president. The particular weakness for Contractor A was that despite his moniker of contractor, there was no contract. Couple this with our being ninety days in arrears already and his needing to fully believe in our good faith (we ultimately did make good) while he was paying his subcontractors on a seven-day or cash upfront basis, and you had the ultimate weakness. Contractor B was often hurt by his tendency to fly off the handle and do erratic things that tended to get him fired from different jobs. While it is one thing to be the low-price contractor in the region, it's quite another to be the most obnoxious.

In true Go fashion, I followed the Four Questions, and the answers led me squarely to the right thing to do under the circumstances. My greatest weakness was my uncertainty about many things, but it was a certainty that the shed needed to be removed. Not doing so would mean trouble when the president got back and trouble from the power company when it arrived. My opponents' weakness was my power in the relationship and their inability to marshal their strength against me, from the perspective of their connections outside our corporation, as long as I stayed clear of any external entanglements. My strength was that I held the pocketbook and the strategic vision of the entire corporation, with which they were in no position to argue. Staying away from my strengths and theirs (not holding the pocketbook threat over them, not driving them to external parties who might cause us problems) and playing closely to my weaknesses and theirs (fixing the power company obstacle and giving them more confidence we'd make good on the work they'd done thus far) made a lot of sense. My initial decision from the morning seemed sound. The plan was set. Unfortunately, Go and life are not so easy.

The situation changed after I had left them in the morning. While going with Contractor B was right from the whole-board perspective, taking into account global and local concerns and weighing them appropriately, there was a new move on the board. When you're walking the razor-thin tightrope of the middle game, you have to respect the rule that "every stone counts."

LADDER BREAKER

In Go, you can capture the opponent's stone by surrounding it and choking it off from its friendlies and/or unoccupied intersections. The particulars you can discover by reading the Appendix, but directly capturing a stone is not nearly as interesting as the various ways you can indirectly capture a stone. In most advanced games, players don't go around capturing stones, despite many stones being primed for capture. Since the game is about territory and not capture (à la chess), the two sides will clash and the de facto captured stones remain on the board. At the end, these stones are repatriated into their opposing territory, thereby reducing whatever the opponent had before. This is a civilized sort of Geneva-like convention for Go, where those captured or surrounded remain unharmed but are returned to the country of origin.

One particular method of indirect capture with interesting global ramifications is what is called a ladder. A ladder is a way to capture a stone by chasing it either into the side of the board or into your friendly pieces. The position, if played out, can spread all over the board, and some professional problem makers have these capture ladders form words and pictures the same way one might with dominoes. The point is that if you've done your local tactical analysis, you can see if the ladder can capture the stone or if it cannot. In fact, this is one thing computers can do faster than humans can in regard to Go. The particular rule that ladders rely on, more than any other aspect of the game, is that "every stone counts." Whether a ladder works or not is determined by the environment on the board.

Following the ladder pattern through to its final conclusion, a computer ignores strategic complications and can tell if the ladder will crash into the side of the board or into sides friendly with the other side, and thereby perish, or if it will crash into friendly stones and thereby live. Put an opposing stone in the path of a ladder and the ladder ceases to capture; that stone is thus called a ladder breaker. It doesn't matter if this stone is important at all in what it is doing in its particular place; if it happens to be in the way of the ladder, it can prevent the ladder from capturing the stone. When people talk about luck in Go, this is often what they mean. Sometimes you'll happen to have a stone in the right place so that a ladder works or breaks, sometimes you aren't so fortunate as to have a stone in the right place.

The ladder breaker for my decision at the mill wasn't part of any of the analysis I did regarding the Four Questions. The new move, the ladder breaker for the mill decision, occurred as many ladder breakers do, far away at the reservation—the EPA visit. While the local analysis was sound and I thought I had captured the situation appropriately with my analysis, I had not captured the situation with my Four Questions analysis.

What if there was asbestos in this shed? What if even the small shack attached to the shed, used formerly to power the shed, was asbestos-laden? While I certainly was in the dark about what the president knew or did not know about the quality of the wood, I knew that the president had no idea about the EPA's visit and its investigation of the debris from the building that was allegedly showing up on the reservation. We'd had the previous owner's environmentally clean bill of health for the entire premises—we had to in order to put this land into trust for the tribe—but this wasn't stopping the EPA from investigating. While I had the proverbial stone to capture to make the old plans work, the local situation alone had to be looked at in light of the global reality. Neither plans, nor good decisions, nor enlightened insight can keep the bogeyman of reality from foiling your plans. Respecting reality, not looking at things just in their tempting, narrow, safe, local context, the real tactical situation can be affected by the global situation—a global situation or move, in this case, that could care less about whatever you decided earlier.

So, ol' wishy-washy VP went back to Contractors A and B and said that the shed would not come down. Not just for the sake of the power company, not even for the removal of the fine wood products that made up its walls. The potential risk of asbestos removal, even if we were totally in the clear, at this point, was too great for us to do anything but get our ducks in a line and see where reality was. You can think you are in the clear, but the middle game demands brutal honesty, not honesty of intentions. If we weren't terribly clear about the materials that composed it, we dared not let it compromise us.

You can probe in Go to test your understanding of a situation. My quick probe into the situation bore out the ladder breaker. "Is this material asbestos," I asked Contractor B. "Uh, not sure, really. It looks like normal wallboard to me." "Well, what's the difference between the two?" "Not sure, really. I guess it could be asbestos, but I thought the former owner cleaned this building out." "Yep, that was my thinking too." This exchange was sure to become part of some exhibit before a grand jury, I thought, should we have continued to plow this old shed under. The original plans, schemes, and designs that led to a good decision in siding with Contractor B before were now ladder broken.

In the middle game you're forced to respect every move or you will suffer as a result. While the global goal has to be the direction and trajectory you follow, the power of localized situations is such that when something is wrong, no matter how small, your entire game can be thrown off if you pay attention only to the big picture. The small, local picture can be a cancer. If not stopped at first notice, it becomes a much bigger problem that may be unsolvable later. The rule in Go is that "small leaks can become a great river."

LOCAL LAND

With the contractor and EPA situations concluded for the day, there was still a bit more work to do. I called to check on the flooding in the basement. The contractor had arrived onsite and had let the building manager know what had happened and how we had contributed to its flooding. The claim was that runoff from the incomplete landscaping around the assisted-living facility had plugged up drains that would otherwise have worked.

Should we expect to have the drainage system break down whenever enough foliage fell due to storm or otherwise? Would the building have no protection from exterior water or runoff? While the floors were still concrete and the Sheetrock was replaceable, the flooding was mostly an annoyance, but these claims about contributory factors seemed rather disingenuous. The nice thing about this particular battle was that as long as the discussion stayed on this issue and things didn't get too heated in the bickering, this problem was largely one of end game, where local rules rule.

END GAME

For the person not steeped in bureaucracy or the love of administrative processes, the end game can prove to be a challenge on a personal level. It is attention to detail that makes or breaks someone in the end game phase. Miss a beat, time things incorrectly, and you'll suffer a point loss. You can play brilliantly in the middle game and create a masterpiece Go record against an equally matched opponent and still come into the end game and lose. Horribly.

With a typical Go game lasting 250-some moves, only 150 take up the beginning and middle games. With nearly 100 or more moves remaining, the situation is still critical. As the final boundaries between the opponents remain, each side jockeys to reduce the other's territory as much as possible while increasing its territory. But, unlike the globalness of the beginning and the Global-Local-ness of the middle game, the end game is almost strictly local. Toward the end of the end game the feeling is analytical, bureaucratic. The later stages of end game have no room for intuition, and in this, its final throes, a mathematical science of end games dictates the absolute best way to play.[2] While not sexy, the end game is a critical part of winning.

What championship golfer is good at driving, fairway irons, chipping, but not putting? None. What great sales rep gets scores of potential clients to go to all the fancy sales events, generates all sorts of interest, but cannot get the deal closed? None. The end game is about sealing the deal. It's a nitty-gritty and oftentimes plainly administrative part of the game. Until it's complete, the game ain't over. Nearly all great Go professionals profess having a great end game. When you're moving from the razor-thin tightrope of the middle game, the tension and width of opportunity of that tightrope are pulled into even thinner opportunities in the end game.

If you are too far behind going into the end game and your opponent is strong, it's best to resign. While there's an entire art to resigning in Go, suffice it to say that the end game rarely swings the point tally by more than five points, if at all, in a professional match. By the time the end game starts, both sides have taken the big opportunities on the board and all that's left is to eke out the final border tangles before calling it a game. That said, there are still plenty of opportunities about which one can be pennywise.

Not one to be pound-foolish, I went into the negotiations with the contractor about the flooding. Every move he made had to be

2. Once most of the areas on the board become independent from one another, typically rather late in the end game, there is an actual advanced mathematical solution to the game that was discovered by mathematicians Elwyn Berlekamp and David Wolfe and is discussed in their book, *Chilling Gets the Last Move*.

judged for its merit, its timing, and its relative value to other end-game-like moves. If I stayed on the defensive the entire time, answering his line of questioning, I would run out of time before this thing was all mopped up, and then the onus would be on me to foot the bill. In a global sense, there is still the comparison of local moves and deciding which is the more valuable, but still that's the only function at this ending state of global reasoning. The local moves and their timing and value were the main determiners of where to play. Do the calculations right and you can basically wrap it up. If buying into the contractor's stories about our culpability were sound, then what were the costs? Again, global perspective is not going to help at this point. You can wonder if your analysis is worth it, you can wonder if spending time on the problem is worth it, but in determining how to react, it is a matter of the probabilities of culpability, the costs of the various scenarios, and then doing your math. If settling the issue costs less than the analysis, don't bureaucracy your way to better decision-making by costing more than the benefit.

How much was the bill going to be for cleaning this up? Five hundred dollars. Oh, and the GM had already rented the equipment to clean it up and the job is basically done. OK, remove four hundred dollars from the cleanup and how valuable is my time talking to the contractor? If I get the contractor back to work and I get back to work, don't I make up the other one hundred dollars, at least? Sure, there are other utilities that come into play. You don't want to be a chump to the contractor and seem like you'll bend on stuff like this. "If we cover this cleanup cost, are you going to guarantee me there aren't going to be any more finishing-up-the-building SNAFUs?" If he agrees, you are netting in the positive for more than you paid in total. That's getting down to the nitty-gritty. That's end game. Besides, there was a certain value in reducing the probability of heart failure. Water on concrete wasn't the end of the world.

HOME BASE

Heading home with a new appreciation for being the buck-stopper, the decision-maker on what battle to fight and when, I could see things more clearly. Would I still make the mistake of rushing into a decision based on a simplistic understanding of global rules? Probably. Would I still suffer the ignominy of being too local in the face of a diet, wanting to be too helpful to the long arm of the law, or accepting the placebos of small wins? For sure. But did I gain in strength and experience that reinforced and bridged learning I knew from Go, but had to transplant to management? Certainly. While I continue to make global mistakes and suffer the slings and arrows of outrageous fortune from the tiniest of local perspectives, I at least can suffer knowing that the probability goes down with each trial.

If I was going to be a better player in management, I would need to build both my local and global perspectives and make sure they were in balance. That said, it was easier to come into a new situation and be a good globalist, because lack of experience doesn't take as much of a toll there, but if you are out of balance, with a weak local understanding, without the experience of multiple fights and losses tactically, a global perspective for the Four Questions is not well informed. If you're an expert at one thing, don't spout the obvious global issues before you get under the skin of something else. Look closely and get burned a few times locally. Your global perspective can be good in new contexts without local understanding, but you'll get burned hard without bringing your local knowledge up to snuff. Beware the contractor, consultant, salesperson—kibitzer—who promises otherwise.

But having interchangeable Global Local lenses and abilities is not enough to see you through to mastery. It's the first crucial element, but without an idea of risk, safety, urgent, or big, your analysis will be flawed, your steps toward the goal will be away from goodness. You need Owe Save to give you depth in your Global Local views.

CHAPTER TWO

———— • ————

OWE SAVE

Owe Save exists on the spectrum of risk and safety. Risk in Go, as in anything, is the element of bad that can occur in a situation. Distinct from chance, risk implies that something can potentially go awry. When you're playing Go you will not always be on par with your equally resourced opponent, who can take advantage of your past mistakes and move ahead in this most balanced of games. In these instances, if you still have a chance to win, you had best play with an eye toward taking more risks, by playing moves that are slightly askew from the balanced tightrope of perfect play. You're going to have to come from behind and force the opponent into the murky chaotic waters of a complicated middle game if you're going to regain what you've given away. By playing risky, you're departing from best practice to take a shot at making the opponent screw up before you do. Since you cannot create more opportunities on the board than already exist, you must hope that your play causes the opponent to play off-balance and create those opportunities. The rules in Go are "Adjust risk according to the score" and "The board does not confer advantage, the opponent does." When you owe, the only way to get back the advantage is to force the opponent to screw up.

The opponent in this scenario sees things much differently. The opponent who is ahead wants to save that win. Instead of looking for opportunities to complicate matters, this opponent will look to make things simpler, even if it costs some points, to make the route sure. The proverbs we use for Go are just rehashes of "Safety first," "A stitch in time saves nine," "An ounce of prevention is worth a pound of cure." Roll up all your old safety maxims into a bundle and ship them insured. When you don't want to lose what you have, when you want to save, you reduce risk as much as is practical. You know the opponent is going to look for an opportunity to bring you down, so don't give him or her one.

Another crucial aspect of Owe Save is the way it complements Global Local and spawns a child between the two rule sets that is another key part of the game—Urgent Big. When you owe greatly or have invested greatly in a position, but have not secured it, you're in debt. If the opponent, after your next move, can come in and pull out the support beam holding this investment up, you'd best play there first. That's what's called an urgent move. It can be the tiniest move. It can be a local move that may not increase your score in the slightest. But, if you don't play it and give the opponent the chance to take it, it may decrease your score considerably. The rule in Go is "Urgent moves before big moves."

On the other hand, if you have scrimped and saved across the board and are everywhere strong, you don't owe your opponent a dime. You can go after the big fish, the big territory, the all-encompassing Global biggest play. The maxim in this instance is "When there are no more urgent moves, take as much territory as you can." To do so is to get closer to the goal of surrounding more territory. Because you have no risks elsewhere, your new investment in something a bit risky is defensible. Even with only one move per turn, because you don't have anything you need to go back and patch up when you don't owe, you can defend this new investment with every move. You're free to attack, invade, or reduce the opponent's bounty or increase your own. Of course, it may cost you some potentially rewarding risks that you did not make earlier, to be this free.

OWE SAVE BALANCE

Owe and Save are always competing against each other. The balance between these two rules is tricky business when the accounting needed to determine what is risky and what is safe is so difficult. Be too safe, and you're like the child that never plays, not wanting to scrape a knee. Be too risky and you'll always be at the mercy of the law of balance: in life, the law of the land, in Go, the opponent who can see weaknesses that you cannot defend simultaneously. Finding the balance is an indication of your strength in Go; finding a rhythm between Owe Save is a sign of mastery.

In Go, many players like to play risky move after risky move and then try to settle down later in the game. But like a party-loving bachelorette or bachelor approaching a first marriage, how do you know when your risky times are up? How much more will you try to stretch things before you enter the stolid world of playing it safe? How much can you? There are players in the amateur ranks who cannot stop that fun-loving risk-seeking behavior, always trying to get more from the opponent. Never protecting, instead relying on brutal fighting instincts, these players taunt, push, and prod their weaker opponents into submission. The nature of Go, however, is such that you cannot be a bully without reason. If you attack without the proper buildup, you are vulnerable to counterattack. If you stretch the pendulum back and back, the opponent will have the opportunity to use that force to swing things back in your face. The nature of the game is balance. Not that bullies cannot thrive against weaker foes, but against an equally matched, more balanced opponent, all-out aggression won't fly. The rule in Go is "Fighting is a sign of strength; fighting for fighting's sake is weak."

Counter to the bullies are the cautious. Never stretching their positions beyond what's safe, never venturing into the proverbial left lane, they follow the rules according to Hoyle and any others that come to mind; they're persnickety. If you attack them, you'll pay, but if you leave them alone, they will let you win on points. Because they never stretch and never put their positions at risk, you can stretch a little here and there to come out ahead without a fight. More worried about order and administration than the true goal of the game, they win in their own minds, but leave the real victory to their opponents. The rule in Go is "Don't be safe to be safe"; William Shedd's more colorful non-Go expression is "Ships in a harbor are safe, but that's not what ships are built for."

Strong Go players may have tendencies toward either persona, but the stronger you become the more you need to balance between the two.

Being too far on either side can be problematic. There are two types of small companies I've seen that have exhibited the polar opposites of the spectrum and were a bit too close to the extremes for their own good. The following story is not about any two specific companies, but is an amalgam of many different companies and experiences. The scary part of this fairy tale is that all of the elements are true examples taken from real companies.

A TALE OF TWO COMPANIES

They were the best, at times; they were bested, at times. Once upon a time, there were two little companies that could, but did so quite differently. One company, a spinoff of a huge multinational corporation that was a household brand name, ran a tight ship. The other, a small entrepreneurial company, bootstrapped and propelled by the moxie and credit cards of its founders, ran a loose ship. Two little companies, two very different parents, two utterly different styles.

ANYCOMPANY

The spinoff was the idea of a huge multinational that decided it wanted to start a little company that could compete like a small company. It wouldn't be burdened with all the large corporateness of the big company in attacking a new market that the big company wanted to go into. So, one day, a little company was born. They called it AnyCompany. AnyCompany would be nimbler, quicker, and able to take chances that the bigger company would never dare dream of. AnyCompany was a wonderful idea and a wonderful dream.

For years, AnyCompany, the little company, was the poster child for those huge corporations that were looking to spawn a little company. The little company was playing in a smaller pond, but was still the big fish in this smallish pond. No one dared challenge AnyCompany's supremacy in its market. AnyCompany was a model for forward development and innovativeness. Everyone said so, even AnyCompany's competitors. Everything was going gangbusters. That is, until one day, it hired Pat Shmo, a Go player, from NewCompany, the very different other small company.

NEWCOMPANY

NewCompany was the product of its genius founder. Brilliant, eccentric, and with enough business acumen to be dangerous, the NewCompany founder launched and built a small company that could and did in a market formerly dominated by bigger companies. NewCompany outmaneuvered and outdeveloped companies one hundred times its size by the founder's sheer will power.

While the NewCompany founder probably would have been happy just keeping NewCompany a one-person machine, the founder realized that if the market value of NewCompany were going to get stratospheric, NewCompany would need to take on more employees.

Pat Shmo was one of these new hires. Pat had been a serial entrepreneur/GM for small companies like NewCompany. Pat was bright and quick and knew how to get things done in NewCompany's markets. With experience and the right degrees, Pat joined NewCompany after a single meeting with the brilliant founder.

While NewCompany did not compete with AnyCompany, it did seem to compete with itself. Because NewCompany was growing so fast, there were a lot of pluses and minuses. For instance, on the plus side, Pat was able to make things happen, and fast. If Pat wanted to go into a new market and had a good idea, Pat walked down the hall, convinced the founder, and then off Pat went to implement. Another plus was the stock options and pay. Pat was well compensated; the founder knew how hard it was to find someone like Jo.

The drawbacks, unfortunately, were always on the periphery looking in. Being good friends with the accountants, Pat learned that the company was any number of times on the verge of running out of cash. While the investor relations expert the founder had hired was able to convince new investors on a regular basis that the current state of NewCompany was a grand opportunity to get in on something big, Pat knew that it'd probably be another six months before Pat's first product would ship.

Another minus was that the hiring process left something to be desired. While Pat knew Pat was good and really enjoyed the founder's interest in Pat's family and potential love interests, wasn't the founder interested in Pat's background? Wasn't someone going to call Pat's references? The founder, when asked sometime later, said, "I knew, right away, that you'd be great. Why do I want to spend time going through all that headache when I needed you working yesterday!"

Overall, the experience was a good one at NewCompany. Pat really did own the product and Pat did good work. At the end of six months on the job, Pat had not only delivered the salable product, but was now going to meetings with clients who thought it was the greatest thing since Spam. With this success, however, came other problems.

While Pat got along with just about everyone because Pat got in good with the founder and most of the other employees were either friends, colleagues, old roommates, or friends of friends of the founder, Pat continued to see money spent imprudently. An Aeron chair here. A bust of the founder there. Neon overhangs of the company logo about the office. While the product Pat made certainly wasn't cheap, Pat had a sense for how many were sold—not enough to support all this new "infrastructure."

The founder, a workaholic like Pat, stopped in to ask Pat how Pat was doing one long weekend night. Pat relayed concern that the fixtures might not be the best expense at this early stage of the company. The founder laughed. "You're great, I'm great, our products are great. Sales are picking up. People are starting to track us in the press. Any day now, we're going to be rich." Pat appreciated the founder's attitude, but the founder was staying all weekend to finish a product before a company demo Monday morning. Apparently, one of the founder's not-so-brilliant entourage, now an employee, screwed up and the founder had to come in to "fix things." Again.

MASHED SHINOGI

This model of management wasn't a completely foreign thing to Pat, a Go player. There are times when a Go player is forced to employ such a strategy. In fact, the dominant player throughout the 1960s and the player with the most Japanese titles to date, Sakata Eio, made this his style. For Sakata, greed was good. "Greedy" Sakata, as he came to be known, got to be the top player in a game rewarding balance, so Pat was not terribly alarmed at the actions of NewCompany.

In Go, it is possible to spread your stones around everywhere on the board, preventing your opponent from getting any large territory, and leave weak group after weak group about the board, completely disregarding the Four Questions maxim. This flavor of Go is known as "amashi." At some point, however, the opponent can go after one or many of these weak groups and try to kill them. The more weak positions the opponent can kill, the worse off you'll be. Of course, the other pain the opponent can inflict is by hurting one or more positions enough so that the opponent can get a leg up elsewhere. One leg OK, two or more legs bad.

What the amashi strategy player is respecting in the game is the resiliency of the stones played. Because there is a strong bias in Go to defense and because the multitude of uses of each stone is so great, you can really push the envelope on taking territory with an almost reckless disregard for your weak groups. Of course, this style of play requires one to be tremendous at getting out of this huge debt.

Sakata was famous for taking territory (the so-called greed) despite the opponent's making the rest of Sakata's positions weaker and weaker. Even in the midst of the opponent's sphere of influence, Sakata would ignore move after move, until at the point of almost no return, Sakata then started what's called "shinogi" tactics.

Shinogi is what the amashi strategist must perfect—the ability to live deep inside the opponent's territory with little to no resources for life. It's a survivalist strategy. Sakata had a number of self-admitted glaring weaknesses for a professional Go player, but his genius was at making the seemingly impossible live, a green thumb in an otherwise black and white world. While the rest of the Go world would need at least a dozen potato-filled pierogi to get by, Sakata was getting by on the Go equivalent of a couple of blades of grass, for weeks at a time.

HANDICAP GO

This technique is nowhere more useful than in handicap Go. No matter your rank, even if just a rank beginner, you can play an even match against the world's strongest Go player by adding stones before play. Doing so, you can adjust the probability of winning to 50-50. Rank beginners should expect to place some forty-odd stones in order to challenge the top player.[1] With each stone approximately worth about eight points, on a 361-point board, a forty-stone handicap is equivalent to giving 88 percent of the total points on the board as a head start. For the strongest player to come out of this gigantic lead with even a chance to win will require shinogi to be sure. Overcoming such a handicap is the ultimate in debt reduction.

Moving around the board in a seemingly random fashion, the stronger player will probe for weaknesses, play moves that can be left alone to die or that when tied with other stones can really inflict some damage. The two main Owe Save rules governing handicap Go are "Don't play heavy in the opponent's territory; play light," and "You can't play slow with nine stones."

Not playing heavy means that you don't need for any particular piece to survive or thrive. Each stone played is a test, a probe, a small investment in something to see what happens. It's light. Like

1. Normally, nine stones is the maximum handicap, because at nine stones you still get an even game's feel without too much artificialness to the play.

a simple question to a witness or suspect, a small purchase of a stock, or giving out a small responsibility, it's not costing you much, but the information you get back can lead to more investment. In handicap Go, when you need to play in the opponent's area, you need to play lightly. Would you go into a hostile environment where you are outnumbered, outgunned, and outflanked and start making demands? Can't recommend it. Likewise, in Go or life, you should not start making big investments without first treating things lightly.

Although for film buffs, a good example of not following the "don't play heavy" rule shows up metaphorically in the Akira Kurosawa film *Seven Samurai* (spoilers follow). Bandits had plundered a small village for years and the villagers were finally fed up with their plight. A few of these villagers went out and found seven samurai who would come and defend them against the bandits. The samurai cleverly created a moyo—a structure common to Go—that would force the bandits to enter their village a few at a time, so that the bandits entering would be outnumbered at that point. In the midst of the villagers and samurai, the few bandits who made it into the village would be slaughtered. Repeat as needed until all bandits are vanquished.

The bandits, apparently not Go players, entered this hostile environment with complete disregard for the opponent. Instead of sending in a scout to ferret out the situation and treating this situation lightly, the bandits attacked full bore. The result was devastating. While the villagers and samurai also sustained considerable damage, the bandits, outnumbered, were vanquished. There was much rejoicing, but smarter bandits might have proved troublesome.

What does it mean to "not play slow with nine stones"? What is faster play? Faster play involves a form, a pattern of stones, that is missing a few pieces. It's a quicker step. Weaker Go players are usually familiar with the normal patterns; indeed, it's their livelihood. But, unfamiliar with why the pattern is the pattern, they are not really in a position to take advantage of a stronger player who breaks the pattern. When a stronger player plays in a way that is "fast," what is really going on is that that player is skipping a step or two in the normal pattern so that that player's moves are lighter, less heavy.

In real life, the comparable situation is the phone call you make when a person gets on an airplane and you can only talk for a few seconds. If you really need to get a lot of information across and your connection is clear, you skip all the pleasantries. You say things like "Car's out back, keys under the armoire." "Call Landlady. Tell her garbage disposal broken." "Djeechet? [Did you eat yet?] No? Order pizza. Money's in top kitchen drawer." It's the same kind of English we're expected to understand in classified ads—"1999 Make/Model. Beauty. Rides well. New tires, exhaust, and tranny. All the extras. $5,000 Blue Book OBO." This is what the stronger Go player is doing in a well-played handicap game— abbreviating. Important elements are missing, but unless the opponent is at your level of understanding, your position is playable, even if there are holes. As any used car buyer will tell you, best to check it out before you buy.

As Pat looked at the founder, plowing away over the many weekends the two worked together, Pat wondered if the founder's play was more the survivalist Sakata strategy or more the bandit getting a break against a constant influx of villagers, or investors as the case was. These weekend moves smacked of heaviness, not light play. Likewise, Pat's inside information that they needed dough quickly to survive—week to week—was shinogi as a result of misappropriation, not amashi. Even the Great and Greedy Sakata was not unprincipled. Of all the Go styles, Sakata's was the most gut-wrenching, but again, it was deliberate. In amashi, heavy debt requires tremendous lifting to get out of alive. In stupidly misappropriating investor money, NewCompany would require not just the heavy lifting, but also the luck of staying in the game based on a good flow of new investors. There is a big difference between a deliberate amashi strategy and a nonstrategy needing shinogi to survive because one gets into multiple bad positions. NewCompany seemed more the latter.

RESIGNED TO GREATNESS

One Monday, things started to unravel at NewCompany. The founder had finished the product, but apparently had slept late. The FOF, friend of founder, unsure of how to use the new product the founder had made over the weekend, was now in the meeting room trying to go through features with a very important new client. Getting the founder on the phone from bed, they tried to finish the pitch, but the two former friends started to argue and the situation got ugly. The client left, saying, "We'll get back to you." The founder called an emergency meeting for later that day.

At the meeting, the founder laid it on the line. From now on, if you wanted to make it in the company, you could no longer screw up. Either you produced or you were out. Just then the investor relations expert comes in. "Can I talk to you?" the expert said to the founder in the midst of the meeting. "We're in an all-hands meeting. You were supposed to have been in here twenty minutes ago!" The expert started to whisper into the founder's ear, but the founder cut off the expert's attempt. "Tell 'em whatever you want. I don't want any more secrets." The expert, a bit put off by the founder's brushoff, told all employees, "We won't be able to pay you for the next pay period, but we should be able to pay you double the following pay period. We got some new investors, but they want our accounts up a bit before moving forward with us."

Pat knew it was time to go. Amashi/shinogi was one thing. Not getting paid, despite the claim that the "company was going to experiment with a one-month versus two-week pay period," a semireversal of the story, was another. Surviving from month to month was something to which Pat was accustomed, but it was getting tiring. Pat started looking. This other smallish company, AnyCompany, looked great with its small feel and its big-company funding. Pat applied.

After six months, Pat's product at NewCompany launched, some money started coming in, and then AnyCompany decided to bring Pat on board.

Leaving a company where you are an essential player is a tough choice. For Pat, however, the founder made it much easier. On leaving, the NewCompany founder made Pat a deal. If Pat wanted, Pat could come back within six months and Pat's old job would be waiting, same pay, same team, same everything. While nothing ever stayed the same at NewCompany for six months, Pat was nonetheless tickled by this gesture. Pat knew enough to be careful with resignations.

Owe Save in Go and elsewhere is about risk, reward, safety, and resignation. Resignation is warranted when you need to take on so much risk with prospects so negligible that you cannot possibly come back. That's when to resign. Don't fly to Mars, don't start that project, don't do that program, don't start that sport, art, or practice. Leave it for someone for whom the odds will be better. Walk away. Life's too short to be mucking up someone else's win with scattered ugly moves that can't go anywhere. Risk, when it gets to be too risky, is termed differently—foolhardy, stupid, insane, inane, reckless, temerarious.

When you're down, sometimes it's just best to resign, friends notwithstanding. Giving up is an art. In Go, there is an entire art to resignation. In professional matches, you can struggle to catch up when behind, but before it's a certifiable certainty, there's a moment when it's right to resign. In the top matches, you'll often hear "At this point, I was looking for a way to resign." That may sound strange, but it's an honest appraisal. While there might still be one more chance, if it doesn't work, there's no sense in looking for more opportunities against a well-matched opponent. Even for the Sakatas of the world, resignation is sometimes the only remaining option.

Unfortunately, stronger Go players teaching weaker ones often wish that their students would more quickly realize when a game is beyond hope. It's not that weaker players are evil and want to continue beating a dead horse, it's just that sometimes weaker players think the stronger player will screw up like their weak opponents do. Sometimes they just don't know how lost their game is. For weaker players looking to play more with stronger ones, having a better understanding of Owe Save gives you more opportunity for review and advice. How? Without this understanding you'll frustrate stronger players by not knowing when to quit.

This is tough to do at times, but in Go, it's a very honorable thing to quit when there's no hope. There are all the emotions wrapped up with the struggle, the need for the win, in some instances, but knowing the precise moment when to resign and walk away is a valued skill. The rule in Go is "Resign when ripe." In the Global sense, it's important to think of Go as more than just one game.

In the midst of a relationship, one-gamedness often rules. All things fall on this one relationship. The sun, your health, the moon, your dignity, the stars are but minuscule backdrops for your hopes for this relationship. After it's gone awry, when it is beyond saving, say good-bye and realize that the one game is not the end. There will be other games to play. While it is nice to keep one game going for an eternity, it's not always in the cards. It is, however, hard to see the Global picture when part of the game is also emotional. In your game of life, when your emotional calculation is that the value of staying in the relationship and trying to "make it work" is a million points, and all other things in life are worth a hundred, even a .011 percent success rate seems rational.[2]

The other edge of the sword is that in trying to time a resignation right, there's a danger that you resign before the game is really over. Losing two or more important battles is not enough reason to resign if you're still in the game. The emotional letdown is powerful, but you cannot let it consume you. There have been games where I was so far ahead that despite two big losses locally I was still ahead in the game. That was the unemotional view. In reality, my

2. It doesn't help that many Disney animated features reward the poor decision-making of the hero or heroine with the most improbable and advantageous resolution to the situation. For instance, in *The Little Mermaid* (warning: spoilers ahead), Ariel signs her life, voice, family, and fins away to a Sea Witch. This horribly bad decision is rewarded with her ultimately ridding the ocean of the Sea Witch, marrying the prince, recouping her voice and her family's love, and being given the choice to live on land. This poor decision-making and inhuman luck are not only handed down to her daughter (as evidenced by *Little Mermaid II*), but to most of the future Disney animated features.

emotional upheaval clouded my thinking, and I resigned thinking that the game was over. Dumb. The rules in Go are "Fight to the end" (meaning you need to know when the end is) and "When you're ahead, don't be happy; when you're behind, don't be distraught." As with all things, easier said than done.

Nonetheless, in Western society, there's a perceived weakness in resigning that compels people to not want to resign. "Never say die" is a dangerous maxim. It's great when there's still a shot, but when there's not, it's a brutal mistake and at times a brutal teacher. In sports, it's keeping your star player in too long, risking injury, when the opportunity to catch up has passed. For NASA, it was the launch of the *Challenger* despite warnings to slow down, postpone launch. In business, as in many relationships, it's a love affair with sunk costs. For Nixon, Vietnam.

The Owe Save battle going on in the art of resignation has consequences on both sides of the equation. There's the very real risk of job security—if I kill this project because it doesn't make sense, don't I get fired? Killing a project that doesn't make sense, makes sense, but does calling in bombs on your own job make sense? At times, yes. At times, no. At NewCompany, Pat was cut a break. Resigning was low-cost with the founder's offer to come back. Or was it?

ANYCOMPANY IN A JAM

Pat was drawn to AnyCompany because AnyCompany was certainly the player in its market and Pat, an entrepreneur, and a successful one at that, saw AnyCompany was well aligned with Pat's ultimate desire to do good in the world while still making money. Although the hiring process to select Pat, the decided front-runner for the position, took some time (six months?!), Pat finally joined and moved to the headquarters of AnyCompany. Pat thought that this slowness to hire occurred because the economy was so good. "The company must have many Pat Shmos to choose from," Pat thought.

Pat's first day was filled with excitement. Being a serial entrepreneur, Pat loved the thrill of jumping right into the fire and getting down to business, and this day wouldn't disappoint. Thrown into the midst of a marketing meeting, Pat had to make the call on an extension of a campaign for a product for which Pat would be responsible. Pat had problems with extending this campaign, as a Go player and as a successful entrepreneur.

Although AnyCompany was the eight-hundred-pound gorilla and its product had all the promise and worthiness of vision that Pat came to Any Company for, the product was still in its infancy. Despite the $50 million ad campaign, the product wasn't quite up to the billing promoted on the airwaves, on the Internet, and via direct mail. Pat believed that the product could ultimately fulfill the CEO's vision, but it was not ready at this time. Certainly an extension to an already elaborate campaign seemed like the wrong direction, at least for the next two quarters.

From Go, Pat knew the rule, "You never want to owe your opponent." As with most of Go's rules, Pat knew, you could take the rule out of the context of Go and apply its elemental structure to other things. Generalizing the rule, Pat thought about the extension of the marketing campaign. "If we keep promising something that we can't deliver, we are essentially violating the rule never to owe your opponent. While our customers are not our opponents, pissing them off will put us into competitive debt somehow." Pat spoke up and asked that all marketing related to Pat's product be stopped.

"Are you sure?" AnyCompany's marketing director said as the creative director and sales lead from the expensive Ad Agency looked on, mouths agape. While stopping the campaign upset the Ad Agency and the marketing director, Pat made them happy again when Pat assured them that the money forgone in the immediate two quarters could be added to the marketing blitz Pat wanted when the product could deliver on the promises of the campaign three quarters from now. "Take all this money, all these spots, all this direct mail, and save it for a big push in three quarters." Now everyone in the room was happy, even Pat.

Pat was happy because Pat had heard that AnyCompany, despite its market-leading preeminence, was terribly risk-averse. In this instance, not only had the CEO of AnyCompany supported and built the vision for the product Pat would manage, but the CEO also had bet the marketing dollars on the hope that the product would come to fruition. This seemed like risk-seeking, not risk-averse play. In Go, Pat knew that you need a good balance between risk-aversion and risk-taking to succeed. When Pat saw these practically foolhardy moves toward this ad campaign, Pat knew the rumors were far from true. Or were they?

BUREAUCRACYLAND

Back at Pat's desk, Pat looked out from the avant-garde-decorated office of glass and titanium and saw a huge plasma screen that faced the inner working area. On it was a PowerPoint slide showing the tremendous impact AnyCompany had on its stakeholders. Pat sat back ergonomically in the fifteen-hundred-dollar chair and waited for the next slide. Pat waited and waited. The slide never changed. Back to other work, Pat spent the first day thinking about how to deliver on the marketing campaign's promise. "Yes," Pat thought, "here is a company that is certainly not risk-averse with its fancy chairs, plasma screens, elaborate advertising campaigns, and posh neocubicles."

The next day, Pat came back to the office and saw that the screen was showing the very same image as the day before. "Hmmm," Pat thought, "I could put this screen to better use. No one really sees it except me anyway. I could put my project schedules up there, progress reports, or just about anything." Pat asked for control of the screen from IT, thus starting the first of many adventures in Bureaucracyland.

Pat called up IT. Apparently, this was a no-no. But because Pat had yet to go through new employee training, this was easy enough to explain, said the IT person on the other end of the line. To create a request from IT, you had to use the COAT system—Customer Order And Tracking. After reading through the manual, Pat clicked on the link permanently embedded on Pat's desktop screen.

The screen seemed simple enough: "For technical issues, press here. For e-mail problems, press here. For phone problems, press here. For all other IT-related issues, press here." Pat, not being someone familiar with the entire IT vernacular, thought this was probably a technical issue. Turns out it wasn't. So Pat had to resubmit. After resubmitting, Pat found out that certain approvals were missing. To get the approval, Pat had to use a different system—ProcessSoft—that would authorize and use requisitions and other mumbo jumbo.

Entering the request into ProcessSoft, Pat watched the process start. After sitting on many different worklists of people who only occasionally logged into ProcessSoft, Pat waited nearly a day as each approver approved and then sent the request to the next person down the chain. After waiting through multiple iterations and recycles for more information, Pat finally got all approvals. Pat waited. Nothing happened. Pat clicked the COAT link and asked what had happened since the approvals went through in ProcessSoft. "Oh, it's in our priority queue. You marked the item as a priority three—not urgent, quick request. There are two hundred priority one requests in line, followed by zero priority twos, and yours is the first priority three." "Hunh?" "Well, we don't really even get anyone submitting anything but priority one requests, so you're going to have to wait." Pat, at this point, gave it up and let the screen sit.

Some weeks later, Pat received an e-mail on how to control the screen. It detailed the login for the computer and the settings for monitor and so on. As Pat started to take the image off the screen, which had rested there for the last year and a half, Pat found that the image had burned itself permanently into the screen. The screen, forever unusable for anything other than displaying that one image, was a living twenty-five-thousand-dollar testament to the protectionism and risk-aversion that shut down more than just stray risky proposals from internal employees.

While Pat was given near complete autonomy to run Any-Company's well-marketed but not quite finished product, the process for exercising this autonomy was fraught with procedures that protected the company from graft, lawsuits, spelling errors, workman's compensation claims, you name it. Pat appreciated the depth and thoughtfulness that were part of the hiring process, but now that process was suspect.

Indeed, at almost every turn, Pat spent twice as much time getting the paperwork done as Pat did getting the work done. Simple weekly messages went to General Counsel for editorial review. Amazing talent that Pat could hire was summarily dismissed because of policy concerns, despite there being a policy, instituted a year before, that allowed such hires. Conference room scheduling was a sixteen-step process. Supplies? Fugeddaboutit: hoarding was the method of choice.

What surprised Pat about this whole thing was that the people at AnyCompany were really good. Not only that, they were doing good work. Fortunately, someone five years ago had started the process to get this work started and now it was coming to fruition. But how did great people in the company grow accustomed to what Pat called the stereotyped-Soviet-Russia-like treatment and not raise a stink?

"Vee have one laundry 'tergent. It's not vorking best, but vee don't complain. Vee aren't boorden vith too many choizes. Vee like having only one 'tergent." That's all fine and good, but what does that say if someone knowingly joins this company fully aware of the bureaucracy keeping it slow? When you can draw top performers, drawn to your brand name and eight-hundred-pound gorilla leadership in your industry, you have to be in for a shock when Pat Shmo, the person you yourself identified as top-notch, starts raising a flag.

Sure, the people perpetrating this bureaucracy and participating in this culture are not evil. Nonetheless, after a rather frustrating process of writing thirty e-mails to support a project that had already been through strategic business planning, budget planning, an RFI (request for information), an RFP (a request for proposals), review from internal and external partners, contract negotiations, contract signing, and ProcessSoft allocations against this project, Pat penned the following: "Often, those skilled at the bureaucracy are just able readers of the map of the minefield—not a minefield of flesh-destroying metal, but the shrapnel that pierces the hard-working employee's soul." Pat wondered if NewCompany had found new funders this month.

AnyCompany was both in debt for the risk-seeking behavior associated with marketing Pat's product and in debt for the internal machinations needed to get even a pen ordered, much less a contract signed or an employee hired. What was saved? Certainly Any-Company didn't have to worry about getting bad press from bad decisions made by employees—a top concern among the board members. However, that risk was more due to lack of implementation than to any lack of good decision-making by its skilled employees. AnyCompany did not have risk. AnyCompany was safe.

As Pat learned, AnyCompany was indeed founded as a small company so that it would not have all the burdens of the larger bureaucratic parent. It was smaller and was created to be more nimble than its colossal parent. But, as the parent company was pruned, the dream of the small company was grafted.

This is Go at its worst—focused on the nitpicky details of a local position, but losing the attention for the big picture, a Global Local disaster fostered by a misguided implementation of Owe Save rules. Yes, it is important to avoid lawsuits, but it is not OK to do so at the expense of any progress. Yes, it is important to ensure proper accounting and controls, but it is not OK for this to take up the majority of an employee's time. Yes, it is important to Save—to control risk, to practice safety first, to be preventive—but not at the cost of negating why you're in business. If investors, shareholders, parents, and teachers want a risk-free investment of their time, capital, or child's upbringing, then they can invest in bonds or a lo-jack for their child. But, is this life? Is this really playing the game? You can make a living playing this safety game, but you can't play (Go, anyway) for a living making only safe moves.

Sure, we all want to play the right moves, follow the known patterns. You'll often hear Go players say, "Oh, I forgot the joseki" (a researched, balanced, and standard opening pattern). So what! If you cannot get into the mess of the form, the form has no life for you. In the old days, companies would buy IBM products because "you can't go wrong with IBM." The thinking was that this was the risk-free choice, and even though it might be wrong, it was safe. Fifty million Elvis fans can't be wrong? To a heart that strives to play living Go, risk-free is likewise growth-free.

STRETCH GOALS

To really excel, you have to spur growth. To spur growth, you have to risk your current understanding and position. In that sense, strong Go players are like NASA. The Go rule for improving your abilities—"You have to risk to gain"—is NASA in a nutshell. While NASA doesn't publish its expected death rate, the actuaries that compute life insurance for astronauts will let you know what that rate is. And it's not the case that NASA is trying to kill anybody. In fact, it is pushing the limits on the knowable, the doable. With every project or initiative it undertakes, it goes to great lengths to do the risky as safely as possible. That's balance.

Ratcheting up the Global perspective of things, you can look beyond the game you are playing now—your current job, relationship, or struggle—and look at the bigger game you are playing. Are you playing to improve? What are you striving for? No matter the challenge or goal you have before you, the balance between Owe and Save will make a difference. When the game you're solving for is not just this company, this job, or this skill level, the answers you get back on how best to make use of the limited resources available to you will be clearer.

In Go, when your goal is to improve, you don't treat each game as the end all and be all. If your goal is to improve, then each game is but a step on a long path. The particulars of your emotional investment in this game, what's riding on this particular game, don't matter in this longer-term perspective of your goals. When your long-term mastery is what is at stake, you can take more risks. When you are weak, to break free of your understanding, you must stretch your mind, your play, and your ideas about the game to gain the bigger perspective.

A WEAK FOCUS

It's a pain to focus on your weaknesses, but that's where the biggest opportunity for improvement normally is. The child learning to play piano might be good at improvisation and not scales. Practicing scales will make the most improvement in the child's total piano-playing ability. If you are taking a standardized test and you are good at the verbal section, it is going to be tempting to study what you know really well. Instead, work on the math sections. Your ultimate score depends on how well you do in both sections, and the progress you make in math gets you the farthest in the Global sense.

Go is like this as well. If you are an excellent intuitive player, your biggest improvement will come from learning how to read out situations in your mind before playing on the board. If you are good at reading, memorize more games to get a sense for how pros look at the game. If your reviews continue to show a weakness in one area, that's where your time and effort should go if you want to improve, not to the things you are good at and enjoy.

In a localized expression of this way, I learn best from abject failure on the Go board. The humiliation and sorrow one experiences when one puts forth one's best effort only to see one's work collapse is great fuel indeed for improvement. Early in my Go career, I had the opportunity to play against an American-born Go professional. He was playing a simultaneous match against ten or so players, and I was fortunate enough to be included.

I had played well and was on the verge of victory when this pro played what I later learned was a trick move. The proper response to this move was counterintuitive. Instead of making a move that has a nice shape, a "tiger's mouth," one needs to play a solid connection. I played the "tiger's mouth" and my entire position crumbled. But, because of this horrible feeling associated with the mistake, I never forgot the position, or the response and the nuances of proper play associated with it. While I didn't have to be told to focus on my weakness, the key takeaway is to not let your winning games and great plays become the fodder for your improvement. The other takeaway was that pain teaches indelibly.

Those who safely reside in their strengths don't grow. Those who challenge, probe, and torture their weaknesses know how far they still have to go. For Go masters, this is also true. When I asked the top player in Japan at the time, Cho Chikun, what he knew of Go, he replied that he knew nothing of Go. Certainly Cho knew much more than me or most anyone else, but in comparison to the ocean of Go left to learn, he responded that his knowledge was like nothing.

Likewise, Cho's play at times seemed reckless. Playing moves against the established patterns, doing uncanny things in the midst of tournaments, during play in our study sessions, he stretched what he knew all the time. Even today, his moves reek of experimentation, discovery, and mystification. True Go cannot be bottled. True mastery is an everlasting quest. Individual games are the proving grounds, the furnace of living Go. This is contrary to one-gamedness.

Again, it is easy to get caught up in one-gamedness. Instead of being happy for the employee who's decided to work elsewhere, you get caught up in what this means for you now, in your current game, and then chew her out for leaving you in the lurch. Instead of letting a sale go for the sake of doing the right thing for the customer, you swindle and emotionally pressure the customer into buying. Instead of tucking your kids in, you go through another twenty e-mails. In a Global sense, it is often a good thing to Owe, to be behind—one game down in tally, but one game ahead toward a more important goal. Focus on your weakness. Focus on the bigger goal.

ACCOUNTING

To build your understanding, you need to understand how you score, what constitutes strengths and weaknesses. How do you know if you owe if you don't know you're behind? How do you know if you need reinforcements when you think you're just dandy? Why will you go forth and charge into the unknown if you think you still owe? In Go, you can make a mistake and all that will happen is that you'll lose the game most of the time. In real life, you're asking for trouble.

Getting to know what is strong, weak, risky, or safe is again a matter typically of the Four Questions explored in Global Local. There is safety in numbers. There's risk for you being in your opponent's neck of the woods. The polar nature of things also exists in Owe Save. There is no safety in numbers if the number of weak positions you have is more than one. How can you defend both when you get only one move at a time in Go, and only one thing to do at a time in life? Just as there's risk in being in your opponent's neck of the woods, there's nothing to it if you have an escape route or if the opponent has the opponent's own risks.

There's no mystery about what to do once you have the information, if you're measuring for the right things. If you owe, you have to pay. If you're all paid up, then it's time to get back out there and take some risks. Sometimes what you owe is a move to the opponent, thereby losing the initiative. Sometimes what you owe is the entire game and you had best resign instead of beating the dead horse. Sometimes, the cost is even greater. In life, where the stakes are usually much higher than in Go, you make a mistake and people may pay with their lives.

If you are controlling a bit more territory than your opponent, but you have three weak positions and the opponent has no weak positions, then you are most likely behind. You cannot defend three positions with just one move, normally. Although there are moves throughout Go's history that have done this, they're rare at best. Strength and weakness are determined by the number, coordination, shape, and timing of the positions relative to the opponent's, the board, and your own prior moves. Much as with armies on multiple fronts, you have to know the local situations and their relative merits globally. You have to determine where you owe and therefore what you have to protect, what risks to take, and where if anywhere you can stretch things, especially if you're behind.

If you're ahead, the situation changes dramatically. You can afford to take risks, but why bother? The borrowed Go rule is "Rich people had best not pick fights." When your positions are safe and you're ahead, you should sit back and wait for the stretch move from the opponent. If the opponent never makes the stretch move, you win by playing steady. If the opponent goes for the stretch move, don't panic. You are safe everywhere and you are allowing the opponent to throw the game into chaos by complicating the situation and playing out-of-balance moves. That's a good thing. You need to have faith that your strengths are a foundation for thwarting the opponent's attack. Because Go has remained a faithful rewarder of good play, if you've made the right moves, you have nothing to fear but the complications that the opponent throws at you. If you can't deal with complications, that's a different issue; you owe your development.

Go is a game of territory, and to control more of it, you have to make a greater claim to it than the opponent does. If it is your move, you have an opportunity to play in such a way as to claim the most territory you can with this one move. The rule in Go is "Play to the biggest area." Because of the nature of the board, you will find that in the beginning of the game, the two players will normally each play moves in the corners. This is following the general rule of playing to the bigger area, because you have borders to build that act like natural rock or sea borders that you can use to corner territory. The subrule to this is "Corner, side, center." It is easiest to surround corner territory because there are two sidewalls helping you surround the territory. It is easier to surround side territory than center territory because there is at least one side wall helping you surround territory, whereas in the middle, you have only your own stones to encompass center intersections. In Go, the rule is "Leave no cannon unspent in battle." If you have a natural advantage, like a corner in Go, use it.

The danger of misreading whether you owe or save can be tragic. Go back to the game in which I resigned while still ahead. That's careless evaluation of the score and territory. It's silly to invest so much, to have so much, just to throw it away on your ignorance, but I would wager that this is more prevalent elsewhere than you'd think. Think of some of the cataclysmic failures of companies that were once darlings of Wall Street.

In a variety of businesses, and going gangbusters in each, Enron was a darling of analysts and the media. All over the map, Enron was moving, extending, pioneering at the forefront of its industry. But, such "attacks" in all directions take management's attention away from such issues as financial due diligence. Overextending was not the right move. At some point, you must balance forward success with calm. When you are ahead, when you attack everywhere, when you knock your opponents backward, you need to take stock (not literally, please). You have to appreciate the balance in the game and figure what you owe. For Enron, it owed more attention to the nonsexy part of its business, ensuring that its positions were safe.

Financial and managerial accounting is boring for a lot of people. We joke about the bean counters, the accountants, and their slide rules. In that anal-retentive world, one bean misplaced and it's as if the whole world were turned upside down. Yet, without knowing the score, you cannot play appropriately. Information is power. Just one bean counter among the bandits attacking the village in *Seven Samurai* and the bandits might have won. One bean counter in your own head, focused on measuring the score, where you want to go in life, is a good expenditure of time and energy.

Yes, it's a sacrifice to lose even a moment of the glory-filled life of someone who never watches the score. Yes, it's painful to have to get out of attack or defense mode to see if that's really the right thing to do at the moment. Yes, the bandits would probably have to lose a scout to learn that the villagers had in fact a rather mighty little moyo going on in the village. A cheap sacrifice for the value in all instances.

SHORE UP

As Pat thought back on NewCompany, life seemed much better. Maybe the grass was greener on every side. Although there were plenty of skeletons in both closets, at least neither company's skeletons comprised the foundation of their businesses. It's just that AnyCompany's skeletons were the ones pooling time and energy away from Pat's entrepreneurial spirit now.

The pluses at AnyCompany were that if Pat could convince them to do business a little differently, they were in a great position, with a great brand and with great people who could get the job done. Back at NewCompany, the opposite situation existed. Built on a castle of cards, NewCompany needed a lot of reinforcement to survive the winds that AnyCompany could. While the founder was brilliant and some of the other geniuses were great, there was no bench.

Sure, with a small independent it is possible to go all out and build and build without shoring up. Most startups do this naturally. But, if you don't come back and patch up, if you don't come back and hire that General Counsel, implement the sexual harassment policy, you are staring risk in the face and laughing. Risk strikes in its own time, and a strong opponent will strike at a time of his or her choosing. NewCompany would learn the hard way if any of the risks ever manifested.

Again, the rule to follow in Go is "Play urgent moves before big moves." Following the rules from Global Local and the Four Questions, coupled with measuring the cancerous potential of small debts that can turn into large ones, you are asked to follow the admonition "Safety first." The urgent move on the board is the one that has the ability to lever the game. Because timing is such a vital part of the game, the right move at the right time can be cancer or cure.

An urgent move is like a small lump. Surely, work, life, and love are bigger, more important things than a pesky bulge, but if not caught soon, an unplayed urgent move festers into a loss. In Go, with much of the board still unplayed, it might be tempting to walk away from a fight in one section to take a move elsewhere that lays claim to a large unclaimed area, but if the situation must be resolved, it cannot endure one move away against a strong opponent. Urgent moves in life can be equally subtle and not be the most massive or expensive thing, but like an o-ring on the space shuttle

Challenger or a piece of foam on the *Columbia,* the smallest, cheapest items can make the difference between life and death. The urgent move is always the biggest move, no matter how small, when you're in debt. The rule in Go is "There is no such thing as a small urgent move"—that is, you can't consider an urgent move small.

Urgent moves are great because they really address hot situations on the board. But what if there were no hot situations on the board? What if there were no fights going on, no weak groups to attack or to shore up? Go is a game of territory, and the bigger the territory you can affect, the better. When you've addressed the main issues and done the preventive maintenance, don't forget the objective—to surround more territory than the opponent. Play big. You have to see the duality from both ends to get at the heart of the matter. AnyCompany, while safe, had played all the urgent moves. They'd finished with the 80/20, but seemed intent on doing the 85/50, the 90/66, the 95/90, and the 99.999/99, when all their customers wanted was the 70/15.

Urgent moves in a theoretical sense are the right moves. Any move that strays from the true Go solution is away from perfect play, is a nonurgent move. In the theoretical sense, if you knew what perfect play was, you wouldn't need any rules, you'd just play the best move and that move would always be urgent. However, that set of moves is far from being discovered.

In the practical sense, an urgent move is a move that seems away from the goal of winning the game, because it seems insignificant, but indeed is terribly significant. It's the how-do-we-keep-from-running-out-of-cash move. It's the how-do-I-save-myself-when-a-runaway-train-is-heading-for-me move, but in a less glamorous guise—how do I save a little now, so I have some later; how do I do this stitch so that I don't have to do ten later? The small thing may have large consequences.

In Go problem books, you have an easy measurement system for what's the right move. Given a choice of four moves, labeled A, B, C, and D across the board, you are supposed to pick the move a pro would play. A takes the most territory. B is obviously wrong because it doesn't build on anything. C protects a weak group in the corner. D takes some territory and potentially threatens the opponent. Make your guess, and when you turn the page, the labels will have numbers by them telling you how you did. A was a 9-out-of-10-point move. B is worth 1 point. C was worth 10. D was worth 7. C is therefore the urgent move.

That's great after the fact, but what about before you turn the page? In a game, you don't get to take back your moves and say, hey, the game didn't turn out as I expected, can we go back to this decision so that I can protect C? Although there are some unscrupulous people who attempt this live and online, principled play and etiquette suggest that undos are best left to Microsoft products.

PICKING

As six months crept up, Pat was going to need to decide. AnyCompany was showing signs of letting go of some of the bureaucracy. In long conversations with senior management, Pat asked things like "How precious is life?" The answer: "Priceless." Pat's retort, "How much do you insure it for?" That seemed to move the point along. Pat's new posting on the forever-slide-etched plasma screen was a quotation from Mario Andretti, "If you're in control, you're probably not going fast enough." Pat wasn't sure if people were sick of the picking on AnyCompany's problems or if there was a change of heart happening.

NewCompany was likewise looking up. After taking on some loans, the founder had to enforce discipline and sadly had to let go a large part of the entourage of friends and family. This also required policies and procedures being in place before the loan terms were completed. This former risk magnet was becoming less risky and would have been a better private stock pick for new investors, if NewCompany had needed them.

Both companies were pushing the envelope on Owe Save, albeit at opposite ends. The struggle to mitigate risk with safety, propel forward as risk-free as possible, and improve by embracing and challenging one's weakness while simultaneously wanting to succeed by focusing one's strength was alive. Was it better to make a weakness stronger, use a strength to win, or use this one game for working on a personal weakness?

Pat went to coffee with the NewCompany founder/CEO/president/chairman. Pat got the full sales pitch. Pat was sold, but just not on rejoining. The founder knew Pat was good and wasn't about to pressure Pat to move back to NewCompany. Instead, the founder said that the door was always open, the pay was always good, and the opportunity sublime.

Pat was expecting the hard pitch, the unrelenting shadowing of a salesperson on the hunt to meet quota. How refreshing that this wasn't the case. This is the tension that can kill a sale, dash the hopes of ever getting back an old employee, or even lose a fisher the fish. That tension is a key element in battle, sales, sports, and Go. As with the other Go rules, the duality of their parentage is reflected in the tension between Slack and Taut.

CHAPTER THREE

SLACK TAUT

Slack is one of the most poorly understood concepts among beginning Go players. Slack and its opposite, Taut, are vital concepts for Go. Slack is how much play you leave in a situation, Taut is how much tightness or closeness you leave in a situation. If you think of slack as the amount of leash you let out while walking a big untrained puppy, you can understand slack in Go. Leave too much slack for the dog and you are bound to get tangled (rule: "Don't play loose"). Leave too little slack, keeping the leash taut, and you are a candidate for shoulder surgery (rule: "Don't play too tight"). Optimizing slack is the balance between the two. In Go, you need to consider your opponent like that dog on a leash.

Your opponent, like the dog, has an independent mind. Give the opponent the opportunity to tie you up and you've left too much slack in your positions (just as we saw in "Don't owe your opponent"). Play too taut and the pressure you are applying on the opponent may get judoed back in your face ("Pressing too hard sows the seed for ferocious counterattacks"). The best way to approach slack comes from understanding globally what needs to be done on the board, understanding locally what is possible, and then optimizing for the situation. Be neither hard nor soft, supple nor firm, tight nor loose: Flow.

For instance, appeasing the aggressor is not often the smartest thing to do. History is replete with examples of slack play. Hitler in Germany before World War II could be dealt with slackly or tightly. In response to Hitler's military buildup, the soon-to-be allies can both appease him and allow him to build up his armies or they can force him to make concessions and not allow him to build up his influence. Should France, England, and their allies have forced Hitler not to build up militarily or consented to face numerous panzer divisions like a cresting tidal wave? In retrospect, it's easy to say what one should do. Mastering slack and taut is not simple common sense, one has to watch this tension always and learn how to use it. Without experience, you're bound to make mistakes.

This rule also functions on a spectrum. Playing tight might be right sometimes, but that doesn't mean you should play tight all the time. Sometimes playing slack and letting out the leash a bit is the best idea (rule: "Only the right tension is balanced Go").

Oftentimes teaching people that they are doing something wrong is best done through nudging and not by outright approaches. If you can find some common ground as a starting point for leading the person to the correct answer, this is much better than shoving someone's face in it (rules: "Don't remove guesswork for the opponent; allow the possibility for the opponent to make a mistake" and "Leave enough rope for the opponent to hang him- or herself"). Psychotherapists use this technique frequently. Instead of saying "Hey, you need to change this," the path to helping someone is setting the groundwork for what constitutes right things, nudging the person toward asking the right questions, and then allowing that person to arrive at the right answer without holding his or her nose in it. Sometimes slack, sometimes taut.

Expert comics are pros at this tension. Stringing in story after story with seemingly disconnected themes, the comic doesn't go for the big laugh all at once. The pro plays in the margins, keeps the audience loose. There's no crescendo, just vignettes of funny stuff. That is, until the comic tightens the noose, drawing the audience closer to the crescendo. You're too busy listening to the jokes along the way, although you sense something's coming. Tension builds, all the while the slack ebbs like the receding water before the cresting wave. What can the possible resolution be?! What are the ties! With one fell swoop, the comic wraps up the ties that held the various vignettes together and unleashes the torrents of built-up tension; the master fisher brings in the now hysterical audience.

You can experience this same sense of helplessness in Go. Playing against a pro, a strong amateur may think "Hey, this pro is not that much stronger than me." All the while, the pro is just playing with you, ignoring your big mistakes, letting you go along thinking how strong you must be. It's not until the pro reels in the weaknesses that they are revealed. "You mean all this time I had to protect?" The pro just nods, and you had best get back to your studying.

GROWING TENSIONS

Growing up, you learn to take advantage of Slack Taut discrepancies. Even a one-year-old has already mastered many of the techniques that are indicative of stronger play. Leave a computer to go read a book and the second you're out of sight of the machine, you can be sure to come back to find a baby typing. Leave something out the night before—makeup, drink, cell phone, indelible marker, anything within reach is fair game—and any slack between an orderly household and something not quite in its place is sure to be toddled.

Moving from diaper to preschool, you realize the value of Slack. If your guardian is out of the room, you are free to do as you please. While you're still at an age where you like to entertain and be entertained by your guardians, you start to appreciate the freedom afforded when no one's looking. Indeed, a parent's first indicator something's wrong is the silence of the nonpresent child. "Why don't I hear anything?" "Why is it so quiet?"

As you enter school, you're taught, typically, with a variety of Slack Taut techniques. Memorizing times tables, taking tests, hall monitors, and turning in homework are all examples of a Taut scholastic experience; a most worthy way to learn. Left to work out problems in class or at recess on your own, the Slack you are afforded becomes another way of figuring things out for yourself, a proper complement to more taut techniques.

In Red Rover, the game where two lines of children stand opposite each other and each line requests that someone from the other team run over and attempt to pierce the line of those calling, you learn the value of the tight grip and the loose hold. A tight grip is good for keeping the line together, but giving a bit as the person tries to pierce through is a better way to ensnare the opposition than trying to keep taut.

In the egg toss, you learn the value again of not trying to grab an egg thrown to you. The more of a cushion you provide the egg, the more likely it is to remain intact, good for another throw. If the egg has nowhere to go but your firmly held out arm, you're going to break it. Where you want to stay Taut during the egg throw is paying attention to the trajectory and speed of the egg in flight. The tighter you can stay to the inbound flight of the egg, the better you can meld your soft hands to mirror its flight to a soft landing.

Picking up tacks from the floor by hand is best done with a Slack approach. Grabbing the tacks from the floor is most likely going to do damage to the hand, if you're not going to go to the trouble of using some sort of implement. When picking up tacks from the floor, you'd best cup them as lightly and loosely as possible so that their points don't pierce. This is likewise not a job to be rushed. The nature of the tack is to pierce, and being taut with with tacks is counter to most people's hand treatment. With slack, you can get them with a free hand. Not getting pricked is a good thing.

In Go, there are a number of different settings that dictate one side of Slack Taut over another. When you are in the midst of a fight, you must stay taut. With each side pressing the other to go one way or another, you have to keep up the pressure. Any backing away and the opponent will take up the slack and you'll be worse off. The rule ingrained in every insei's head is "Push, push, push"— don't give in when the going gets rough.

In preparation for fighting, as in the late beginning stage or early middle game, you want to leave room to deploy your forces in multiple directions. You want to leave some play in the situation. When your pieces and the opponent's still have not come to blows, you need to be able to keep the Global goal in mind, meaning that the direction for where you want to go can shift dramatically from how you initially set up your stones. If you've been too tight in the goal, you've lost flexibility to maneuver the fight the way you'll need. In Go and in aikido, controlling the position and slack in a fight is called "ma-ai."

MA-AI

I discovered aikido on my way back and forth between football practices. Passing from the locker room to the practice fields, there was this flyer showing one man in a long flowing white and blue dress doing some sort of spiral thing to another person, upside down and in midflight, in a white and black dress. It seemed a bit strange, but the geometry of the blue-dress guy in relationship to the upside-down black-dress guy had a certain true quality to it. Growing up as a multisport athlete, I had an eye for good-quality athleticism, and this photo seemed on the mark. The relationships between football and aikido I picked up later made the picture even clearer.

For football linemen, distance is a key element to success. The distance between you and the opponent across the line of scrimmage is all the prep you have between the snap count and what you need to get done. With running plays, the offensive lineman needs to get into and under the opponent's body as soon as possible. The more slack between you and the defensive lineman, the more likely it is you will lose control of him. In passing plays, you have to master the slack between you and the defensive lineman and you and the quarterback. Get in too tight with a defensive lineman and he'll pull you in and shuck you aside. Too loose and it's easy to lose your center position between the quarterback and the pass rusher.

The distance from the locker room to the aikido sessions was about a hundred yards, and after a day's practice, I stopped by to check aikido out. I was amazed. Frank Doran, the guy in the white and blue dress, was performing some kind of magic on his senior students, the ones in the black and white dresses. For all I knew of pass protection and run blocking, what Doran was doing was a magnitude more powerful, but also more beautiful, than any sort of blocking or shucking I'd ever seen.

Enrolled, I gained an even greater appreciation for what Doran was doing. Gearing up the body to create these art forms was no two-week excursion. Just learning how to absorb the kind of throws he was doing was going to take three-quarters of semiregular practice without even coming close to performing the techniques he was doing. And just as you are taught Go, by hand, you get your ass handed to you over and over again in most aikido sessions.

As I progressed what little I did, I was introduced to the concept of ma-ai. Its literal translation is space-harmonious, or the harmony of space, but its implications were something much deeper. Just as in football, there were advantages and disadvantages to being in close and being far away. Being in close, you can blend with your attacker's energy better and when centered direct the attacker to your liking. Being in close also means that you're prone to counterattacks, strikes, blows to the head, groin, knees, and so forth. Remember, when trying to take the knife from the attacker, it's best not to leave any gap in your approach. Getting to the Doran-level, where you could bring an attacker right up next to you without risk of injury to yourself, was a large part of the art of aikido.

Too close in to the opponent and certain techniques don't work. A spear is not the best weapon to use in battle at very short range. Likewise, nuclear weapons are poor short-distance weapon choices. Too far from the opponent and it is too difficult to say your position has an effect. Ma-ai is the right distance from the opponent for attacking or defending. How far away to be and what works at what distance is something you have to learn, but the concept is important to understand. Once you enter someone's periphery, you metaphorically appear on that person's radar screen. Once there, there may be no escape from having to fight, to kill or be killed, share or be shared, bring harmony or discord, dance or flounder.

An example from business comes from the many startups that

have claimed that they fell prey to Microsoft once they appeared on the giant's radar screen. In Jerry Kaplan's book *Startup,* the reader finds that the famed startup working on pen computing, GO Corporation, felt it did not keep a proper distance from Microsoft. Microsoft signed all sorts of partnerships and licensing deals that essentially gave it rights to much of GO Corporation's intellectual property, customers, and financials. The claim is that Microsoft then dismantled the relationship and took whatever it found valuable while leaving GO Corporation in the lurch. One of the key lessons from this story is to watch your distance. Another key point is that a simplistic understanding of being close when attacking and keeping distance when defending, and vice-versa, is an ignorant route for Go, business, or life.

At a distance, the attacker can plot, scheme, or generate a stronger attack than in close. With that distance between you and the attacker, however, you are also able to discern what the best response to the attack should be. Not being in the attacker's face, you are also giving the attacker the option of not attacking. These were abstract parallels to the world of football. Having trained in both football and aikido before learning Go, I was ready for what Go had to say about ma-ai.

As your run-of-the-mill offensive tackle or aikidoka (someone who practices aikido) might suspect, you defend yourself in Go by coming into direct contact with the opponent's stones. Outside football and aikido, I learned the opposite. "Stay away from your enemies," "Defend by not being there," and "Don't get too close" were all rules of thumb I'd learned to steer clear of trouble. Now, again, I was being shown that the proper way to defend against attack was to get close, not far away.

The idea of defending up close is that you're in a better position up close to understand what is going on. Its cousin is "Keep your friends close, keep your enemies closer." That is, with friends you really don't have to worry about them, you can keep things slack. With enemies, you had best keep taut to their plans or you're bound to come under their attack without any forewarning. In aikido, there is an entire set of techniques called irimi, or entering, where you learn how best to get in close to the opponent to neutralize an attack.

Likewise, proper Go attacks typically occur from a distance. The rules are "Attack from a distance" and "Don't touch the invader." Contrary to the defensive point of view, you don't want to give the defender more information or leverage than necessary. You want the defender to have to find a way out. That's attacking with slack. By not attaching to or touching the defender, you force the defender to commit to the way out of the attack. Forcing the opponent to defend from a more taut perspective commits both you and the opponent to only one way of progressing. If you've read out all the possible variations, then by all means, attack by attaching, but, in a game replete with multiple aims and means to get to the goal of winning more territory, forcing the opponent into a corner or attaching to the defender's pieces must be a very sure path to the opponent's destruction. Otherwise, the cornered opponent can escape and counterattack your now-too-close pieces.

Playing virtual Go across different fields in life, you find the value of this counterintuitive rule on attack and defense and the underlying power of ma-ai.[1] When you find that an employee, colleague, or fellow congressperson is getting out of line, it's your team that needs help, you need to defend; it's irimi time. When you're certain where you need to be and you need to redirect the course of things, you need to run block, get in close, attach attack. When you need to attack, not physically, but perhaps in other ways, you need to add the uncertainty that comes from attacking from a distance.

Another aspect of ma-ai has to do with shape. In Go, there are thousands of pat shapes for better play, attack and defense with

1. The key to the metaphor is to look at the language of spacing. We use space metaphors and their connotations in most everyday speech. For instance, "Stay away from that in our conversation with them" does not mean that you want to stand far apart while discussing, but that you don't want to discuss a controversial topic. "We are close to a decision" does not mean that there is an envelope nearby with the answer but that soon a decision will be made. Go is a game of spacing, but to make effective use of it, you need to abstract the spaces and distances to their real-life equivalents.

cool names demarcating the good from the bad to the ugly. A move that has a good shape is one that is far enough away from your other pieces—not overconcentrated, thus violating the Four Questions rules—but close enough to be strong, flexible, and resilient. Good protective shapes have cool names from nature like tiger's mouth, bamboo joint, and small horse enclosure. Good attacks have names such as ladders, nets, and crane's nest. Bad and ugly shapes are their opposites. Inflexible, overconcentrated, and weak, bad and ugly shapes have indicative names such as empty triangle and dumpling. Efficient shapes, proper ma-ai; inefficient shapes, improper ma-ai.

As a consultant and MBA, I have gotten a firsthand view into the power of shapes and distance on life. There are many examples from consulting and operations research that show the power of cutting down on distance. When you can cut down the distance traveled on an assembly line—in some instances companies have been able to pare down thousands of yards—you reduce your floor space costs and increase your production significantly, all with no increase in workforce. Just being mindful of distance and spacing things more efficiently, you can do the same work with less effort.

Just as space and distance are keys for understanding Slack Taut, time and timing bow to Slack Taut considerations.

THE ORDER IS EVERYTHING

Aside from the coordination and spacing of your stones on the board, the other means to victory in Go is the use of timing. With each player getting only one move per turn, whoever holds the initiative has the ability to either keep it, lose it, or use it in such a way as to influence the rest of the game. Timing can mean the difference in Go between life and death of local and even global positions, and the rhythm of play can be used to evaluate the quality of one's play or to draw the attention away from positions that need attention. As much as Go is a game of territory, it is also a game of timing. Just as Owe Save dictates what is urgent or big, Slack Taut dictates that timing and sequence matter.

In Go, the rule is "Order is everything." Groups live or die because of it. Professional matches, with hundreds of thousands of dollars at stake, are often determined by it. Just one move out of order can ruin an entire analysis, an entire game. How can you make the opponent commit before you do? When do you take a profit from the customer or opponent? When is it time to run, invade, make life, or build? Most every issue in Go is a timing issue. Likewise in life.

Think of visiting your local car sales lot. You drive up to the lot with that please-don't-interact-with-me-I'm-just-looking worry on your face. You're spied by four to five sales "representatives" who start rock-paper-scissors to see who gets the honor of selling you value. As you step out of the car, you're quickly greeted with the aw-shucks-take-your-time-here's-my-card line. Your first salvo is "I'm just looking," and the unstated sales response is "Sure you're just looking . . . that's why you just drove up and parked in our lot; you're looking to buy," but what you hear is "That's fine. Take your time."

Inevitably, you need to ask a question. You try to resist, but you truly are looking to buy a car and want more than the information from the Internet, *Consumers Digest*, or *Blue Book*. You ask, "Don't you have any green ones in stock now?" The sales rep's sales alarms ring stridently. Not only have you just indicated a preference for a particular model, color, and price range, aside from general fear, you have further cemented your intent to escalate your commitment. "Why don't you come into the office and we'll see what we have."

Your heart sinks. Do you really want to enter this unspecified level of hell? Buttressed by the fact that you've done your homework, you amble on in. Throughout the dealership, you see the many cubicles of hell. Each sales rep has his or her own private torture chamber for wreaking their magic, person-by-person. It's a big purchase, you want and need the reassurance that someone is going to bat for you. Your sales rep, your personal tormenter, is typically the good cop; the dealership management, bad cop. Surveying the premises, you see the tormented in their various contortions. Some are waiting for the rep to go back to the manager for approval of this low low figure. Some are on question forty of the new customer profile. Some are haggling with the used car buyer ("Really, it's never made that noise before"). Some are being escorted from the rep cube to the next, more sinister level—financing and warranties.

"Would you like the rust package?" "This paint protection plan guarantees your paint for five years." "Our roadside maintenance agreement is tops in the industry." "Our wheel guard . . ." "Our no-maintenance maintenance program . . ." "This insurance program . . ." All the little extras, the protection of your newly inked agreement to buy, come flooding in once you've graduated from cubicle hell. And it's at this stage of damnation that an epiphany strikes. Suddenly, the order of this monstrosity all makes sense.

KEEP TAUT ON KEY POINTS

In Go, there are key shape points to most positions. Playing on those points typically does considerable lifting toward your goal. That is the nature of Go's shapes. The problem is that without the right preparation, the shapes and key points are unable to do their magic. Try to invoke their power without the right setup and not only are they powerless to help, but they can be used against you. The rules in Go are "Order is everything," "Timing is everything," and "Sequence is everything." Note: Some of the rules of Go are prone to hyperbole.

The key points are much the same at the car dealer; proper setup is the key to profit. These days, most anyone can get the invoice, shipping price, the day the car left the factory, and maybe even the assembly line's softball team photo, all online. When the market is not hot for a car, the price will typically reflect something close to the invoice price, plus some smallish profit for the dealer. If you've never heard the line "I gotta feed the kids on that five hundred dollars over invoice," then you're in for a treat at some dealers. For cars that are hot, dealers can make a rational microeconomics pitch, "Yeah, that's the invoice, but the market's paying X over invoice. Someone will come in in the next day or two and take it at this price. Why not make that someone you?"

The car sale is an ordered event. From visit, to discussion, to test drive, to sales cube, to financing, to walking off the lot, the dealer is in the best position if you follow the sequence as intended. Imagine how many fewer cars would be sold if the first thing you were sold was the rust package or the extra warranty up front. You'd certainly have questions about the car's quality and longevity. But put that sale at the very end of the process, when the buyer has typically sat through hours of negotiation and has bought into the value of the car, and you find the most profitable part of most car dealers' sales—the financing sales. Timing is everything.

You can have all the invoice stuff and try to beat the price, but how many companies are publishing their rust protection online? Not many. And not many buyers are even bringing in the full informational arsenal of what is possible. Without a detailed invoice price list of all the options and their costs, you're likely to hear "Oh, yeah, that's what the price is for the base model, but with a sun roof, auto-tint, and CD player, you're getting a lot more value than that baby." Got a complete price list? "Oh, that's the old price list. See, this car has a different CD player than that list."

Remember the rules from Owe Save. They come into play here. You walk onto a dealer's lot, you are in the dealer's territory. The dealer has the advantage. Just as in Go, you'd best play light. The heavier your play, the more likely you are to take the full brunt of their advantage. The order of the moves is important for doing this.

The first rule of any sale is not to sell price. What is price, anyway? Some financial mumbo jumbo that hardly conforms to anyone's idea of what they want. A want is a value that rarely has an exact price tag. Salespeople are trained to sell value. Get the customer into the car. Let the customer experience its benefits, its new car smell, the ditching of the old and the turning to the new. Bring the customer into the dealership, see the car in lights, see the car's shared legacy, prestige, and pedigree. This car has won awards.

This car has been featured in the press. Fifty thousand Brand X buyers can't be wrong, can they? Price is the last thing you want to sell.

By putting value first, the sales rep can probe the customer's value points (read, weaknesses). "I noticed when we took the car out that you really were looking to see how the car handles from the stop light." If the buyer's a lead foot, the seller might need to turn him to another car. "You were asking me about air bags and crash tests . . ." If the buyer wants safety is this the car that's going to put him over the top? The order of events, however, is to take up all this slack given by the customer and save it. Yes, you want to move someone to a new car if this particular one doesn't have a chance, but if someone's already in love, you'll find uses for that information later.

CONTROL TIME

The second matter of timing you want to control is the customer's time. The longer someone is at a dealership, the more likely it is he or she will buy. The natural human weakness is to attribute value to one's time, even though it has already passed. In Go, it's a natural inclination to want to save stones you've already played. Beginners will try to save positions from death as the stronger player subtly attacks them, all the while aiming at something else. The rules in Go to redirect such attachment are "Once a stone has done its job, it's served its purpose," "You can't undo the past," "Don't throw good stones after bad," and the pair "Don't give up key stones" and "Give up superfluous stones."

It's the whole notion of sunk costs. Even in very smart businesses, people want to get a return from products in which they've invested, sometimes despite themselves. Astute financial minds are still prone to human weaknesses. Made a huge investment in some technology, person, channel, or ideology? You really don't want to let it go. You know it could be so much more. You've already invested so much. The literary maxim for this kind of love is "Kill all your darlings." No matter the investment, don't throw good money, time, effort, or stones after bad. If nothing good is going to come of it, stop!

At the dealership, your time spent is your time spent. If you've already done the dance with the test drive, the brochure, with the haggling and the value pitch, you've come to a good stopping point. It's as if one song has ended and another is about to begin. What? What about price? Sorry, if you want to get to price, you need to enter the catacombs of the dealership. You're going to have to dance into the next song. Just as you have spatial ma-ai in a fight, there's a timing ma-ai in a fight.

It's like the acts of a play. In Go, you have the beginning stage and then multiple fights, sometimes one big fight, that last throughout the middle game. Each of these fights has its own tension that defines its fight's life span. It's the moment in the boxing round when the fighters are regrouping. It's the time during a relationship when you give each other room to breathe. It's the time in Go where groups are not coming into direct contact. These are the splitting moments between acts. As in a conversation, there's a time to be engaged and listening and a time when you can get up and leave. Getting into price is getting into the next act without intermission.

But, out of your area of expertise and into the car dealer's moyo, you know that you can handle yourself.[2] You're a smart, well-educated, or clever person in whatever you do. Up against the sales rep you should run mental cartwheels around the poor sales rep who's barely feeding the kids at five hundred dollars over invoice. If this is your thinking, think again. It is not the case. Not only is it bad at Us Them rules, as we'll see later, but it's just dumb. This person makes his or her living on people who think they are smarter and think they'll run circles around the dealership. It's the ultimate disrespect of the Owe Save rule. Yes, in handicap Go, the stronger player comes into the game with knowledge that can turn the tables on a huge advantage given the weaker player, but unless you also sell cars for a living, this is not even the same game as whatever

2. See page 78 for an explanation of moyo.

you do. Indeed, the very best salespeople can sell you down the river, and all the while, you think you've made the salesperson cower on every detail.[3]

REELING 'EM IN

Whatever happened to all that saved-up information the sales rep was collecting while you were on the road? When it's your time to hit Cubicleland, you'll see it. What about price? Well, what about that safety value? Your protection and safety cannot be replaced. What about the price of the car? Well, what about that performance? You could pay a lot more and get a much slower car. What about the cost? You know, although there are thousands of these on the road, I think this metallic color is one of the only ones I have seen; I know you don't want to be driving something everyone else has.

In Go, you are constantly trying to achieve perfect play, kami no itte. Any variance from perfect play leaves slack on the board for either you or the opponent to take up, although some of that opportunity is forever lost with each passing move. Measuring slack from perfect play, your moves could be scored 100 percent for getting it just right to 0 percent, not hitting it at all. With each move potentially influencing only so much of the board, each move has a value (for example, Black's last move was worth eight points). The cost of each move is your forgone opportunity to do other things.

During the car sale, the forgone opportunity is not getting some other car. The way you measure whether the car is right for you is a matter of those values the sales rep honed in on: safety, performance, individuality, less the cost of the car. If another car, within

3. To be fair, not all car dealerships are looking to sell you down the river. Many realize the value of repeat business and that once people leave the lot, they are going to learn from others what kind of deal they received. In the Global Local sense, if you're playing strictly Local sales games looking to take each customer, you essentially kill your repeat business, which is the cheapest business to get and the cheapest way to gain new customers. Imagine the power of a friend coming up to you and saying, "I just had the best car-buying experience of my life."

your budget range, delivers more of those values and at less cost, you're buying the wrong car.

Now that's a great Global perspective. Look at what you really value in something you're buying, figure out what values all those intangibles have, and then compare costs against benefits. In Go, it's picking between five or six different battles and choosing where to spend your one move. "This move helps the most locally, but globally, it has a bit less effect than this other move."

The sales rep's job is to give you no slack toward that Global evaluation. Preying on the momentum of the situation, the sales rep, if you're starting to head toward the door, will ask that ever-present car sales question in its various forms: "How can I get your business today?" "What do I have to do to get you into a car today?" "How can I earn your business?" It is fine in the beginning stage to let the uninterested come in and go, and it's OK to let the brochure gatherers pick up their wares, but once you've taken someone for the test drive, gotten into that person's skull and extracted the key value drivers, you cannot let them just leave.

Now is the time the sales rep will unleash all those trump cards saved up in the test drive and the casual discussions, and, if you're shopping with someone else, start to play the two or more buyers against each other. Now is not the time not to close. The bait has been taken, now is the time to set the hook. Now the sales rep will see how strong the tie is between the buyer and what the sales rep has read in the buyer's face, fears, and frustrations. Now, the tension between you and the sales rep can become uncomfortable.

In Go, this kind of unleashing can come when you least expect it when playing a professional. Your amateur moves have been error-prone since the start of the game, but the pro, knowledgeable about all the slack you left on the board, knows how far ahead or behind you are. If the pro decides that you need to feel the pressure, it can be unleashed. Usually happy to play the casual game, the pro can turn it up a notch and give you the real tension in the game.

With your sales rep, normal human distances and etiquette can be stretched. The rep has a wide arsenal of strangle points that can make you uncomfortable when you want to turn away from this deal. "I thought we were friends." "Were you unhappy with my service?" "I have given you everything any other car dealer in America could give you . . . is it that you don't want the car after all?" Bringing on the heat, slowly bringing in the slack, the rep raises the stakes of your basic human decency.

TRICK AND FINISHING MOVES

Not all Go players are honorable. Against weaker opponents it is possible to play moves that are poor, with the assumption that the weaker opponent will move in a way that does not take advantage of this purposeful misplay. It's playing a move that would score in the perfect play ledger as a 50 percent move, but should the opponent not take advantage of the trick play, the score for that trick move becomes something more than 100 percent. This purposeful creating of slack to take it up, with complete disregard for the opponent, smacks of foul play.

The stretch of etiquette, the use of Slack Taut tension in the sale, and the nefarious actions of sales reps have tainted most people's experience of buying a car, so much so that now there are more than a few dealerships that have a no-haggle price, and the terms and packages are set in stone. While there can still be wiggle room in the financing and other options, the general dissatisfaction with the hard sell is proving to have legs.

There is an important distinction, however, between trick moves and moves that occur naturally and are quite sound. One particular Go rule that stems from a parallel but sound stock is "Take your profit before leaving." Toward the end of a battle in some area of the board, with your next move, you can settle the battle and move on. Before leaving this area and this act of the greater play, there are often opportunities to take some profit before settling the situation. In Go as in life, the rule is "Strike while the iron is hot." If you can force your opponent to respond, while this area is still urgent, you can get a small advantage before moving to another part of the board. In a game characterized by incremental advantages, this can be key.

Barbara Walters, Mike Wallace, Perry Mason, Michael Moore, and Columbo all share a penchant for timing in interviews that uses this "profit before leaving" technique. Call it sneaky, call it callous, but it's more an artifact of timing than of trickery. Contrast this with the performance by Connie Chung with Newt Gingrich's mother, Kathleen. Connie, hearing that Newt might have some choice description of Hillary Clinton, told Kathleen, "Why don't you just whisper it to me. Just between you and me," getting in the little dig, the subtle slight, the almost imperceptible tone that can be left for the audience that forwards an agenda and shifts the scene ever so slightly. What Connie Chung did was for sure a trick move.

The master of the finishing ploy was Columbo, the TV detective. Indeed, it was his calling card. He would probe and interview the probable perpetrator with a barrage of innocent questions and then, not getting anywhere, he would begin to leave. Just before he left, he would say, "Oh, there's just one more thing . . ." and down came the hammer. Often this question was the searing probe that struck right at the heart of the matter, and its answer would often lead to resolution of the episode's mystery. In Go, better players always try to find some profit or potentially irritating leftover (called "aji," the Japanese word for taste—that is, something that lingers) for the opponent before resolving a local situation and moving the battlefront elsewhere. The point is that before the battle is over, things are still smoldering and the opponent must still respond. The moves in the local region are still urgent.

By taking some smallish area in the midst of this act, this battle, before it is finally over, you have gained a small advantage that could be considered end game amidst the middle game. These opportunities don't come up all the time, but when they do, they're a stunning, nontrickery way of gaining an advantage in the end game before it ever starts.

In more reputable showrooms, you still get the same sort of treatment. Yes, you've finally negotiated the price of the car, understood its value relative to other cars, and are finally feeling good about your experience, having not gone back to the pressure cooker shark tank of that other dealer. But still, the final level of car-buying hell is Finance.

Just as the grocery store puts the candy, gum, and tabloids with no table of contents at the checkout stand, the car dealer knows that just offering the opportunity will compel some people to buy. This brand-new car that satisfies all the criteria for a well-oiled, well-heeled, and value-prudent expenditure of your hard-earned dollars now needs rust or paint protection? An extended warranty? A premium roadside assistance package? Probably not any more than you need the candy, gum, and tabloids at the grocery store checkout line.

LIFE AND DEATH

Training in the order of moves is done in Go through life and death problems—local situations where it is either Black or White to play, to kill or save the local group. These problems are largely about the standard life-giving shapes in local circumstances, but they are also all about timing and sequence. As you look at the problem, you weigh your first move. Should it be A, B, C, or D? A is the shape move that looks critical to the group's life or death, but play it first? Is there some other move you need to make before you play A? The rule in Go is "The route is forged through thick jungle." You might think you see the path, but given all the possible retorts, you cannot be too sure. Order dictates that you'll likely have only one way to victory. One move that starts the hunt. One move that finds the way. One move to kill them all and then in sequence slay.

This is exactly what transpired during the saving of the *Apollo 13* mission. With the normal craft out of commission, the astronauts had to rely on the two-man spacecraft's power to get them back. Some two hundred thousand miles from Earth and speeding away quickly, they had fifteen minutes of electricity with which to get back to Earth under normal operating procedures. Trying all the procedures normally used to bring the craft safely back to Earth, the ground crew needed to find the one procedure that would allow them to power up and get them back, but none of the procedures were working. While Go players don't have the kind of stakes involved that the *Apollo 13* mission did, it's the same kind of tenacity and pressure a professional Go player has to weather to see if there is any way that a position can be saved.

On the ground, without a computer simulator capable of complete replication of what was going on in flight, the astronaut grounded because of a measles scare, Ken Mattingly, and others worked around the clock with slide rules, graph paper, and then a simulator to determine how to cut out extraneous power sucks and still get all the necessary procedures in place. By tinkering with the order of power-up, the ground crew was able to find a procedure to get all the necessary reentry procedures in place and do so under this most severe power budget. Any slack in the procedure would have meant the module would not be able to complete all its necessary procedures to get back to Earth.

In Go, you have to do such simulations in your head. Reading the situation in your mind's eye, you have to account for each stone's survivability for your side and the opponent's while running through various scenarios. When you think you have the plan worked out, you play the first move that will test your read of the situation. The rule "Order is everything" is the key to the survival of borderline local positions.

Likewise, foods prepared in an improper order or without the proper attention to the preparation order can kill. E. coli has killed hundreds of people whose food did not go through the proper steps and cooking temperatures. Potatoes are toxic when green, and then the eyes are toxic after they have been sitting too long. There are dozens of medicines and foods that are toxic or lethal without multiple steps for removing their dangers. In Japan, one of the most famous examples is the puffer fish, fugu. Should a chef deviate from the taut order of fugu's preparation, the patron who eats it will die.

On the other end of the spectrum, the most expensive coffee is the result of a unique fermentation process. The luwak, a type of marsupial, cannot process the coffee plants it likes to eat. But, because luwak do eat and process these cherries of a rather exotic coffee plant, the result is a gourmet coffee drinker's booty. At anywhere from $120 to $150 a pound, you can buy Kopi Luwak, coffee made from the "processed" beans of the luwak.

The acorn, a staple food of the indigenous peoples of California, likewise is a mystery of discovery. Acorns as they hit the ground are full of tannins. In order to make acorns edible, the indigenous people of California would dry the acorns for a year, remove their skins, pound (not grind) the acorns into flour, and then leach their tannins out in a stream. It makes you wonder how people ever came to think of eating acorns in the first place. In heavy acorn fall, cows will die from eating too much of the tannins of the raw acorns. Amazing how order changes things.

RIGHT TENSION

Knowing how taut or slack to keep the leash, student, or lunar module startup procedure is a measure of your strength. In the midst of a fight, giving ground is virtually always appeasement and is going to lead to a loss. In more peaceful times, slack dominates, so that positions can be flexible and able to go in either direction. Moreover, there'll be times when the order matters, as on *Apollo 13*, and times when it doesn't (brushing one's hair or one's teeth first).

But let's say you've determined how slack or taut you should be in a situation, addressed local and global concerns, have a good mix of owe and save going, how do you arrive at the right plan for your next move? What if you were thinking globally and you should have been thinking locally? What if you were thinking save, when you should have been thinking owe? What if you arrived at slack, when you should have been playing taut? The key is to keep in mind that all rules live in a duality of reverse and forward. Indeed, most any rule in Go can be turned on its head.

———— • ————

CHAPTER FOUR

REVERSE FORWARD

Look forward, you see what's ahead. Look backward, you see what's behind. Most of us are comfortable planning forward and reminiscing backward, but some of the more powerful techniques Go players use require you to plan backward and reminisce forward. Backward planning starts with the goal and then looks at the steps needed to get there. Forward reminiscing is visualizing the steps you're going to take and living in that future by putting yourself into that mind frame. Thinking each step into the future, the farther you can read on the Go board, the stronger you'll become. The clearer the goal in the distance, the easier it is to trace backward from that goal to what the right steps will be. In tandem, Reverse Forward gives you the forward-looking steps coupled with the backward-looking map.

The other benefit of Reverse Forward rules is to know that doing things one way and doing things opposite are more likely the scope of possible opportunities than just one side of that spectrum. Because GO'S RULES are dualistic, sometimes doing the opposite is as good as or better than doing things the "right way." Many people have proven that the right way to get ahead in middle management is not to kowtow to one's boss or just sing the company's praises, contrary to popular belief, but instead to stand up to the establishment and challenge the status quo. While the risk of getting fired increases, the risk of not staying at your same level likewise increases. It's important to consider Owe Save when throwing things into reverse.

TALK TO THE HAND

The dualistic nature of GO'S RULES is a confusing part of learning Go, especially since this is the first introduction to such a system. Just as sometimes you are told to be aggressive, to "push, push, push," there are other times when you are told to be more passive, to "shore up before striking" and other rules to the contrary. For many people, Go is beyond description, and indeed this is something it shares with its ancestral cousins.

Indeed, one of Go's nicknames is "hand talk." One rationale for this moniker is that you don't need your mouth to communicate in Go, just your hands. Perhaps because Go grew up with the ancient Chinese philosophy of Taoism and the practice of zen, Go was primed for similar treatment as an indescribable art. A concomitant to yin and yang, its yin-yang colored stones wrapped around each other inside a board's intersections made the game enigmatic. Go is on a par with the mystery and the close-mouthed-ness of these other Ways, but is there a need to be sympathetic to the unspokenness?

Many of the patriarchs of the various Ways have shown their great distaste for trying to describe their Ways rationally. Moreover, they'd say, because even the duality is an illusion, you had best not try to speak what something is, you had best just experience it. The third patriarch of zen, Hsin Hsin Ming (c. A.D. 606), once said, "Words! The Way is beyond language, there is no yesterday, no tomorrow, and no today in the Way." Nonetheless, millions upon millions of pages have been written on zen, Tao, the Way of Tea, archery, and karate.

There's a zen Buddhist story of a Westerner going to a zen Buddhist temple. Having heard that the Way was beyond words, he came to Japan without learning Japanese. Upon entry he was taken to the head priest, who asked what he wanted. "I want to learn zen Buddhism." The head priest asked how his Japanese was. The man replied, "I thought that zen was beyond words?" The response was, "Indeed, it is, but until you can unlearn what you have learned with those words, you cannot see it."

IN HEGEL'S DEFENSE

One thing people learning Go should comprehend rather soon is that most every Go rule has its antithesis. Likewise, the direction of one's thinking should span forward thinking and backward thinking, direction and misdirection, direct and indirect. Sometimes this is discovered much like snake venom antidote: The rule exists because of the poison of its opposite. More to the point, the duality of GO'S RULES and the universal rules of thumb of other fields suggests that you might find what chemists call stereoisomers—mirror images of compounds, or in this case rules, that likewise are effective, but are complete opposites of their mirror image counterpart.

Maybe you too have been bludgeoned with the "Hegelian dialectic of thesis, antithesis, and synthesis." From time to time, the sagacious among us will spout "just like Hegel's . . . ," "as Hegel relayed in his dialectic of . . . ," "yes, it's the antithesis that leads to the Hegelian synthesis of. . . ." I cringe to hear that from the nonjoking. There is no Hegelian dialectic of thesis, antithesis, and synthesis. It's urban philosophy legend. It's like the legend of Mikey the kid from the Life cereal ads who died from Pop Rocks and soda. While the philosopher from Germany back in the nineteenth century did have a triadic structure to his works, while these structures did seem like a progression, Hegel was not trying to say that there is a progression from thesis (a rule) to antithesis (its opposite) to some transcendent rule (the synthesis of the two). More like a Go player, Hegel realized that the spectrum exists and the experience across that spectrum is dynamic, not progressive.

Because of Go's close association with things like yin-yang, Taoism, and feng shui, Go's Reverse is bound to get coupled with those who like to talk about judo-this and judo-that. Certainly, judo has cornered the market on Reverse. "Use your opponent's strength against the opponent." "Take your opponent's momentum and use it against the opponent." "When the opponent looks to lock up, that's the moment to strike." This is great stuff in business, judo, Go, what-have-you. It gets at the nature of Reverse Forward, but is judo just about reverse? I wonder if people who talk about judo this way ever watch a judo match? The gold medal match of the Olympics is not a staring contest with the two opponents looking at each other, each waiting for the other to flub, each knowing that the ultimate victor only uses the opponent's strength against the other. It's just not the case that there aren't Forward moves in judo.

THE FUTURE IMPERFECT

Remember Pat from Bureaucracyland? Pat leaves Bureaucracyland and moves to a company called Torrential, a leading technology company with marquee clients. Indeed, half of the Dow 30 were customers and Torrential's opportunities to upsell and keep these customers was strictly in Torrential's hands. A pioneer and innovator in its industry, Torrential, like many companies toward the end of the twentieth century, was a hot commodity and an M&A target, despite having only seventy employees. One of Pat's first tasks on arriving at Torrential was determining the strategic plan going forward. In order to raise money for growing the company, Torrential would have to go to investors with a business plan, unlike in Go where you don't really have strategic or business plans in the same way. Go's planning is more like football's. A football coach can scout out the other team, know something of what his own team can do, and think of how best to react to the situation and circumstances before him, but providing a road map to what you're going to do on each play is an impossibility. It's just not a good practice to say, "In the third quarter, twenty minutes in, we are going to punt." After kickoff, you can be at the eleven-yard line, which keeps you from running some plays, or you can be on the opponent's twenty-yard line, which suggests other tactics, since you're close to the end zone. While there have been great coaches who have put together a list of twenty plays to run, no matter what, to open a game, beyond that you had best read what the other team is doing in relation to your moves. That's not to say that you cannot prepare, but we'll get to this later.

Likewise, in Go, you don't know what the opponent is going to do, and with the number of possible combinations of plays in Go numbering into the near infinite, you'd be wrong to say beforehand what intersection you were going to play on after move twenty. Although many players have their own unique opening style, it is possible for the opponent to counter that opening, should the opponent want to do so.

Nonetheless, as a former consultant and MBA, Pat knew what the strategic plan elements were, even in relation to Go. Just as in Go's Four Questions, you do a SWOT (Strength, Weakness, Opportunity, and Threat) analysis. Just as you need to know in Go your abilities and weaknesses, the opponent's, and the two's relationship to the board, the three Cs (Company, Competitor, and Customer) were the analogues for business. Strategy wasn't foreign to Pat, but providing a business plan for investors that could stand the test of inking it was something Pat had practiced more with other people's companies, either in cases at biz school or as a consultant at the client site, than in person. It's my understanding that Oprah likewise does not resort to elaborate written plans or spreadsheets.

READ

Look into the future. What do you see? One's ability to read ahead is tantamount to success. In Go, whoever's view of that future is clearer, all other things being equal, will win. But, what about winning? If a move is clear to everyone ("the 'fog lifts' "), then you've lost the opportunity to exploit a strategic opportunity. You will be in a competition to exploit the same opportunity. If you can take a move or opportunity that the opponent doesn't see, then, in Go, the advantage goes to your side.

In Go, one's strength is largely determined by one's ability to read. The better you are at reading, the better you can solve life-and-death problems. The better you are at reading, the better you can see reality. The better you can see reality, the more impact each of your moves will have. The skill is quite difficult. To put all the variations in one's mind, to play out in one's head what will happen forty moves out, is something that separates the strong from the weak. The rule in Go is "Read, read, read."

In professional matches, it is not unheard of for a professional to say "I read it out to the end game" or "In twenty moves the ladder won't work." Of course, the professional is not reading out every possible variation till end game or all the variations possible within the next twenty moves, but if one could play perfect Go, this is indeed the skill one would need to have. What pros are saying is that their experience looking forward can cut out a lot of pointless reading and get to the essence of what needs to happen in the game, taking into account the various balances needed. It's a visual, kinesthetic, and intuitive knowledge and pattern recognition that separates humans from computers and it's what keeps humans far ahead of computers in Go.

Reading out the future for Torrential wasn't going to be easy. The industry itself was in tremendous upheaval with every technology company getting crazy valuations. CBS Marketwatch, a billion-dollar company. TheStreet.com, a billion-dollar company. Pat's colleagues at Torrential, those bright, high-Q folks, had lived and breathed Internet IPO frenzy and were convinced that Torrential could be the next billion-dollar company. Unbeknownst to them, Pat came prepared with Pat's own valuation of the company. Based on standard non-IPO-frenzy economics and finance, Pat's estimate was that Torrential was worth, maybe, $11 million. Of course, Pat was soon told, "Pat, you don't know about Internet economy valuations." While we can get into the nuances of Lead Follow later, suffice it to say that reading the map correctly in these heady days was difficult.

Pat's job then became not value setting, but operationalizing the operations to achieve the highest value. Since the metric was revenue (for some, it was "eyeballs," the number of people who'd view a web page), the more the plan grew revenue, the more likely investors would invest, the more opportunity Torrential would have to get rich, and the greater the likelihood that Torrential would be able to reward its investors and founder with a bigger slice of the pie. Not the most admirable goal, given what Pat already knew from Go. Better Go would dictate taking a more Global view and managing for the long term versus revenue growth alone, but the times were heady. When reading what to do, remember, check back with the Global goals. Pat missed this one, but Pat was also under the gun.

Strong Go players will let beginners know that they shouldn't "try to read too much, but play more games instead." The point is that when you're a beginner, you don't really have the stuff to be reading out the situation ten or twenty moves ahead. The time you spend trying to read, you could be experiencing more of why a less well-read situation doesn't work. In Go, the trial is not too costly. In this instance, Pat didn't have the luxury of failing multiple times to learn something. With Go and a few hours a day, you can learn a lot and fail all you want. Pat's situation at Torrential was either sink or swim. Pat was committed to swimming without substantial trials or errors.

Pat's read à la standard strategic consulting and MBA best practices was not reading in the right direction. Pat would have been better off employing what Pat knew from experiences working at other startups. The success of Torrential would only partly rest in the business operations. The bulk of the reading needed to be done in the politics, relationships, and mess of how to get this company into gear. The rule in Go is "When you read the wrong things, it doesn't matter how far out you can read." While the business plan needed to be done, Pat was going the wrong way with Pat's thinking.

REVERSE

Reversing polarity in your thinking is key to understanding the duality of nature and finding when to use the opposite of what you need to do, to get what you need to get done. It's like turning your wheels in the direction of the skid when a car is out of control. It's like going two steps back to move three steps forward. Thinking about the opposite of what you want done to get something done is often the key insight to solving your problems. As we've seen before with "Attack from a distance; defend up close," what seems natural often is the wrong course.

This kind of reverse thinking is one of the first conceptual blocks forward-thinking Go beginners have to bust. "To attack, defend" is a Go rule that asks you to shore up before striking. Don't Owe before you go. "To take territory, take none" and "to gain, sacrifice" sound like zen riddles, but in fact they are sound Go advice. It's often a matter of context. It's often a matter of having the experience under your belt to see what the rule is leading to. But the general abstract concept is that there are two ways to do the same thing—Forward and Reverse.

In one of my first marketing classes at Kellogg, we were shown commercials and asked to raise our hand if we felt that each was good or not. Sitting in the front row, I watched as the commercials passed by and like everyone else raised my hand for the good ones and did not raise my hand for the bad ones. Since I had come to Kellogg from southwestern Oregon, the home of chip truck drivers fishers, crabbers, and loggers, I did not have the same pedigree career- and locale-wise as many of my classmates who hailed from prestigious investment-banking or management-consulting jobs. I suppose I should have expected what happened next.

On the screen was an ad of Roseanne Barr, the star of the iconoclastic lowbrow sitcom *Roseanne,* chowing down on a piece of pizza, eating it rather sloppily, smacking her lips, and getting the grease of the pizza all over her hands and face. I thought, "What a great commercial!" As the commercial ended and this gorgeous pizza-eating shtick came to a close, the professor asked, "Show of hands of people who thought this was good." I raised my hand quickly and high.

The laughter occurred before my turning and finding that I stood alone in judging this a good ad. Apparently none of my classmates felt likewise. As the professor turned to me, smiling, she asked, "So, why did *you* like that ad?" Well, as far as I knew, people who loved pizza the way that Roseanne seemed to would probably appreciate this ad. After hearing any number of times from my esteemed colleagues what a bad ad it was, we learned how the ad had performed.

Despite the slovenly approach, this ad got people eating the advertiser's pizza. Whether it was the pizza-eating style or the actress was not clear, but as far as the effect of the ad on the intended audience, the results were clear. This ad was a good ad in the sense of its success as an advertising vehicle. This ad apparently was not a good ad for driving first-year MBAs to its places of establishment. While there is a lot to be said here that we'll wait for Us Them to address, the reverse approach worked.

What we normally think of as the right way to drive food sales—entice people with the sights and sounds of an appetizing meal and then exhibit people enjoying their food—works in opposite as well. And it's just not a principle for pizza anymore. Better marketing research, as we would learn, occurs backward. Instead of asking a bunch of questions forward—"How do you like our product?"—you start your market research by asking backward.

TEWARI

In Go, this is exactly the kind of Reverse approach that is the hallmark of better players. Just as solving a maze backward is easier to do, solving your marketing research or Go problems is easier done if you just look back. In Go, this is called "tewari." In chess, it's called transpositional analysis. In business operations, it's reengineering. In market research, it's called, cleverly, backward market research. But you get the point: Tewari flows in a different direction.

Where tewari is most useful in Go is in analyzing inefficient use of one's stones. After five plays in a local area for each side, the analysis is to go through each of the five moves and evaluate them out of order. What crops up typically is the move that is not adding value. You could leave the bad move unplayed and the situation is often the same. Likewise, in all other fields, you do much the same thing.

Business reengineering is famous for this. Take any process that is potentially problematic and could be more efficient. Map out all the steps. Are there any shortcuts? Is any particular step just there because of long history, someone not doing his or her job and therefore necessitating a longer process, or did it make sense before technology or *after* technology? By mapping the process flows out, you can then go through each one and deduce the value of each step. That's the same tewari that's been around for centuries.

Even in driving down the freeway, you will increase your ability to get there faster if you are looking behind you as much as in front of you. Looking forward, you know what cars are in front of you and, if need be, what lane to change into if things look stymied. Looking backward, however, will tell you if the processional of cars is going to close off any lane changes. By looking backward, you can see what options you'll have in the future. The more options you have to move, and not get stuck, say, behind the processional, the sooner you will have the opportunity to arrive. If you don't look backward, you don't lose anything, but by looking backward, you gain. This is entering into the Expand Focus discussion, but before getting to that discussion, you often need to look back.

Backward market research is even cooler. Everyone knows you have to do market research. It's the key to understanding one's customers, and we all know how valuable that is. Asking customers questions, you can get into their heads and then plan appropriately. Backward market research does not do it that way. Instead of going on an interesting fishing trip around the bays of what customers feel and think, backward market research demands that you have some useful question to ask—the so what.

An example of forward market research would be "What kind of soap works best for you? A) bar soap, B) liquid soap, C) goopy soap, or D) powdered soap?" What would the point of the answer be? What are you trying to get at? Perceptions of the efficacy of soap? What would you do if you knew that people answered goopy soap? Would you change your product? Would you go out and buy stock in goopy soap companies?

An example of backward market research starts with what you are trying to answer. If the question is what will generate the most money for your company, what will give you a unique advantage in the soap industry, you need to ask a different question. The first thing you need to get backward to is the goal. Solve the maze backward. People aren't buying soap, they're buying clean. What if you could get clean without the soap? Wouldn't that be a unique selling point! How you get to clean is what people want typically from soap. If you're a soap seller, you had best know the first question to drive the second one.

Obviously, some soap manufacturers have done this. When asking what the first question was, they figured out backward that people weren't even buying clean. People were alternatively looking to buy an attractive bathroom ornament, an aromatherapeutic experience, or a way to moisturize skin. Moreover, when people were looking to get clean, clean turned out to be low on the priority list. Stopping acne, stopping aging, or stopping oil were higher-priority issues for soap buyers.

Some of the most famous Go games are great examples of this. No matter what the peanut gallery says, the pro about to play has no way out. The consensus is that the pro is going to have to either resign or give up something that will turn the tide of the game. Then, something miraculous happens. The pro plays something that no one foresaw, but that now is clear. In each of the variations from the peanut gallery, this move was always four steps down the chain, too late to save the situation. But, if you reverse this fourth move and make it first, the opponent is put into a dilemma. Suddenly, the tide has turned and what was a lost game is saved.

While this happens infrequently, it happens often enough that people will try this as a last resort in an otherwise broken situation. The natural order of things and the normal flow of things is good Go, but not creative or innovative Go. Innovative Go challenges and dashes the status quo and finds moves that are a bit out of order, but thereby more ripe with opportunities. Turning the status quo on its head and asking the question in reverse, top players find moves that reverse or change the standard order and make a move earlier in a pattern that is more appropriate to a situation.

This innovative approach occurs outside Go as well. In baseball, the Oakland A's are famous for ditching baseball's long-standing play or selection criteria, based on a player's look, body, speed, and form, and putting in their place base on balls. This is a great reverse innovation. Not only did it look at things from the goal backward—What's the most probable way to win a game and what players will do this?—but it turned the status quo on its head and did so cheaply.

Innovations in business happen the same way. Instead of making an incremental forward-flowing idea tinker—make the product faster, cheaper, or lighter—look at what people are trying to solve, understand the goal, and then work backward from there. Sony did this any number of times with, among other things, the transistor radio and the Walkman. The question Sony asked was, "What problem do my customers have now with the solution my products provide?" Reversing the questions sheds new light on how to move forward. That's tewari.

REENGINEERING

Tewari in the business-consulting world seems like one of those New World things that is actually very old. Reengineering took this concept, not unknowingly most likely, and created an entire industry of operations- and process-improvement consultants. The typical engagement would be something like the following.

Let's say you sell large machines to mom-and-pop manufacturers. The sales process is lengthy, but lucrative, if you get a sale. You are the operations consultant. Figure out if there are improvements that can be made here.

1. Your salespeople make a number of sales calls.
2. You send brochures to the interested parties from the calls.
3. If a manufacturer is still interested, your sales representative visits the manufacturer to meet and greet the decision makers.
4. The manufacturer thinks about the purchase.
5. The manufacturer decides to buy.
6. Your sales representative brings a contract.
7. The contract is signed.
8. Your sales rep sends the contract to accounting for billing.

9. Your sales representative gets a commission on the sale.
10. The accountants do a credit check on the manufacturer.
11. If the credit is OK, the accountant approves the purchase order.
12. The accountant approves shipping a large machine to the manufacturer.
13. Everybody's happy.

Tewari looks at the process with the steps out of order. In two instances above, the process seems broken. By changing a few steps, you can see how the process might be improved and where time might be wasted.

If we perform steps ten and eleven, before step three, what is the impact? If we do not approve the credit of the manufacturer, do we go on with steps four through nine? Probably not. How much time will be spent on sales reps visiting this client, spending time on the phone, on the plane, or in restaurants visiting potential clients who are not creditworthy? As you might guess, credit approval, when possible, should probably occur farther forward in this process.

What about step nine? When commissions are paid on a signed contract, what incentive does a salesperson have for making sure that the client is creditworthy? If you put step nine after step twelve, then the salesperson is much more inclined to ensure that the manufacturers are creditworthy and the order is delivered.

Although the art of tewari in Go predates reengineering and operations consultancies, the tewari method and approach to understanding processes—be they business or Go processes—is just as sound off as it is on the Go board.

A NET ONE STEP

Just as you should employ reverse techniques in planning, thinking, and looking, you need to realize the power of moving backward to make forward progress.

Don't be discouraged if it seems as if your improvement is waning and your progress is stymied. With a good coach and the proper mindset, you are actually growing. Nature works even without evidentiary support; no matter if the bloom is early or late, each timing can be fruitful. Likewise, don't expect to improve faster than your effort and detachment. Your effort is the impetus for change and, unfortunately, also the seeds of attachment that frustrate you when you think there's a lack of progress. Detachment is just doing your best and letting nature take its course. If you have the right teacher, way, or mentor, trust that nature will take its course. You will not walk before crawling, leap before walking, or fly before running, but you will progress with the right direction, effort, and detachment.

In my own progress, I learned that one's strength is like a spring. I had actually learned this while weight training for football. You try and try to lift more weight, but even with great struggle and time invested, you lift no more than you did before, sometimes even less. But, then, one day, pop! You can lift not just a little more than before—you jump a couple of levels at once. The longer the plateau with serious work and time invested, the greater the pop in strength.

When training at the Go academy I experienced this as well. I would study eighty hours a week minimum and would still trail behind my child opponents for months on end. But, after I knew I was leaving, my strength went pop! Go became much easier. The moral is don't give up hope when stagnating. With continued serious effort, diligence, and proper direction, your spring will pop and you'll see the fruits of your labor.

DO THE OPPOSITE

The reverse principle, unfortunately, is not well known, but its forward-seeming polar opposites are well known. Perhaps you've heard the expression "Absence makes the heart grow fonder"! Note the opposite expression is likewise, at times, true, "Out of sight, out of mind." We need to recognize the universal value of these expressions. But, as with most maxims and principles, they are often used, but no thought is given to their underlying relationship.

The Go expression "To defend, attack" says that instead of just defending yourself, attack the opponent in such a way as to shore yourself up at the same time. In Go, you are always trying to keep the initiative, because without it, the opponent is driving the game (see also Chapter 6, Lead Follow). But with a number of weak positions across the board, it is difficult to keep them from attack unless you approach defending them by attacking the opponent. The key is not to attack the opponent too fully. The Go rule is "Don't attack to kill, attack to gain a small profit." Better to keep the opponent comfortable in the attack, while gaining defense for your positions and keeping the initiative, than to attack too hard and find yourself with not just your original burden, but also the new one, the position created by new attack, that is now coming under counterattack.

Lennox Lewis did a great job of "to defend, attack" in his match against Mike Tyson. Always watchful of Tyson's considerable power, Lennox jabbed and jabbed, not to knock Tyson out, but to keep Tyson's power at bay. The Forward strategy, "To defend, defend," trying to bob, weave and avoid Tyson and get punches in when he could, probably would not have worked as well. In the same way, Lewis also kept up the initiative throughout the bout and was able to choose the moment to strike fully at Tyson. The jab was never the clincher, but it was used to gain a small profit and keep Tyson on the defensive, attacking to defend.

In zen, Reverse is par for the course. There is a story of a student who goes to the master and asks how long it would take to become enlightened. The master says that with ten years' study, the student should achieve enlightenment. The student then asks the master how long it would take if he worked twice as hard at it, and the master replies twenty years. Shocked, the student then asks how long if he worked four times as hard to achieve enlightenment, and the master says forty years. The master was cutting to the heart of Reverse.

If you're focused on a goal like enlightenment, as in this story, you are always checking, is it here yet, is it here yet. As with picking up tacks from the floor, you should not grasp so hard; as in letting someone free, you profess your love. You often need to be focused on the opposite goal to get the thing you want.

HOG HEAVEN

Reverse is often seeing something backward and paying attention to the opposites. Back in the mid-1990s, when Harley-Davidson was under attack, it used another version of the Reverse to get its job done.

A number of Japanese motorcycle manufacturers were looking to eat into Harley's share of its big-bike motorcycle buyers. And why shouldn't they? This segment of motorcycles was the most profitable and lucrative, and the competition for the smaller-sized motorcycles had virtually no margin. Not only that, but their initial forays into this market had brought Harley's share down from 61 percent to 56 percent.

But, of all the brands out there, Harley was unique. There were very few people who'd sport a Kawasaki tattoo on their bicep, or even Coca-Cola, Kraft, or Joe Camel, but a Harley, that was a whole other ballgame. Of all the brands in the world, people had a true affinity with the Harley-Davidson motorcycle. In the Way of the Harley, it's more than a product; it's a way of life. Once a Harley rider, always a Harley rider. The Harley Owners Group, its members therefore known as HOGs, was a strong proponent of the Harley way.

Harley, the company, was about ready to bring some new capacity into manufacturing production and it knew that it could compete with the Japanese entrants in this segment. Ramping up production for the bigger bikes would help Harley compete, as the Japanese had already announced their commitment to building more of these bigger bikes.

However, the plan before this plan for new Harley production capacity was to go to the smaller bikes. These smaller Harleys were not going gangbusters. The word at the dealership was "Why not try one of these smaller bikes to start out?" which was sure to raise the ire of the Harley-wannabe. As well, the Japanese had dominated the smaller-bike segments since their entry into the American market some time before and now were looking to extend that dominance into the more profitable category.

Many executives at Harley were pushing for dedicating the new capacity to bigger bikes. It would continue the existing good coordination between advertising and brand, it would stay away from playing against the Japanese strength—their smaller bikes—and the capacity would come in time to confront the Japanese head-on. It was also Harley's most profitable segment. A strict Four Questions–like analysis seemed sound.

Obviously versed in the Reverse, Harley knew the value of the indirect strike. Victim to it many times before, it had learned that a better practice in defending is to attack indirectly at first and then go after the target directly. To do this, you make the opponent stronger where the opponent is strong, the anti–Four Questions approach, and cause him to violate the stay-away-from-strength rule. When the opponent has reeled back from the feint attack on the strong positions, you are then in position to attack the opponent's weaker positions. And Harley did exactly this. Despite considerable protest from a number of executives, Harley dedicated the capacity to the smaller bikes. Pressing on the Japanese manufacturers' strengths took the focus away from bigger bikes. Despite the vastly smaller profits Harley would receive from the smaller bikes, the customers who would buy these smaller Harleys would be back buying bigger bikes later. Once a Harley rider, always a Harley rider. By pressing on the Japanese manufacturers' strength in a compelling way, committing plant capacity to smaller bikes, Harley kept the Japanese from stealing share as they had done in years prior. By moving away from forward planning to reverse planning, Harley realized a greater share of the bigger-bike segment with the smaller-size bike capacity decision.

IN-DIRECT

The English prefix "in" has a Reverse Forward life. Sometimes, it means against or opposite, as in incompetent, inoperable, or intolerable. At other times, it means more or pro, as in innumerable, incredible, or inflamed. It is this dual nature that is the compelling part of indirect techniques.

If you want to catch a feather, don't try your hardest to grab it, for it will bob and float away. Instead, if you want to catch a feather, hold your open hand out and move it carefully below the falling feather. Slack Taut meets Reverse Forward. In Go, if you make obvious efforts to surround the opponent's stones, you will fail. Anyone can see such attacks. Instead, let your stones surround the opponent's when the balance of the game dictates it. If you want to win more territory, don't try to take more than the opponent; flow carefully in such a way that when the balance is tipped, your stones are in the right position. That's direction without direction. In a sense, indirection.

For years, military strategists have employed indirection as the primary means for beating an enemy strategically, as opposed to fighting him face-to-face. When General Norman Schwarzkopf attacked the Iraqis after their invasion of Kuwait in 1990, the general feigned the invasion one way and then brought the big guns another way. Of course, military leaders are not the only ones privy to its value.

Doctors use this technique on kids about to get a shot—"Oh, wow, did you make that drawing?" as the nurse plunges the needle into the arm out of the child's view. In tennis, when you know the opponent's backhand is no good, it is often a good idea to hit shots to the forehand repeatedly and then hit to the backhand when an opening to win the point materializes. Otherwise, the opponent improves the backhand, rushes the net, or runs around the backhand when you least expect it. You indirectly lean on the forehand.

In conducting phone referral screens of employees, this is also a great ploy. Beware when screeners come on the phone and say

"This candidate is the greatest ever, we really enjoy him and we all really want to get this person a job here." When you hear that on the other end of the phone, as a referrer for the candidate, be careful. The next question is likely to be "Since we both just love this person, what areas do you think this person would most likely improve in while here?" This is a nice indirect push against your strength, your positive feelings about the candidate. To get at your weakness, the screener wants to catch you off guard. It's an indirect and very successful way of saying "Come on. Give me a weakness other than 'just works too hard' or 'much too honest.' "

Of course, indirect actions do not need to be hostile or sneaky. A great example of a benign indirect move is in the movie *Karate Kid* (warning: spoilers ahead). The kid is compelled to learn karate to keep the local thugs at bay. His instructor, therefore, asks him to sand his floors, paint his fences, paint his house, and wax his cars. After a couple of days of this labor, the kid is frustrated that he's been a servant, not a karate student. Unbeknownst to the kid, the way he was taught to paint, wax, and sand embedded the karate techniques he wished to learn. After discovering his new talent, he learned a lesson he would not have received if he had been instructed directly—just because the tasks the master assigns are not obviously useful, don't assume that they aren't; the master's perspective is much deeper than yours is.

THE PLAN

Back at Torrential, the forward planning was going along well, but the reverse flows of Pat's company's problems were becoming manifest. The CEO, the programmer and empathetic head of the company, the one who when he coded made the birds sing, tended to enthusiasm and emotion when stoicism might have been the more advantageous approach. Much of Pat's role at the company was balancing stoicism and conservatism with the CEO's more liberal tack.

Despite the CEO's nonprogramming leniencies, things were

going well on the forward progress. When Pat joined, the processes were out of control, the people weren't given the opportunity to finish one project at a time, and the product was unreliable, but Torrential still had a product on which millions of people relied. Besides, the errors were all things Pat knew how to fix—nuts-and-bolts-type things. After a few employee changes and some fixes to some business processes, Torrential was on its way to becoming a more reliable supplier of products. These were late beginning stage Go moves. They were moves that sketched a framework from which Torrential could compete, and they were moves that corrected mistakes; at least the ones Torrential could see itself. With the house and business plan largely in order, Torrential received its funding and marched on.

Strange things happened on the way, however. Torrential did not follow the business plan, with a few exceptions. Torrential was undisciplined but did good business and hit its marks, despite the plans.

Plans are localized around the time they are made, but globally relevant in the exercise you go through. Plans are not operational mandates. In Go, you can read forward all you like, but if the environment changes enough to warrant a change in direction, a change in direction is warranted. While it is good to plan, it's good to know when to ditch the plan.

That said, there are few things worse than concocting a plan and insisting on enacting it, despite all global necessities and goals. In the episode of *Seinfeld* called "The Comeback," George Costanza was in a meeting chowing down shrimp when his coworker said, "The ocean called. They said they're running out of shrimp." George sat there dumbfounded and was unable to come up with a retort. Later, George thought of what he felt would be the ultimate comeback: "Well, the Jerk Store called and they're running out of you!" But, by the time he had thought of the line, the perpetrator had already moved on to another job. George wasn't so easily dismissed.

He fabricated an elaborate scheme to see the perpetrator again so that he could deliver his comeback. He went through all sorts of machinations to set up the situation again so that the perpetrator would again deliver the original putdown so George could deliver his prepared comeback. Unfortunately for George, while the perpetrator did repeat the barb, when George delivered the comeback, the perpetrator trumped his comeback with "What's the difference, you're their best-seller!" George, hoping not to lose face entirely, made a crack about the man's wife, who, unbeknownst to George, was in a coma, which left George persona non grata.

While even the most beloved plans hardly ever get this much babying, there are a lot of situations that get close, and with much more at stake than just one person's losing face. Another reading of the rule might be "Don't fall into your plans; the one goal is all that matters." In this sense, Torrential was still OK, despite the plan.

PLANNING STRATEGIC

Don't get the idea that good Go players do not plan. Don't get the idea that planning and Forward thinking are for suckers. That's certainly not the case. While it is true that you can solve the maze easier backward, you need to have a view of the whole maze in order to do that. In business, life, and Go, you don't have the future laid out for you and therefore cannot just paint by numbers. That said, the clearer you can make what you're going to do, the better. In Go, your strength can be partially assessed by how clearly you can see stepping forward without the moves already on the board.

In doing any sort of strategic planning or improvement, visualization of the result is a good practice—not just in Go, but in most anything. The clearer the image, the more focused you can be toward it. An unclear description of a goal might be "Sometime later in life, I want to be a better person." A better description of a goal is "Before I am forty, I want to help more homeless people get into homes, raise money for three charities, and be healthier." Better still would be "Within three years, I want to help thirty homeless people get into homes; raise money for the American Go Association, Red Cross, and Help the Homeless; and improve my BMI from X to Y."

Before a professional Go player makes a move on the board, the pro will often sit and think. It's not that the pro Go player is trying to psych out the opponent by not responding to an obvious threat, but that sometimes obvious things are not so obvious. With each move on the board, some of the uncertainty and difficulty in visualization are removed. The former picture in the pro's head of how the game is going now needs readdressing. It's not that the response won't come, but where the game goes next and what the answer to the threat means is the pro's business. When you practice that discipline of stepping back from the flow, even momentarily, you can find good things.

SWIMMING WITH THE FISHES

Toward the end of 1999, Torrential had a number of suitors. As one of the last independent companies focused on the entire technology chain from soup to nuts in its industry, Torrential was in high demand. There were a number of media companies and Internet portals interested in acquiring Torrential with their astronomic valuations. Most of these suitors bought this technology elsewhere and oftentimes from one of their competitors, who had already bought or built their Torrential-like competence. After dancing around with a number of acquirers and talking to investment banks about going IPO, Torrential finally, and fortunately, stuck with the sell route.

In early 2000, Torrential had a final letter of intent from a major media company's interactive business unit spinoff. Just as Torrential was about to sign a deal with the spinoff, Pat got a last-minute telephone call from a friend. He had another buyer for Torrential. Pat told him that Torrential was expecting a term sheet the next morning from an unspecified media company. The friend said he would call Pat back in the morning. Pat informed the rest of the executive team at Torrential and wondered if indeed the call would come. Just as promised, the call came. One of the most revered companies in Silicon Valley was interested in buying Torrential. Let's call them Bates.

Where Bates was weak, Torrential was strong, and vice-versa. The match seemed to complement both sides. Bates would get strong technology that it could use in its various channels and as a complement to its current services. Torrential would have the ability to apply its techniques and competencies, developed around its own customers, on Bates's complementary set of customers. It was a great match. Torrential walked away from the term sheet with the spinoff and signed a term sheet with Bates.

In Torrential's exuberance, there were two careless reading errors that were not even five moves out. First, Torrential did not read out its own cash position properly. Not anticipating recruiter fees due, not anticipating accrual versus cash differences correctly, and therefore not making commensurate hiring, payable timings, and other changes, brought cash down faster than expected. Not reading your cash position properly makes cash the opponent—guaranteed. The rule in Go is "Always know the score." Torrential did not. While Torrential could have raised money, it could hardly bring in new investors while in the midst of a deal. Forward Reading error number one.

Without an adequate understanding of Torrential's cash position and its commensurate longevity, the term sheet was signed in ignorance. Reading error number two. Even if Torrential did not read out the cash correctly, Torrential should have read out the possibility of the deal's taking longer to consummate than Torrential's reserves could hold out. As a result, Torrential signed a term sheet that did not provide it with cash if the deal was incomplete and Torrential were insolvent; there was no exit fee if Bates backed out; and, since the term sheet was nonbinding and mutable, Torrential could be in for a bumpy ride.

As negotiations after the signing of the term sheet continued (organizational designing, meeting the teams, and so forth) through

May, Torrential's coffers were coughing. What's worse, Torrential was still in the midst of due diligence, and that fact was abundantly clear to Bates. Not only was Torrential drained cashwise, but the April 2000 wakeup call to the Wall Street bears and the crashing of the market and companies all around Torrential were still stridently ringing in everyone's ears. Market valuations were plummeting. Potential clients had that deer-in-the-headlights look in the eyes. Torrential's worth relative to Bates's worth was declining. Everyone worried about tech revenues, Torrential's main source of revenue, but no one worried, yet, about the kind of revenues Bates brought in.

Torrential took its first hit. Bates wanted to capture some of this slack and asked to alter the deal. What choice did Torrential have? Getting back with the spinoff Torrential had pissed off after working on the term sheet for so long and the backing out at the last minute was certainly not going to happen. Finding another suitor before the coffers choked was unlikely. Pat could go back to Torrential's investors and ask for more money, but after April 2000? No way. Torrential had put all its eggs in this basket, and the term sheet was not an ironclad document Torrential could use as muscle to keep Bates in the deal. Reading Error number one's head was rising. Reading Error number two's was a close second. Poor reading leads to catastrophe. Pat was stuck. "Don't owe your opponent," one of the fundamental Go proverbs, was working its nastiness in every direction. Torrential owed everybody if this deal didn't go through. This was a wonderfully awful lesson for Pat.

In Go, time is another potential opponent. Time can kill you as fast as the opponent can. At the Go academy, we were encouraged to play speed matches. We would get only ten seconds a move to think, play, and hit the electronic clock. At the academy, the room would be full of the tenth through sixth second "beep, beep, beep, beep, beep" of the countdown and then the fifth through first second "booooooooooooop," and then silence. At the end of the boop, if you haven't played and hit the clock, you lose. That's it. Them's the rules.

In this negotiation with Bates, time was definitely in the boop phase. Market values weren't getting better, cash was becoming more scarce, and the deal, while not changed too much, was certainly looking like so much fast-flowing magma . . . right over Pat's head. At any moment, the deal could change again and Torrential would be stuck in its flow. Think Lando Calrissian dealing with Darth Vader in *The Empire Strikes Back*. Pat was half-anticipating the line "I am altering the deal, pray I don't alter it any further." Not wanting to play victim, Torrential saved its hide by indirection.

TESUJI

In Go, you can play a balanced game with a number of weak positions. As long as you are clear about the final goal—to control a greater share of the board than the opponent—you don't need to fret about weak groups if the real overall score is moving in your favor. Remember amashi—play at the edge of Owe, where you pray you can save your major outstanding risk. That said, too many weak groups can implode on themselves. A clever opponent will move one weakness toward another and then play in the middle before they meet to kill two birds with one stone. In such dire straits, there are occasionally moves that save your hide that have remarkably similar characteristics, called "tesuji." They have familiar names to Go players, such as the nose, the ear, the peep, the wedge, the crane's nest. At this point of the game, Pat needed some sort of tesuji or there was a great possibility that Torrential'd be negotiated down to nothing, or that Torrential'd be out of the negotiation and left for dead.

There was no compelling reason why Bates needed to get the deal done. It had not announced the deal to its employees. Everything there was kept "close to the vest." It could continue to use a competitor's technology to supplement its content, even if that meant not doing what both Torrential and Bates dreamed would be a wonderful complementary product. The time Bates spent working on this with Boardvista, its investment banker, could probably be forgiven as long as Bates did another deal. Where was Torrential's leverage? Was there any weakness Torrential could exploit in timing or order that could tip the scales in its favor? Where was the tesuji?

Indeed, there was a most wonderful tesuji to play. The natural and typical order of moves in a M&A deal had been followed to date. Meeting, initial term sheet, due diligence, negotiations. In looking through Bates's strengths, Pat remembered to include that they were partly an editorial firm, but Pat forgot to put it also in the weakness column. Weakness? Editorial firms are very sensitive to the timing and order of moves. You never want to get scooped.

Thinking about the order of moves led Pat to remember the ear tesuji, a move famous for how it plays a move seemingly out of order, but is actually correct. If the order of moves in this deal had continued as scheduled, it would have gone one of three ways: meeting, initial term sheet, due diligence, unfavorable negotiations, sign, announcement; or meeting, initial term sheet, due diligence, unfavorable negotiations, unfavorable negotiations, unfavorable negotiations, sign, announcement; or meeting, initial term sheet, due diligence, unfavorable negotiations, no deal, Torrential death. The remaining advantage was the ability to influence the order of moves.

Pat mentioned to Bates that Torrential was not so close to the vest with its employees. Indeed, just one week before the first meeting with Bates, Pat's eager and ebullient CEO had announced to the employees that Torrential was going to sign with the media company spinoff that Torrential ultimately ditched. Pat also mentioned that the day after the initial meeting with Bates, the Torrential CEO had announced to the firm that he looked forward to becoming a "psycho"—Bates slang for its employees. A complete 180 degree from the CEO from the prior week. Pat wondered, openly, about so many people knowing the story and what havoc it could wreak if someone talked to the press. Obviously, this would be an easily scooped story.

Bates knew what Pat was saying was true. After a brief pause, Bates's CEO immediately got to work on a joint press release announcing the merger. With its release soon thereafter, Torrential had some security that this deal would not disappear.

This tesuji struck right at the heart of the order of moves. Not only was this move like an ear tesuji, but it also shared common elements with the more so-called judolike aspects of Go strategy. Taking Bates's strength and momentum as an editorial firm, and with one phone call, Pat put it to use to save Torrential's hide. Within four months of the press release, and a couple of loans from Bates to continue Torrential's operations, the deal was closed without further renegotiations. Forward thinking and movement would have sunk Torrential; Reverse order brought things forward.

One key lesson from this is that Pat certainly did not play perfect business Go regarding the M&A deal. Pat's counterparts and Pat made several key errors along the way. But one of the most important aspects of Go, also true of business, is that when you make a mistake, thereby creating Slack on the board, if the opponent does not take it up, the potential for 120 percent correct moves exist. That is, with one play, you not only take up the slack left behind, but you can take the initiative of the game away from the opponent. Would you call this a trick play? I don't, but it does show the power of Forward thinking about the order and the Reverse of that order leading to the finding of tesuji. When you take up slack left behind either or both players—in Torrential's case, the slack left from Torrential's misreading the crisis in cash and negotiating position and Bates's desire not to be scooped—you can make a move that makes those bad moves seem good.

MIRROR IMAGE

While you are looking in the mirror to go down the road faster, while you are looking backward to find inefficiencies or errors, you also look forward to see what you can see. In order to get a better glimpse of who is doing the work, you need to see not only what's out there ahead, but what's staring back at you when you look in the mirror. The forward image you project is the reverse image you see. You're always at a disadvantage in seeing yourself when you're forever looking forward at others and backward at yourself.

But what does that image matter? There aren't really two yous, are there?

CHAPTER FIVE

———•———

Us Them

Paraphrasing Sun-tzu, "If you know yourself, but don't know the opponent, you will win only 50 percent of your matches." The other 50 percent comes when you are able to see things from the opponent's point of view and understand what the opponent wants to do. In professional Go tournaments, the two players will often ask the game recorder for the game record and flip the paper diagram of the board over to look at the board from the opponent's perspective. In "seeing through your opponent's eyes" you look to see what the opponent's best move is in a given situation. More often than not, you and the opponent want to play in the same general area.

The Us perspective or identity is the proponent, the collaborator, the company you keep or belong to. The Them perspective is the opponent, the competition, the others. Shifting between the two perspectives provides a good balanced vantage point in decision-making and strategy. With just one perspective, you'll miss half the potential view.

Football has incorporated this practice for years. In preparation for an upcoming game, coaches will study game film, analyze the opponent, and coach second- and third-stringers to simulate the plays and styles of the opponent. Pitting the first-string offense and defense against the simulated opponent in the days before the actual contest allows the first-string players to get a feel for what's to come. The better the mimicking done by the second- and third-stringers, the better prepared the first string will be on game day. Whether football scrimmaging or military wargaming or business scenario planning, seeing through your opponent's eyes is vital to getting a perspective you would otherwise miss.

Seeing through your own moves is your ability and confidence in your reading ahead. At the highest levels of Go, you cannot do without thinking ahead and cannot be influenced by the opponent's moves, which could be feints, probes, or other indirect diversions from your real problems. It is always tempting to stop the opponent from doing anything on the board, but you must remember that Go is first a game of balance. You can see only so far into the opponent's mind from the stones on the board. You must build and have confidence in your own ability to read situations out. The farther you are able to see through your own mind's eye, the better your game will be. Of course, when you're a foreigner in a foreign land, it can be difficult to get your bearings.

US GAIJIN

As someone not born in Japan and not part of the widespread Japanese society, you are "gaijin," meaning outside person or foreigner. Gaijin are not expected to know how deeply to bow, how to speak Japanese, or to have proper Japanese manners and etiquette. In Japan, a mostly homogeneous nation without much diversity, you feel your gaijin-ness. No matter if you are white, East Indian, black, or Coquille, you are gaijin.

As I entered the Nihon Ki-In's Igo Kenshu Center, or Japanese Go Association's Professional Go Training Academy, I was placed in the gaijins' dormitory area up on the third floor. Right next door was my gaijin neighbor, who had arrived a little before me, Hans Pietsch, from Hamburg, Germany.

Hans was a serious student of Go, and my first match at the dormitory was with Hans. He had been drifting back and forth between B class and C class (C class was where all newbies started before the advent of D class), but was making good progress. Hans spoke English fluently and I knew just enough German to be dangerous. Together, we shared a common gaijin plight.

Whenever we encountered a more traditional non-Western

dish, which could range from fish ovary sack to oh-I-still-don't-know-what-it-was, we would both chime in unison, as if happy, "Mmmm, just like Mom used to make!" When the dorm's head-master had trouble explaining something to one of us, he'd then go to the other and try again. Since neither Hans's nor my Japanese was that good at the time, the headmaster thought that perhaps his English would work on one of us. It usually didn't, but it was fun to laugh about the attempts.

As gaijin, we were encouraged to do things gaijin would do while also getting pressure to be more Japanese. For instance, gaijin at the academy were encouraged to help people practice their English, but we were still mandated to follow the center's rules. If you played your cards right, you could try to get the best of both worlds—speaking English and flouting the rules because you were "just a gaijin who didn't know any better." Sometimes this worked, sometimes not, and sometimes never.

Bathing in Japan is an example of cultural differences. You don't get into a bath to get clean, you get into a bath to be part of the commune, of the society. In order to get clean, you need to wash before entering the bath. Gaijin who attempt to use the bath before cleaning are quickly corrected. No exceptions. Sullying the bath water is a big no-no; you must bathe and rinse before even thinking about bathing.

It's assumed that gaijin cannot learn to bow. Bowing is a language only partly about deference, and as such, it cannot just be picked up and spoken fluently. While there are some basics—the more senior person or person with more power usually bows less than the more junior, more subordinate person, who's supposed to bow more deeply—they don't always apply. There's sorry bowing, sarcastic bowing, greetings bowing, and oh-thank-you bowing, among thousands of other nuances. Getting sick of all the formality of bowing, Hans and I would bow deeply and humbly before starting our matches and shock the locals with what seemed like very serious bowing. Over time, we conformed more, but we never lost the tinge of irreverence.

This irreverence was sort of quid pro quo for Japan, since many Japanese words in everyday speech are borrowed English words. Since Japan has a strong relationship with the United States culturally as well as politically, you could actually find quite a bit of U.S. culture scattered around Japan. The problem for Hans and me seeking these spots out near the academy was that the Japanese translate English into "katakana." Katakana is the way Japanese write foreign words, and because there is not a one-to-one correspondence between Japanese and English sounds, you can imagine the comic horror of reading something in katakana that said, phonetically, "Rubba Me Tenda," which was supposed to be the title of the Elvis Presley song "Love Me Tender." Two very different meanings.

But without getting into the perspective of your foreign host, you become the "ugly foreigner"—someone who assumes that things will be the same in the foreign country as they are at home. When you try to move your perspective from Them to Us, taking on the host country's perspective, you notice more of how you should behave, what things mean, and where you have latitude as a foreigner. For most people, this makes visiting or staying in a foreign country a richer experience. Putting yourself in someone else's shoes, even if they are Japanese wooden geta, can make a world of difference.

"SHU, HA, AND RI"

Before you can start putting your mind into Them, you need to know something of yourself and how to improve in an art, sport, or other field. Once you've got a handle on Us, then you can start taking on Them. There are many people who are quite satisfied knowing only Their problems, never looking at themselves as the We that needs improvement. For those who already know that the greatest enemy is more likely oneself, here's Go's way to improvement—SHU, HA, and RI.

Toyota Motor Corporation has a long history of Go-playing

company leaders. The Toyota Motor Company president from 1975 to 1976, Toyoda Shoichiro, would ask new employees to apply Go mastery techniques to manufacturing cars:

> The game of Go make[s] use of the three basic concepts of SHU, HA, and RI. SHU means to absorb all the basic knowledge thoroughly. HA means to try an approach that is different from the approaches one has used previously. RI means to develop new approaches, unique to oneself. These same concepts can also be applied in work. Your minds should be flexible enough to absorb whatever new knowledge may become available. You should approach work with a burning conviction to do well. And you should remember that you, personally, are creating products which will be useful in society.[1]

In every endeavor, the basic forms have to be learned. This is what Mr. Toyoda called SHU. These are like the three Rs of elementary school, the basic techniques of driving, or as in tennis the forehand, backhand, overhead, volley, half volley, serve, and service return. No matter what the field, there is no escaping the basic forms. Without a basis in the basics, your game is baseless. In Go, there are opening patterns and strategies to understand, middle-game techniques to master, and end-game skills to help finish games and evaluate situations. With gaps in any of these skills, you end up reinventing the wheel when you play. Knowing the basics is the first step toward mastery.

After learning some of the basic forms, you will find that you are stronger in certain areas than others. Certain styles and approaches will be more comfortable to you. Challenging your comfort zones, however, has a number of benefits. You get a sense for where you are strong and weak and may learn that you can also use a different style or form. You should try ways that are unfamiliar to you, ditch your comfort zones, and challenge yourself to pioneer. In Go, if

---

1. From "Open the Window: It's a Big World Out There!" Published by *Toyota Kaikan*, October 1993, p. 17.

you like to play games that focus on influence—moves that focus on the future versus the present—you might be well served playing games that are more territory (present versus future) oriented. This confronting of comfort zones is part of the essence of HA, the second way to mastery.

Each of us is unique. The concept of RI is putting this uniqueness to the fore once the basics are mastered (SHU) and various approaches to the game have been tried (HA). Bruce Lee did this with jeet kune do. He took elements of Chinese gung fu, boxing, and many other styles and formed something truly unique to Bruce Lee. In Go, it is sometimes easy to tell which professional is playing by his or her style. Takemiya plays his initial moves on points that are geared toward the center of the board, and plays what is called a "cosmic style"—outside influence is the hallmark of his game. His longtime rival in the late 1980s and early 1990s, Kobayashi Koichi, plays what has been called "submarine Go," or moves that take territory, geared toward the edges and corners of the board as opposed to outside influence. It was the ultimate clash in styles and, due to their great rivalry, shows that there is no one style that dominates all others. Since everyone is unique and Go is so open to different approaches to play, your own style is your best bet for improving beyond the basics. This is part of RI.

In my own Go career, I tried to follow this path. When I was first learning how to play, I read every technique book I could find. From books on tesuji, to life and death books, to books on joseki and fuseki (opening strategies), to end-game play, middle-game play, how to combat trick plays, no Go book would go unread. As I began to try out these forms, I found that my book learning was not terribly effective, but with time, this background in the basics was a good foundation—SHU. The stronger I got, the more I found that there were all sorts of ways and styles in which to play. I tried them all. Outside influence strategies like san-ren-sei or the Chinese fuseki. Territory-oriented strategies like playing one's initial moves on the 3-3 point, or playing "submarine Go"—HA. Upon entering the Go academy, I found the inspiration and way to develop RI. Cho Chikun, Tei Meikou, Nakazawa Ayako, and other professionals were inspirations to go beyond styles and develop something that contributed uniquely to the game. That could only come from me—RI.

BALANCE

Knowing that you need to start your improvement on the Us side, knowing that SHU, HA, and RI are the path to better play, you still need to learn that balance is an essential element of the game.

In Go, as in nature, balance and imbalance have tremendous ramifications. An unbalanced newspaper article smacks of partisanship. A balanced tightrope walker stays alive. An imbalance in resource distribution makes one person rich, another poor. An imbalance in your inner ear and you'd best not try to pass a roadside substance abuse agility test. Balanced budgets, happy CFOs. Unbalanced hormones, rebellious teenagers. A balanced fighter or running back keeps fighting or running, an unbalanced one falls. In Go, you either respect this balance or suffer from your ignorance.

The Go-playing balance-advice column in a newspaper might read something like:

"Can't I get my cake and eat it too?" Lose both.

"I want to be a great ballerina, but I don't want to give up my weekends." Be the best weekday ballerina you can be, then.

"I love to eat, hate to work out, don't want to diet, but want to look thin. What should I do?" Pick.

"We strive to get our customers the lowest price, the highest quality, and the fastest delivery." Your loss.

The point is not that the questions are necessarily impossible to solve, but that the disrespect of balance is rampant. Go and life are about trade-offs. You can't visit all the good restaurants of the world. You can't view all the good views. You can't tell all the good stories. You always trade one thing for another. You have to respect that nature. Balance is elementary.

In Go, you get smacked in the face with this early in your development. Early on (and even much much later), players will say things like "I want to control everything.[2] The opponent should get nothing." This is an early stage of most everyone's development, with occasional lapses later on. Despite the opponent's getting a move for each of yours, despite the opponent's seeing exactly what you play on the Go board, despite an equally resourced and equally matched opponent (if you are using handicaps appropriately), most everyone who's ever played Go has at some time thought, "The opponent should get nothing."

This is like chess. In chess, it is natural for the game to end with the other side having just the king remaining; all the other pieces on the board are yours. In Go, the object is not to force attrition down to the king. In fact, that sort of thinking can be detrimental to the overall goal. The goal in Go is to win by controlling 50.1 percent or more of the unoccupied intersections on the board. If you are overextending yourself across the landscape to keep your opponent from getting anything, you are everywhere a potential target. In equally matched matches, you learn rather quickly that the one-side-ought-to-take-all mindset is a quick rout to defeat. Balanced approaches that take only what the board and the opponent give you are a more likely route to winning.

Why? Because the only opportunity you have with such an equally resourced opponent and an environment that hides nothing and is equally open for the taking, is what the opponent gives you. You cannot create more intersections. You cannot remove the opponent's stones without forcing them off. You don't get one more move than the opponent. You are forced in Go to compete solely by taking up opportunities the opponent leaves you.

Go is not alone in this. There's a great parallel in aikido. An expert swordsman confronted the founder of aikido, Morihei Uyeshiba. The swordsman had heard the stories of the founder taking on and humbling all kinds of martial artists. Obviously, this

2. One thing to be wary of is the seemingly lax opponent. In my own matches, I have a tendency to fall into my opponent's mood and rhythm. When the opponent plays lax move after lax move, I begin to fall into thinking called the "god complex"— "everything I want to do on the board is possible, I can do no wrong." That's the quickest route to one's demise.

was some sort of rural legend. The swordsman got the founder to come out and at quite some distance the swordsman readied his attack. Against the unarmed founder, he only had to wait for his opening. He only had to look . . . for . . . an . . . opening? After approximately ten minutes, sweat beading his brow, the swordsman understood, bowed, and asked the founder's forgiveness. There never was an opening. Because when you have only what the opponent leaves as an opportunity, and there is no opportunity, there is no attack.

Osensei, as he was known, would often tell his students, "I hit him with the biggest thing I knew, the Earth"—his team, as it were. He was aligning himself with the universe, so any attack, any transgression was felt the way a spider feels every touch on the web. His coordination with the universal ki, or life force, was so attuned that once when fighting as a soldier, as he was being shot at, he was able to dodge bullets. To this day, many people still question the founder's "powers," but in many videos and in many of the stories of his many still living students and witnesses, none question those stories' veracity.

This is Us and Them at a transcendent level. Through his years of martial and spiritual training, he arrived at this enlightenment one day as the universe bathed him in golden light. To this day, many adherents of zen, yoga, and other Ways experience this same sort of universal rapture. Seek and you shall find.

This idea of there being no opening is exactly what you would expect in perfect Go. An attack is an aberration, its assumption is that things are out of balance and that gain can be made. In Go and in life, there is a bias toward defense. The defender is already there. The attacker is moving in on the defense. In some Go situations, the defense has an advantage of 4-1. While there is a distinct imbalance between attack and defense, defense does not hold all the cards. To compensate, the one natural advantage the attacker has is that the attacker knows when and from where the attack is coming. In the game of Go, where there are no hidden moves and every move once played stays, sneak attacks are tricky. Osensei, in tune with the universe, of course knew anything that the attacker might do. Fortunately for the attacker, he was skilled enough to know that Uyeshiba knew this.

Of course, people don't play perfect Go. By our best estimates, top players play four or five levels weaker than 100 percent correct, which is amazingly close to perfect given there are nearly 10^{170} distinct ways Go wars can ensue.

Throughout the centuries an entire vocabulary has been developed to talk about balance and its ramifications for the game. If the opponent takes one of two points within a position, you'd best take the other. This is called "miai." Opening patterns that reflect a tradeoff between the two opponents where one gets power while the other gets real profits are called joseki. Off the Go board, balance is the conscience little listened to but often claimed.

Try to tell someone he's off-balance. Even if you're right, the reception is likely to be partial, unbalanced. Tell your very successful CEO that her programs are too aggressive and that the company could do better under more passive management . . . you're one step from slipping on pink. The issues surrounding these admittedly fringe challenges are that balance is not part of our daily practice and that discussing it can be difficult. Balance is seen as a good idea, but it is not part of our vernacular. But balance is the law. Take some from this side, the other goes down—the law of the balanced scale. Put all your eggs in one basket instead of diversifying across baskets, you're taking chances you don't need to. Add a credit to one side, take a debit from the other. Got your ear fluid out of balance, be out of balance. Be ready and balanced so that you can go in any direction and you're in a better place to return a serve in tennis, defend yourself in your martial art, create a product that more closely matches a customer need, or keep yourself alive on the tightrope. We all understand it, but we deny it when it's not convenient.

Worse yet, there are zealots of balance who are perpetual fence-sitters. Whether the lukewarm folks of religion, the chutto hampa players of Go, or the moderate stone-throwers at every and any political campaign, the moderation zealots are not great because they are in between. In Go, this is easy to see, but how to see it elsewhere?

If you think of balance as a metronome that swings from side to side with a little beanie up top, perfect play is the path of that beanie. The most ardent, but still perfect Go, yin play, the far left reach of the metronome. The most ardent, but still perfect Go, yang play, the far right reach of the metronome. A perfect balanced play in the middle of the spectrum, the top of the metronome's arc. Those moderate, lukewarm, fence-sitting goobers are not even close to the top of the metronome's arc, but there somewhere close to the lowly middle of where the metronome's arm originates.

In Go, you deal with the unbalanced and those straying from the better course by taking what they leave on the board. Oh, being too wishy-washy, let me help clarify the situation. Oh, being too aggressive, that's fine, at some point you'll be overextended and I'll get the opportunity to strike back. But this is seeing things from your own perspective.

THEIR TOWN

You are responsible for your own work. Just as experience comes only to those who do, your game is only what you make of it. You can spout the formulae, you can read directly from the Way of Go, but at the end of the game, it's no defense. If you cannot put the concept to use, it is no use spouting. "Blah Blah publication says that we should implement the X (insert latest buzzword or acronym). It's the latest thing and all the experts love it." "Yada politicians ran their campaign this way and they won. We should do that." "The Johnsons went to a marriage counselor and they were put on a regimen of paraphrasing and cold turkey." Every suggestion under the sun may be true Go for some game, but you control what you play. Your game, your play, your deal.

It's tougher than you first think. Imagine that you're the president. You have all the information under the sun, you can weigh things no one else can possibly see or gather, and when the buck stops at you, you can ask for all the advice, assemble all the experts, but you have to make the call.

In Go, your analysis of the game and the situation is your basis for deciding how best to move next. Paying attention to GO'S RULES, you try variations and look for a way through the opponent, improving on your past plays, and try for the one best move. However, if this is as far as you go, you'll be worse off.

Most times, the opponent is going to need to look at the same areas you are in order to push the game his or her way. The rule in Go is "Your opponent's best move is your best move." Part of the reason is obvious: When you're always trying to thwart what the opponent is doing, your opponent can't piece things together well. The other, almost more important reason, is that oftentimes, the opponent's move *is* your best move. In life and death, in the beginning stage, in the middle game, and even into the end game, the opponent's designs and best approach are usually a good approximation of what's best for you.

It's the same gift-giving strategy your parents or guardian gave you when you were a kid. Instead of getting your friend some random present, you'd be told, "Get him something you'd like." While this was bound to fail sometimes, it succeeded more often than it failed.

WHO ARE YOU?

Most of us have this idea of who we are. Without getting too philosophical about identity, it is a key concept for one's strength in Go and those who want to learn from Go's wisdom to look at identity in a new way. Let's go back to the business strategy idea of the 3 Cs—company, customer, and competitor. Company represents your company, your interests, and your incentives. It is the service provider, the product producer. Customer is the consumer of that product or service. Competitor is anyone or anything that stands in the way of that company's providing that customer that product or service. All three designations can apply to yourself.

Let's say you diet. You diet because you, as the company, have it in your best interest to keep healthy, fit, and the like, because the body, your customer, wants it that way. The competitors to your diet are those working around the clock to keep you from eating healthy and following the regimen of your diet. The customer, your body, is the competitive field over which company and competitor interact.

Enter your favorite food that is not part of the diet's regimen (pretend, if you've never been on one). The competitor, your hunger and longing for that food, wants to provide that food's service and product to the body, the customer. The company, your predilection toward the diet, wants to get other, healthier foods into the body. The company, seeing that food is already in the house, already on the shelf, and within a stone's throw of the body, takes action and starts to throw the fattening food in the garbage.

The competitor, finding the fattening food is about to get dumped, starts a vicious political campaign to keep it. "What's one little morsel going to hurt? It's your favorite!" "This is the last time. After this, you can stop. Imagine the taste, the thrill of eating it." "Wasn't this diet just labeled a fad on that news show? Maybe it's all bunk." "How long do you want to live anyway? I mean, if the meteor hits tomorrow, what was the point of not eating your favorite thing? You die anyway."

Not only does this competition go on, but there are different time zones involved. The company is interested in the long term. The company plan is looking out three, maybe even twenty years. The competitor is looking at the short term. While a lot of people complain about companies that pay attention to quarterly results, this competitor is only interested in instantaneous results. The customer, the body, all the while, is getting hungry.

The company goes to the negotiating table with the competitor. "Let's say we just hide the food from the customer?" "Uh, why?" "That way, you can still get to the food at some point and I won't have to go all out against you." "OK, but can I get a bite in before I put it away?" "OK, but just a small one."

If you think this conversation never happens, you've never really known anyone who's struggled on a diet. Maybe a diet is not your thing, but perhaps this sort of internal negotiation sounds familiar in a different context. There are different roles the same entity can play.

Coordination is stronger than sheer strength. Take two strong Go players against a weaker player. On a one-on-one basis, either stronger player is likely to beat the weaker one nine or more times out of ten. But, if you pair the two stronger players and they are not able to talk to each other, the match becomes more even. With your own thoughts, you might be at odds, but two heads are certainly not better than one if there is no communication. Go, when it is management by committee, is certainly three stones weaker. If the two could communicate in private and at length, they might do better, but it's all a matter of coordination.

PRETZEL LOGIC

As you move in and out of the various personalities and roles, trying to assess who's who and what's what, you are taking a lot of time off the clock if you're playing a timed game. Just as timing is a key element in Slack Taut, your analysis time in Us Them can get tight. Given enough time, you are sure to have a better analysis, but as in most things, the value of your analysis tapers as time passes by. But if you never get to the analysis, you'll miss out on defining what needs to be done.

The pretzel you can get tied into is pretty confusing. Consider Torrential. Who was Pat's competition? The other technology competitors? Yes. Other substitutes for Pat's technology? But what about the liberalism of Pat's CEO? Without the threat of getting scooped, Bates might have never made the move it did. What about one of Torrential's customers who had the nasty habit of torturing himself and Torrential's services? How about time, as it was running out, toward the end of the Bates negotiation? Bates?

Who was Pat's company? Pat's fellow employees? Yes. Torrential's investors? Possibly. What about Torrential's loyal customers who were out there telling their friends to use Torrential services? What about Torrential clients who were giving referrals? Even Torrential's competitors were proving the market to Torrential's investors, driving up the value of Torrential's stock by virtue of competitors' proving that a market was there to take and giving Pat fodder and thoughts about how Torrential might improve its services.

Torrential's customers were easy enough to figure out. The people who paid Torrential for its products were certainly its customers. But what about Torrential's employees? Wasn't it selling them on why they should do this or that? Certainly when recruiting them Torrential treated them all like valued customers. The competition? In three separate private stock offerings, Torrential acquired companies and then was bought by Bates. For competitors to the clients Torrential served, namely the other companies it sold to, weren't these competing technologies all Torrential's customers?

Now, come back to strategic planning. In Go, the competition can be yourself as much as it is the opponent. There's a world of difference between the opponent's winning the match and your giving the match away. Likewise, you can be the customer. Helping your own progress, goals, and improvement, you should treat yourself as you would any customer. It's easy enough to see yourself as you, the company, but sometimes you have to remember not to hurt yourself. Realize that you are not the competition. Treating yourself as the customer is sometimes the right change in attitude.

Across the board, the opponent, by prodding your weaknesses again and again, often helps you more than you could ever help yourself. That frustration at losing might compel you to really understand your weakness. While the opponent's also the opponent and sometimes the recipient of the lessons you have to teach, the twists on who's who is important.

As the game progresses, you might find that you have a peaceful game in which every move leaves plenty of free intersections unplayed. If you cordon off your areas and don't enter the opponent's neck of the woods, the opponent may reciprocate and stay out of your areas. To the extent that the two of you don't disagree, the board is unfilled, with many more vacant intersections at the end of play than there would be if you two were to fight for every point of territory.

In other games, fighting over who has more leads to skirmishes all across the board that leave the entire board covered in black and white stones. With most intersections filled, the total score per side would be much lower. But the goal in Go is not to leave vacant intersections, it is to control more of the board than the opponent.

In this sense, the board is indicative of what happens in a price war, political mudslinging, or spousal fight. The fewer skirmishes, the more vacant intersections there will be for each side. The more skirmishes, the fewer vacant intersections there will be for each side. In the price war, the board eats more stones. In more cooperative competition, there are more vacant intersections for each of the players.

In training, the teacher in Go sometimes does things not for the sake of the Go board but for the student. If the student doesn't like to fight, raise a fight. If the student gives way too often, take as much as the student gives. The responsibility of a teacher is to make it hurt in the lesson so that the student need not learn the lesson when the stakes are for real. For the teacher, the opponent, the They, in a teaching game is not the student, but the student's weakness.

The student has a great responsibility as well. While the student cannot hope to best the master, the master will still make mistakes. The student must try to catch these mistakes when the master doesn't see them. The benefit the master gets is that the student is not entirely versed in the forms, so the student's spirit and understanding are less reliant on pat patterns. The advantage is that that student's efforts and spirit, if honed the right way, can be a hotbed for unique approaches and styles. Just as each student has RI waiting to get out, the teacher has to appreciate and find when the student is introducing something new or pointing out a mistake the teacher is making.

GET PERSPECTIVE

That all said, it is very hard to be objective about your own work. Rank beginners often explain how they played here or there and therefore lost the game. While it is good to review on your own, getting another person's perspective on your games can open your eyes, as long as you are open to it. Many times, it is the "bad move" that actually gave that beginner a chance and the supposedly "good move" that lost the game. Without the right perspective, you are bound to think you are right despite being horribly wrong. They, be they teachers, opponents, or just you at a future time, can be your best helpers.

The order, from best to worst, on getting perspective on your play is: Have someone three or four ranks stronger review your games; have someone who did not play the game, at your rank, do an evaluation; review with your opponent; or wait some time before going back to the game to review it. In life, if you can afford to hire a guru, management consultant, doctor, or lawyer, great. If not, just having people unfamiliar with your situation might shed light on the issue because they haven't been in it. If not, are there any opportunities to communicate with your opponent about the situation? If all else fails, getting some time away from the issue at hand may be enough. All of these techniques beat thinking in the heat of the moment, reviewing immediately after, or not reviewing at all. Getting perspective means getting distance, emotionally, intellectually, and psychically.

This accounts for my progress in moving up the Go ranks. Learning to play Go as I did is the best possible way to learn for an adult. I always had excellent teachers and was always able to get the brutal truth about my game, even when I didn't want to hear it. Weaker player habits were never allowed to form, as I always had a mentor to say, "That is not the way to play."

Employment as an outsider post-Go was also an eye-opening experience. As a management consultant, you are often brought into a company where the problem seems obvious—an "emperor's not wearing any clothes"–type thing. In various engagements, I saw firsthand how wrapped up and myopic we can get in our own world. In most cases, the value of the consultant is easily justified for that outsider perspective.

Of course, if you are the person trapped in your own myopia, you don't want to be sold simple solutions from some management guru who is going to bail after collecting ten thousand times what the average employee in the company makes for telling us "G, U R U." Kibitzers are rarely an appreciated breed.

Traditional Go boards likewise reflect this disdain for kibitzers. When samurai played Go, it is well known that if some commoner were to interrupt their game, they'd slice off the kibitzer's head and place it under the board as a warning to other potential kibitzers. Indeed, on some consulting engagements I have been on, this tradition looked as if it might make a comeback. Even today, traditional boards, which are still lined with a sword dipped in ink, sport a small cutout underneath them. Today, the purpose of this small gap under the board is to improve the resonance of a stone striking the board, although everyone knows its more grisly legacy—to make room for the heads of kibitzers.

Once you have selected a master, *listen.* If the master says play fast games, play fast games. If the master says forget strategy, get better at tactics, forget strategy and focus on tactics. Moving from one master to another is OK in a short selection process, but once you have placed your bets on this master, unless the master is certifiably incompetent, learn, follow, absorb. You might be learning something that you cannot see, but the master can.

IMPROVING WITH THE FOUR QUESTIONS

There is a human bias to favor working on one's strengths and not on one's weaknesses, contrary to the Four Questions admonitions. As previously mentioned, if you ever had to take the SAT, GRE, GMAT, GED, LSAT, MCAT, and so forth, you probably were stronger in either the math or the verbal component. Let's say you were stronger in verbal (transpose math, if you were a math wonk). Every time you'd do the verbal section of the test, you felt good.

Not only did you succeed more, but you felt better after finishing the sections. You were in your element. Not only in the test, but in prep for it, verbal practice was something you could go the distance on. You were so good that you could even start to analyze the esoterica, the subtleties of reading comprehension deconstructionist dilemmas, say. We humans are predisposed to playing too close to our strengths.

If your weakness is really math, then you need to spend time bettering your math, so that your overall score is better. If you are getting 95 percent correct in the verbal, but only 60 percent correct in the math, that esoterica review to move from 95 percent to 100 percent in the verbal component is going to take nearly the same resources as moving you from 60 percent to 80 percent in math, but no one likes to focus on his or her weaknesses. However, a score of 100 percent verbal and 60 percent math is still worse than 95 percent verbal and 80 percent math. Sure, you may be taking the test for the fun of doing verbal questions, but more likely the big goal is to get the best aggregate score; hence, study your math!

Whether studying for a standardized test or deciding where best to locate a new store if you own a chain, you're only half-done if you've looked only at your own weaknesses and strengths. Turning the camera around, you need to see what your opponent is doing. Just as you have your favorite strengths and to-be-worked-on weaknesses, you need to see what the opponent's strengths and weaknesses are.

Take your typical spy movie. Throw the spy against hundreds of goons armed with guns, nunchakus, and rocket-propelled grenade launchers, and the spy walks away unscathed through the mess of goons lying all around. But capture the spy's kid brother, lover, or pet and the spy is helpless. This is the epitome of playing closer to weakness and away from strength. Your opponent may try to thwart your strengths, but in the end the simple move against your weakness proves the thing that can disarm you. If you can treat your weaker subjects or places for improvement like the spy's Achilles heel and put yourself in the shoes of the spy's nemesis, you see what a compelling target that weakness is. Transcending identity and making it work for you, Us Them gives you the tools to do for yourself things that would make sense only to your opponent.

In Go, as in life, you don't get an opportunity to do too many things at once, but to the extent it advances the goal, the more things you can accomplish well at one time, the better. So it is with the Four Questions. If you can find a move that is close to your weaker stones, far from your strong stones, close to the opponent's weaker stones, *and* far from the opponent's strong stones, you will be better off than if you met only one of the criteria. When you become competitor, customer, and company, you see how you can escape our human predisposition to focus only on strengths.[3]

SACRIFICE

Sacrifice, unfortunately, is a fact of life. The Go rule is "Don't be attached to your stones." In layoffs, firings, and breaking up, sacrifices can be tough; despite the knowledge that the move was toward the goal, sometimes it is still hard to let go. One of the keys to Go is to know what to be attached to and what to detach from. As with anything, you want to attach yourself to your one true goal. In Go, that goal can be winning a particular game, making yourself a better player, becoming a professional, or realizing the nature of

---

3. Reality is a bother, but understanding something about it is pertinent for your game. There are common decision-making problems that afflict humans no matter if they are playing Go or not. Two such problems are "anchoring" and "availability" bias. Anchoring is when a first impression lasts too long. For instance, in home sales, the seller's asking price often influences the final price more than the actual fair market value. The initial anchor is that initial inclination or plan that weighs down your thinking. Availability bias is having information handy that you then assume addresses situations in your life. In Go, you might read a column that shows a pattern that occurs frequently in pro play. In a game of your own, a situation may crop up in which that sort of pattern is possible. Availability bias influences you to want to play out the situation like the column, even though this kind of pattern might not be appropriate for your position. There are entire books (for example, *Money Mistakes* by Max Bazerman) devoted to these two biases and others that plague human decision-making. In order to become a better strategist and decision-maker, not only should you know GO'S RULES, but you must confront these biases that affect decision-making in every field. Because we are human, we already have built-in competition.

things through Go. Each different goal necessitates different attachments and different sacrifices to reach each goal. It's always a matter of balance.

Sacrificing your stones, if done appropriately, forces your opponent to play more moves to capture those stones than might be expected. The rule in Go is "Sacrifice more than one." Ditching more than one stone, given Go's bias toward defense, makes the opponent commit commensurately more resources to take two stones than to take just one. Good sacrificing in Go means the opponent either commits to taking your sacrifice or leaves things a bit risky by not doing so. When the goal is to win the game, the Go rules "Give up superfluous stones" and "Once stones have carried out their mission, give them up" provide some comfort when letting go of key positions. The trouble is that there are other Go rules, such as "Don't give up key stones" and "See the interconnections," that balance good sacrifice with bad.

There is a true story of a man who raised his son in the inner city to become a successful leader despite not having all the advantages and there being plenty of examples nearby of people going the wrong way. His son was nurtured and taught how to succeed and thrive in a prudent and righteous manner despite a less than ideal environment. Once his son had grown and was doing great works in the world, he came back home on vacation and was shot and killed in his old neighborhood. When the reporters interviewed the father, who had taken all this time to nurture and foster the best things in his son, and asked if he'd done something wrong, he replied, "Yes, my mistake was in not doing more to help my neighbor's child."

It is too hard to say what would have happened if he had diversified his focus from just his own child to help others in the neighborhood. Would his son have been as successful? Would he still have been shot? Would he have been able to make a significant difference in more than just his son's life? Understanding what is Us, what is Them, drawing the boundary, and seeing the interconnections is a grueling analysis. Doing some initial thinking can often shed light when none has illuminated before.

Oren Lyons, one of the Faithkeepers of the Onondaga Nation, was sitting with multinational business leaders at a conference, all of them waiting to speak. Oren noticed that they were all talking of their grandchildren. Coming from a culture where you think of the needs of your seventh generation, you're thinking of your decisions for a much bigger We. Introducing this concept to the business leaders, Oren pointed out that what their businesses did affected their grandchildren. While these leaders of industry could focus their mind on their grandkids, they did not think of their grandkids in relation to their businesses. Oren helped put the two Thems—Them their grandkids and Them their businesses—together, and that made things a bit uncomfortable. Should they stop their companies from polluting as much? Should they deplete fewer natural resources? If so, do they sacrifice their current profits for the unknown probability of helping their grandchildren later? They could either try to reconcile the divergence or ignore it completely. Either way, some sacrifice was going to take place.

Having clarity of goal is essential for knowing how and what to sacrifice. When the goal is clear, sacrifice is tantamount to focus. My fellow insei and dorm mate Hans, who became a pro player after years of sacrifice and hardship, long after I had left Japan, had a clear vision for his life. He knew he would not become a top pro, despite winning a number of matches against top players, and that his mission in life would be to promote Go throughout the world and help those looking to improve their Go. While he would compete as if he were going to be number one, Hans's Us was a larger Us, beyond himself and his Go. Even promoting Go, however, comes with its sacrifices.

In a weird chain of events (which included my sending Hans an e-mail only hours before the incident to ask how he was doing, after nearly three years of no correspondence) Hans and a touring group of Japanese professional players were mugged at a Guatemalan sightseeing spot. Though they turned over all their valuables without a struggle, the mugger shot and killed Hans after Hans had handed over his money. After years of struggle through the ranks of the insei classes, after accepting this mission to promote

CHAPTER SIX

———•———

LEAD FOLLOW

In Go, you are always trying to keep the initiative. Dictating what is happening across the Go board, if you are smart about it, keeps the opponent's plans at bay and your initiatives closer to realization. If you are always responding to the opponent's moves, following, you will always be reacting to situations the opponent creates and will relinquish rights to your own schemes. One of the first rules beginning players are encouraged to follow is "Don't follow your opponent." This is hard to do because the weaker player assumes that the stronger player is playing a move for a good reason and that not reacting to it is akin to sacrificing something in the area where the opponent has played. Whether following or not, the key is to do what is right for the board.

Sometimes it is better to follow, however, especially when the opponent is violating rules from Reverse Forward. If the opponent attacks, attacks, attacks, by all means, defend, defend, defend. Once the opponent has reinforced your positions all over the board, you can begin counterattacking all of the attacking positions. This is called "Let the opponent drive you to victory" or "Lead by following." Sometimes the opponent forces you into good positions: Let it happen. Sometimes the opponent presses you to take more territory than you should be allowed: Let it happen. When you have no complaints, follow the opponent, but be careful. Oftentimes the sweet-smelling path the opponent lays out for you is a trap. Playing passive, being aggressive, responding or leading are all good in their own right; knowing which is right when is an indicator of one's strength.

Tennis battles with my old doubles partner exemplified this. He had a rather poor backhand. I could win most points by hitting to his backhand and waiting for the unforced error. The problem was, if I kept hitting to his backhand, his backhand would improve. Over time, I'd learn that he would avoid his backhand and play awkward forehand rallies as long as possible. Flipping the rule to "make your opponent follow you," the strategy becomes simple. Challenge him to play his run-around forehand as long as possible and only on crucial points take advantage of the backhand. Because we were evenly matched otherwise, this way of playing improved my record significantly. Of course, once he noticed the ploy, he improved his backhand and consequently I had to improve my game.

As with most things, leading or following is a matter of timing. When you preempt, you have the first-mover advantage. In Go, this is so advantageous that the second-mover is awarded "komi," a point handicap given to the person moving second in an evenly matched game. While the person responding has the benefit of seeing what the opponent is going to do and is therefore at an informational advantage, that information might be that the opponent is ahead. There are aspects to both following and leading that are important tools in Go and elsewhere.

A CHRONIC PROBLEM?

In the 1990s, a major multinational petroleum company, one of the Seven Sisters that were the companies spawned from the Standard Oil monopoly breakup, was a predominant player in any number of markets throughout a particular state. Let's call this company Betsy.

I was part of a team of people acting as consultants to Betsy and we were asked how to respond to the entry of a new competitor into this market. Apparently, the new entrant was starting to take business away from Betsy and Betsy brought us in to give a read of the situation and help Betsy decide what to do.

In Go, when you have the most influence on a particular territory, you control the timing of what happens there. The more influence you have, the more control you have. Just as we explored with *Seven Samurai,* if it's your moyo, you call the shots if an opponent enters. Likewise, if you go into an opponent's moyo, you should expect to follow the opponent's lead as you enter. When you Owe, you Follow; when you've Saved, you can Lead.

It's a matter of what's whose. For instance, there are pat ways one controls a corner of the Go board. With one move, you can control one of the four corners at the outset of a game; unfortunately, this corner-securing move has little influence on the rest of the board. With one move, you can have a lot of influence on the board radiating out from a corner, but for the corner territory itself, you really do not control it. Some moves can split the difference between these two extremes, and with a second play, you can complete the control of the corner and exert influence out from the corner—of course, you spent two moves. As with everything, there are trade-offs.

For Betsy, the first order of business was determining what sort of control Betsy had in this market. Could Betsy really say that she controlled the market and that no one could enter? No. Could Betsy say that the competitor would feel the brunt of Betsy's response to this entry? This was to be determined.

The kind of analysis we did, in Go terms, would be a mix of both Reverse Forward thinking and Lead Follow thinking, which merges into something that parallels what the linguist Ferdinand Saussure called synchronic analysis—looking at language at a point in time ("syn" meaning with or at, "chronic" meaning time) to see more of its inner nature—and diachronic analysis—looking at language through time and seeing how it changes and disperses to get an idea of its underlying nature.

The synchronic look at English would examine the language as it is spoken today, not as how certain English teachers think it should be spoken. The usual way one does this is to diagram sentences and look at the grammar. For instance, it is proper English in the southern United States to use the construction "y'all." The English grammar police might say that such a construction is an abomination, but indeed, it has deeper structure than first meets the eye. There are rules for its use that the Queen's-English-grammar prude is sure to screw up when trying to mimic it. The y'all construction is, in many parts of the country, a form of you found in many other countries, namely the construction for you-plural, referring to more than one of you. Mimicry that uses y'all to refer to just one person is just plain wrong. The internal rules of use for y'all are the synchronic aspects of the term.

In Go, the form of synchronic analysis one does is, at any given point of the game, to ask the Four Questions, find the points of tension, Slack or Taut, look at who's winning Globally and in each local battle, and so on. That's a synchronic view of things in Go. What is the board saying right now about who is ahead? The rules in Go are "The board tells no lies" and "Play to the board, forget the opponent." "Play to the board."

For Betsy, measuring all the preceding GO'S RULES would help determine whether Betsy could attack the newbie forcefully, severely, mildly, or not at all. Instead of positions on the Go board, you could take a snapshot of the competitor's strengths and weaknesses, look at the market's customers and their needs, and determine where Betsy's strengths were relative to the newbie's. But, as you might have guessed, looking at just one side of the analogy would be leaving some of the analysis undone.

Diachronic analysis is doing an analysis through time ("dia" meaning through, "chronic" relating to time). If you trace English back through time, you find that it is partly derived from German and partly derived from French, among other influences. Dig deeper still and there are grandparents for those parents, respectively Latin and Germanic. Go back a generation more and Latin and Germanic have a common parent in what is called Proto-Indo-European (also known as PIE), which is the great-great-grandparent of nearly half of the world's languages. From PIE come Russian, Greek, Sanskrit, and English. How do we know this? Diachronic analysis.

In Go, one does diachronic analysis in Reverse Forward fashion. Look forward and work your way back and vice-versa to see how the future might play out in your head. That's diachronic analysis of the board itself. Another interesting aspect of diachronic analysis is to see what is going on above the board, where the opponent is following what you are doing and where the opponent typically takes a stand.

The rule in Go is "Don't follow your opponent." One should not respond just because your opponent has made a move somewhere. If the opponent enters an area where you have been, you can lose your advantage. As a first-mover there, you can counteract the opponent's encroachment with another move of your own. The problem is that sometimes that particular area is not the most important or urgent. Sometimes, you must give up local advantages to gain a global advantage. That is Global Local. The Atlantic City gaming industry can provide a hypothetical example of what not to do.

If your neighbor's casino decides to give away thirty-thousand-dollar Rolexes to random customers every hour, that neighbor will gain many customers. Do you do the same? What if all the other casinos in the area do the same thing? Do you allow a Rolex gap? You need to ask if the move is sustainable, duplicable, ultimately profitable, and in line with your overall strategy toward your customers; if yes, hand them out. If no, follow one of the thirty-six Chinese stratagems, Ge An Guan Huo, "Let the fire (or cash, in this instance) burn across the river."

The rule "Lead, even when you follow" says it is good to follow when the leader is going your way. If the opponent continues to take less of the board and forces you to take more of the board, don't upset the opponent's plans just because the opponent is leading the situation. The other admonition from the rule is to not play submissively. The clever opponent will seem to give you more territory and more influence and then at a key juncture in the path, pull out a move that changes the flow. The rule "Your own plans are hard to see, the opponent's even harder" means that you need to always ensure that where you are following is where you want to be.

A good diachronic analysis of "Is the opponent following my

every move?" or "Am I following the opponent around the board?" tells you something of how you are doing. If you are never taking the initiative, you need to really have a good synchronic understanding that you are ahead and that the opponent just happens to like leading you to victory. Possible, but usually the opponent's mind is not so clear or generous.

Between your synchronic assessment of the board and a good diachronic assessment of your moves and the opponent's, you can get more of the complete picture of what you should do. Betsy did not just need an understanding of strengths and weaknesses, but needed to know something of the trajectories of the two companies, the customers both might serve, and what else might be coming or going in the industry.

TO FORCE OR BE FORCED

In football, you have a snap count that determines when the play is to go into action. This snap count gives the offense an advantage over the defense, because the defense does not know at what time the ball will be snapped. Having this very slight advantage over the defender is oftentimes not enough to account for a defender's highly attuned reaction time. Moreover, when your own players are the competition, you can trick yourselves into reacting before the ball goes into play, which will result in a penalty. That's when Us are Them.

The longer you control the snap count, the longer you control the ball, the better off you are. Since it is far less likely that you'll score on defense, it is better to keep possession of the football. Retain the offensive. In Go, you do exactly the same thing. While you have the initiative, potentially, every time you touch a stone, real initiative comes when you can compel the opponent to respond to what you are doing and keep that going as long as you can, soundly, throughout as much of the game as you can.

In handicap games in Go, when you are artificially behind from the outset, you catch up with feints and indirections that seem threatening, but might actually be something the opponent should not respond to. The opponent responding to the stronger player's moves is well warranted to do so, but playing without the initiative is purely reactionary and violating the "Don't follow your opponent" rule.

To counter the initiative, you need to "tenuki," that is, play away from the area where the opponent just played. The board is big. The opportunities are not limited to where your opponent just played. Playing elsewhere despite the opponent's last foray is a declaration of independence, but must be judged from the Global analysis of what area is bigger, the Owe Save affects of playing away, and so forth.

While the initiative is important in the beginning and middle stages of the game, even into the end game initiative can make or break a game. When the borders have been determined by battle and fight, the border details still need to be worked out. Encroaching on your opponent's hard-won territory, you'd think that making an inroad at this late stage is a sure way to keep the initiative. But, if you likewise have hard-won territory and the opponent goes after your territory, you need to know your accounting. There are many games in which the territory that was held by one player gets eaten by the opponent because of this sort of end game back and forth. The key is to understand that territory, like anything else, is a means to an end.

If you had a 55 percent market share, would you give it up for a 20 percent market share of something else? Without knowing the details, how could you decide? It might be the case that instead of having a million customers, you instead want one hundred. They could be a hundred senators, for instance, versus a million people gained through a nefarious spam campaign. The initiative is a matter of how much territory you're going to take.

Torrential, as you saw, violated this rule any number of times. The most egregious incident was Torrential's early idea of its valuation. Part of the reason for the ramp-up of Torrential was seeing other companies going IPO and then being able to put cash in the coffers hand over fist. Admittedly, one of Pat's first errors on the job was to follow Torrential's opponents—namely, the comparables going public. In Go, being led by the nose will typically lead to ruin. Fortunately for Torrential, it was still in the beginning stage, where mistakes can be made up for.

The antithesis to this following principle is to try to make the opponent follow your every move. Against weaker players, you can do this rather effectively. Sometimes a weakness is apparent, but you might not have all your pieces together to go for the jugular. Instead, you create situations nonchalantly near the weakness that allow you to build strength while your weaker opponent is none the wiser. By the time you go for the kill, it is too late for the opponent to defend. That's "making the opponent follow you."

However, I usually find that it pays to follow my opponent around after a few moves in high-handicap games. When the opponent is weaker than you, oftentimes the opponent is the opponent's own worst competition (Us Them). The rule in Go is "Follow when the opponent is going your way." If the opponent wants the inside portion of the board and the outside is bigger, by all means, "Let the opponent take the smaller territory."

The other things weaker players are wont to do is pull out all the stops and push you to perfect play. Because of this human need to do things that you're sure the opponent will respond to, when you don't know what else to do, play moves that have an effect. This is the sort of childish thing we never seem to forget how to do as we grow older. "If I can threaten to capture the opponent's stone, the opponent is sure to save it." But, when saving a stone means that the counterattack will be severe, best not attack it. The rules in Go are "Don't force the opponent just to force the opponent" and "Don't threaten or force the opponent just because you don't know what else to do." When you force the opponent, you want to have a good reason. Typically, weaker players don't have a good reason for forcing; therefore, follow the weaker player's forcings.

This happens in business frequently. Smaller companies looking to build their businesses and wanting to take risks the bigger players will not go for will spend enormous amounts of money to grow the entire market or do market testing. The bigger company can gain the informational advantage of the smaller company's hard work, and when the smaller company has proven the concept or the market, the bigger players can step in with their entire arsenal and steal the business, the idea, and more. This is a following attack.

Taking the initiative and keeping it is a big plus. Having a good sense for the diachronics and synchronics of Betsy's situation relative to the newbie and other competitors who might lurk waiting for Betsy to move, we consultants had come to a conclusion: Betsy, the larger player, could force the entrant to pay for entering this market by hitting it with more services, such as convenience stores and restaurants, while concurrently lowering prices, and do it all before the newbie built its next one. This would signal Betsy's firm resolve to defend this territory and make every new store opening a big loss for the competitor. It was a grand strategy. We consultants had saved the day, so we thought. If our solution was truly grand, then it would need to pass another test: Did it have a good next?

THE NEXT NEXUS

The 2003 United States takeover of Iraq was an impressive display of military might. The Iraqi army, long feared as a tenacious opponent, was vanquished quickly. Whether the attack was warranted is best left to historians, who can go back through the facts and see what's there. Despite the rationale, the one thing the United States did not do well is what one calls in Go "having a good next."

In Go, playing a great move is a wonderful feeling. It looks good on the board, has all the brilliance of shape and balance, and can really have an effect on things. But great feelings are not how the game is won. In order to win, you must be able to transcend one-movedness. One move, no matter how strong, does not win the game. A great move that does not create great follow-up moves is not such a great move.

In Iraq, the good next was not packaged well. The buildup to the invasion was marketed as the winning move. "Saddam must go"; "End the tyranny"; "Free the Iraqi people"; something about WMDs. . . . But managing expectations and knowing how to spin things after the one good first move is akin to having a good next move in Go. Without your good next, the first move is questionable.

It's like going up to one of your children and saying, "For your birthday, we're going to go to the bestest amusement park in the whole world! Expense is no object." That's great. Have a great time. What happens the next year? What expectations did you set? What about the other kids? Just as public corporations stay away from upping dividend payouts because it sets up the expectation that dividends will go up again soon, for the next birthday, for the next time it comes to announcing dividends, you are going to be at a loss for a good next without planning for it in advance of making the first move. In Go, you try to plan out as many good nexts as possible or you leave yourself open to the opponent having one more than you.

The situation in Iraq, after the swift military dismissal of the Iraqi leadership, may have been the most probable outcome. If so, then a better move at the outset would have been to decide what victory was in that next move. "If we enter Iraq and vanquish the leadership, we will know we have won if we are hit with a number of suicide bombings and random attacks, the last desperate moves of a fallen regime." After the fact, it is less convincing to say that was a measure of success. Indeed, order is everything.

For Betsy, our grand strategy of making the competitor pay was a great move, but it too smacked of one-movedness. If the opponent has already committed to the region, despite whatever moves Betsy made, there would be trouble. And what if the competitor was not acting rationally? If we were going to be entering into a sort of Rolex gap war, there was no winning. If the next move after trying to thwart the competitor from opening more stores wasn't going to work, the plan would backfire.

In Go, you have to measure your ability to drive the opponent.

Holding the initiative means that you are making progress Globally, while making good decisions Locally, by keeping the opponent Owing, while not exposing yourself to counterattacks. The tension in Slack and Taut and everything else up to this point must be considered. While some moves can be made because they are good in themselves, there is a void after playing such a move with no good next.

The negative potential for our nexts for Betsy, derived from our grand strategy of stymieing the opponent, could be realized in a number of ways: We could start a price war with the entrant, when we'd prefer to charge more; we could introduce new services to follow the competitor's style, but not have the expertise to carry it out; we could weaken both ourselves and the competitor and leave ourselves open for another big player to come in and clear us out; we could set up unreasonably high expectations for the consumer and forever alienate our customers. Nonetheless, the opposite could be true as well. Further analysis was needed.

PROBES

In Go, sometimes it is not clear what you should do. There is a situation on the board that merits either invasion, reduction, expansion, or some such strategy, but without good information about the situation, your one recourse is to do a test or probe. In Go, you probe before you buy. Yes, at times you are sacrificing a stone in order to probe, committing a resource that could be spent elsewhere, but it's better to commit to buying the information when the situation is unclear.

Probes are moves that test what an opponent will do. They force the opponent to commit to a direction or defense before you decide how to handle an area. Instead of entering a new market, you can do a survey or provide samples to the audience. The idea is not to start investing right away, but to see what happens after an initial move.

For Betsy, there were things to try before committing to the overall strategy. Could Betsy afford a price war in the region? We could find out what would happen if we tried it in one part of the market against the competitor. Would we be able to convince our independent store operators to get on board with the strategy? We could try it out with one or two and see. Testing a thing or two is sometimes costly, but can also be revealing.

A probe can also misdirect the opponent. If you start probing a price war, the opponent might read that and think, "Hey, they are starting a price war." While it may be the case in the test market, it might not be the case in the entire region, but the opponent won't know that.

In Go, you try to do the same thing. You want to feint in one direction to get the opponent off-balance, and then you can reveal your true plan. Better opponents are less likely to fall for the initial feint. Some players might think that this is a trick or unscrupulous play, but instead, if done correctly, it is a test of the opponent. Should the opponent fail the test, it's an opportunity for the opponent to learn something. Should the opponent follow the rule "Don't take the bait," then the test tells you something equally important: The opponent is strong, the opponent will commit one way or another to address such plays, and you should play elsewhere and see if another situation comes ripe to your advantage.

"Timing is everything" is a key Go rule that holds even for probing. Sometimes it is too early to probe; sometimes it is too late to probe; and sometimes it's just right. The time for Betsy to do some probing was now, before the situation became too fixed.

STANDARD MOVES

Being in position to lead the opponent is a Go player's dream. Since each player gets only one move per turn, having another move before the opponent plays in an area is a distinct advantage, a mini-first-mover's advantage. When you control the pace in the game, you're setting a standard, playing your game.

Setting up the standard that the opponent follows is not simple. In Go, the opponent sees your every move on the board. While the opponent cannot look into your head, the astute player will not be easily coaxed into letting you set up an initiative-holding position. Indeed, such a situation is more easily set up with a weaker opponent who doesn't quite grasp what you are doing. Nonetheless, setting up the standard comes at a price.

Microsoft's setting up a standard way for people to interact with their computers has paid off handsomely. Nordstrom's standard of quality customer service takes a large investment in inventory and sales commissions, but it works. But not all companies setting out to create a standard have seen their investments pan out to the same success.

Ask any cell phone carrier or Sony's Betamax what it took to develop something that could become a standard and the cost of not achieving that standard. Each takes or took significant risks in setting up a model for their customers to follow, and many did not make the grade and ultimately had to take on losses associated with anticipating being a standard setter without actually becoming one. For instance, Sony invested millions of dollars in production of Sony Betamax players, videos, and promotion only to see a lesser-quality standard emerge in VHS.

The rule in Go is "If you lead be careful, if you follow be careful." You can lead the way, whether with pen computing, the wing-T football offense, satellite phones, SACD/DVD-A, or digital radio, but the attempt to get to critical mass, to get at something that sets the standard for the industry and the customers, is a big risk. Leadership is risk. It is moving before others move. It is betting that where you lead is where people will want to go; in Go, betting where the territory will come.

Betsy did not have control over this state's market, despite its dominance there. However, there were opportunities for leading where the opponent could not yet follow. For instance, introducing loyalty programs where customers build up points in Betsy stations would make a whole lot more sense in markets where customers could build up significant points before an entrant entered. Then if the entrant entered, not only would they have to compete on the price of the gas, but on the attributed value of the loyalty program. Deciding what Betsy should do in response to entry in this particular market was going to demand more analysis.

DOUBLE SENTE

Holding the initiative in Go is called "sente." Losing the initiative is called "gote." Professional Go players go to great lengths to keep sente. While professionals are very good at never throwing away points, they'll do just that to gain sente. The struggle for sente is part of what makes watching a professional match so exciting. As an amateur, you're constantly told the pat patterns, and yet the pros know just when to depart from the pattern, or how to sacrifice to change it, so that sente can be retained.

In Betsy's incumbent market, there were sente moves that Betsy could make. Because people tend to buy gas at convenient intersections and on and off points, the real estate available for naturally occurring gas station spots was well known to Betsy. While Betsy did not have designs to put stations there, Betsy could make lease options for many of them without even blinking. While the entrant had already acquired some of the land, Betsy could retain some advantage over the entrant by controlling areas the opponent would want to control. If the entrant had the opportunity, the entrant could acquire all these locales and then Betsy would need to respond by moving to less desirable spots for new stations. "Your opponent's move is often your best move."

The problem again with taking all the sente is that there is often not a good next. If you can control all the low-hanging fruit before the opponent does, then you raise the opponent's costs and improve your future, but in Betsy's case, the game was still much too complex to rely on quick hits to help Betsy.

DEVELOP A FOLLOWING

Let the opponent walk all over you? Stay still when the opponent enters? Don't move a muscle? If there is one thing Go teaches again and again it is that sometimes doing nothing or following what the opponent says is not only a good thing to do, but some-times the best thing to do. While we have covered following the opponent when the opponent is leading you to victory any-way, what about when the opponent is actually playing the right moves?

The nature of Go is that you often have to concede before at-tacking, follow before taking the initiative, and work your way up through the ranks to gain the respect and mantle of leadership. The giant misperception in Go and in life is that leading is con-trolling and following is being controlled. This is not the case. If you are in control of yourself, have a handle on the diachronics and synchronics of the situation, and can rationally determine that fol-lowing leads to victory, there is no harm in following.

The key is to know when to go after something and when to let something come after you. There are plenty of plants and animals that do exactly this. They wait and wait for the prey to come and then, when it does, they spring into action. It's a surprise party. An ambush. In the *Star Wars* movies as well, Darth Vader starts out Episode V looking for the young Luke Skywalker, but on the bet-ter advice from the emperor in Episode VI, Darth realizes that Luke will look for him. The fiction is based in reality. As we saw in Slack Taut, sometimes the best way to capture someone is to let him or her go.

MOMENTUM OR ANALYSIS PARALYSIS

All this time spent analyzing the situation comes at a cost. As soon as we started the Betsy analysis, the situation on the ground changed. While in Go, the position doesn't move as you study it, sometimes your perception of what is going on can change. In real life, both the perception and the real situation are constantly in flux. Take too long to do a good synchronic analysis and you are likely to not have that snapshot of a point in time to anchor your beliefs on anymore.

At the same time, you don't want to get caught up in the rhythm of the fight, dance, and struggle. It is compelling and natural to go with the flow. Be like water in a vase, cup, or square, conforming to every situation as it comes up. Trouble is, if the opponent is dictating the shapes to which you are conforming, it is more than likely that the opponent will be dictating how the game proceeds. But if you can mix up being water with being a mountain, being wind, being fire, the opponent will never know what vessel will take the game in the right direction.

The skill in discerning which part of the dichotomy you should be on is not a simple one to acquire. Knowing the concepts and their importance will help you know what to look for, but more than likely the rhythms and paralysis will strike again. Balancing the two requires the utmost emotional and mental control, something even professional Go players find challenging.

YOU CAN LEAD A HORSE TO WATER

In Go, you can lead the opponent to follow your standard and buy into your subtle ploys, but that doesn't mean the opponent won't do something you don't expect. You should expect that even if you lead the opponent-horse to water, you cannot make him or her drink.

If you are a consultant, your client is always inclined to follow advice. The client is paying a significant fee, and not following your advice would seem unsound. And, since you have an outsider's perspective, you aren't caught up in the rigmarole of the job—you can be Global amidst all the Local in-fighting. Then too, the client has been coaching you daily on what the right answer is, and if you're heading toward the answer the client expects, the client is willing to take on more work.

In Betsy's case, we struggled to find the right solution despite the client's need for us to get it and to package it for a quick solution. As the client's mentor, you have a responsibility commensurate with your suggestive power. If the client wants you to solve the problem, there's a problem. The client has to own the solution and then treat it like a plan and research. It is information, not a treasure map leading to gold.

If we were to allow ourselves to get caught up in the momentum of leading the client, we'd be falling into the initiative-loving trap. As a consultant or a Go player, you can start to get involved in your own greatness and fall victim to the god complex, that ego-stroking position of thinking that you can do anything and go anywhere and whatever you suggest comes up gold, never mind reality.

With Betsy, we understood where we stood once we got deeper into our research. Trying to delve deeper into the local details and particulars of Betsy's strengths, Betsy led us to the drawer. The drawer represented more than $20 million worth of proposals and recommendations that other consultants had provided over the previous three years. Indeed, while some of what we did was reinventing the wheel, the more telling sign was that despite our hard work and recommendations, there was probably little chance that the company would buy into our analysis. We could only recommend.

Teaching Go feels the same way at times. Some students take what you say to heart and try to make a difference in their game and their understanding of their weaknesses. Other students, however, simply like the idea of having Go lessons. After a while, I will fire a student for repeating the same mistakes again and again. There's no point in making good suggestions to someone when they go unheeded.

A friend of mine would always call for help on managing his career. I would say why not try this or that and do more of this and less of that. After listening to me in a heartfelt manner, he would go off and do exactly the opposite and then come back to me for advice. I would try again making specific suggestions on particular situations and the like. But I should have known that there is no way to give someone in Go a road map for winning a game if they don't have the requisite strength.

FOLLOW-UP

Initiative, following, watching, probing, yielding, and pressing are all ways that we can take the lessons from the preceding rules and make them come alive. For our purposes, it's better to have a mix of Lead and Follow initiatives going at any one time and splice them together, wary of all the pitfalls, than to assume that leading leading leading is going to be the best strategy. If you're always in front, you often don't see what's really going on (god complex).

But how to Lead Follow when you have only one move at a time? For some aspects of a move you are leading, and for other aspects you are following. Yes, you may be leading in territory now, but you are following in influence. You may be leading in unification of troops, but following in number of places you affect. Without knowing which side of the spectrum you should be on, you're compelled to play chutto hampa (see Reverse Forward) in hopes of meeting both, but doing neither. It doesn't have to be this way.

With Expand Focus, the rest of the game comes into focus. Knowing when to do two things at once and when to do just one thing at a time is the last crucial hurdle you have to overcome to reach the upper ranks.

CHAPTER SEVEN

———•———

EXPAND FOCUS

A key challenge of Go and life is that you can't do everything. What then to do with limited time and resources to address multiple situations? While you can pay attention to all the preceding rules, some players get more out of each move than another. The principles surrounding Expand Focus explain how.

Expand is the side of the duality asking you to diversify, stretch out, be open. Maxims include: "Expand your horizons." "Expand the scope of your initiatives." "Expand your perspective." "Expand your mind." "Don't put all your eggs in one basket." No matter what maxim or rule, Expand is diverse, vast, scattered. Expand rules come in the form of portfolios, options, and meanings; the more the better. They are powerful concepts, but just one item in the toolkit.

The fewer the better is the Focus side of the duality. Maxims include: "Focus." "Narrow." "Hone in." "Move to the beat of one drummer." The Focus side is direct, razor-sharp. You coordinate on a single mission rather than multiple missions. It's the strategy of making a beeline, purity, convergence, and fixedness. The fewer the better is the motto, but its narrowness can be a detriment.

The dangers of Expand are spreading yourself too thin, not being decisive, trying to do too much at once. The dangers of Focus lie in pinning all your hopes on one thing, giving one target for the opponent to shoot for, and missing out on opportunities that lie elsewhere because of your myopia.

Us Them provides valuable fodder for Expand Focus—the other side of the competition. Just as you want to expand your options, you'll want to limit your opponent's. As you want to have more options in a situation, you want your opponent to have fewer options. Just as you want to focus, you will want the opponent to get distracted and diffused. All the while, keep in mind the Us Them rules illustrating the shifting sands of who's who in a competition. The opponent you're going after may be your friend later and vice-versa.

But how do you know when you should be focusing or diversifying? Is there a way to measure the value of diversifying and focusing? Go players have been answering such questions for millennia. In a game where you get only one move per turn, but have to address an entire world of situations, the root problems Go players face are the same that anyone with similar constraints faces. Just ask the people responsible for your garden variety lawn gnome.

BANDS OF GYPSUM

Lawn gnomes, toothpaste and food fillers, and the stuff that helps keep your house from burning down all rely on the almost magical properties of a substance known as gypsum or calcium sulfate dihydrate. Mixed with various other things, gypsum can be made into a gnome, a piece of wallboard, or highway filler, or used to provide more calcium in your diet. Mined from veins of gypsum scattered throughout the United States, gypsum is the lifeblood of a company known as US Gypsum, or USG.

USG's number-one product and breadwinner is Sheetrock— the Band-Aid, Kleenex, and Coke of its industry—its brand name being synonymous even with competitive products. The magic of Sheetrock is that it makes for a nice wall (unless the door stopper is missing and you get a hole in the wall at the arc of the doorknob) and that it is very resistant to fire. In that sense, Sheetrock is like a move with many meanings, two of which are its attractive and utterly pervasive use as a wall and as a mainstay fire retardant. Big business.

Outside the Sheetrock machine, which is most of USG's business, there's a division known as the Industrial Gypsum Division (IGD), which handles all the other gypsum requests, be they for the lawn gnome manufacturer, the toothpaste filler, or medical gypsum products, to name a scant few of gypsum's other incarnations and USG product lines. At the time we consulted with IGD, to say that IGD was diversified was an understatement. In its portfolio of products, there were more than a thousand different products IGD could sell. The question on IGD's mind was whether to keep the business expansive or to focus the business more.

In a theoretical sense, for Go or life, you're always at an advantage if you can focus. By focusing your resources to their best and highest use, you will gain the greatest return, earn the most territory, and capitalize on your resources' most effective use. The problem is that in order for you to focus with confidence, the future has to be very clear; otherwise you may be focusing down the wrong path and may make commitments that end up being for naught.

In politics you can see this in the rallying cry of the 1992 Bill Clinton campaign against George Bush, Sr.—"It's the economy, stupid." With people up in arms about the economy, Clinton was ushered into the White House largely by focusing on where the voter sentiment was. If the voter sentiment was not as high with the economy, but more on the menace of Iraq, then George Sr. would have been at an advantage.

Focus not only helped Clinton ride the voter sentiment but also pigeonholed Bush Sr. Once committed, Bush could not say "It's the economy, stupid, too!" In Go, games go the same way. If the opponent commits to the center of the board with tremendous focus, then you should take the sides and corners. This concept of two or more equal opportunities, as discussed earlier, is called "miai." Miai means that if your opponent takes one, don't bash heads. The rule is "Take the other miai."

If you're first out of the gate to the place where the most people are, you've picked well. Focus gets you there the fastest. If soy milk becomes the breakfast drink of choice tomorrow, then those who are making soy milk investments today will be rewarded. But should the market turn sour on soy milk, those investments in soy milk futures would likewise spoil. Once committed, however, it would be difficult for Clinton to go back and say "Well, it was the economy, now it's health care."

The problem, for Go and life, is that you cannot always know what's going to happen on the board. As discussed, the number of potential variations in Go is greater than astronomical. You need to hedge your bets and focus only where things are very clear. The greater the uncertainty of your positions and the future, the more you want to give yourself options. The player who can see farther into the future can focus more and as a result can gain first-mover advantages in areas where things are still unclear to the opponent.

For USG's IGD, it knew a number of things. First, the gypsum deposits that IGD used were still in large supply but could only be taken out at a plant-by-plant rate. While there were variations in the quality of the material coming out of the ground, and therefore in the potential products, the variation was not so large that you didn't know what to expect. Geologists and other sciencists could forecast what quality would be coming next.

Second, there seemed to be a steady stream of customers from all walks of life. From agricultural, to medical, to food industry, to oil well cement, to ceramics, to lawn gnome makers, IGD never lacked for a variety of customers and demand for its thousands of products. While medical and food customers needed higher-quality gypsum, road filler and the like could take just about any-thing.

Third, IGD was starting to see competition from other major manufacturers. Offering fewer products, at a lower price point, these other manufacturers were starting to eat into IGD's business in some of its larger product lines. While the quality of the prod-ucts from the other manufacturers was often lower, the price was making the difference in a number of sales competitions. The com-petitor's focus was getting people to adopt non-USG products by selling below market to compensate for quality and loyalty.

USG had to decide how to handle these competitors and how best to handle its product mix for maximizing return to USG as a company. Because IGD was seen not only as a bottom-line contributor, but also as the potential progenitor of the next Sheetrock, IGD was the diversification of the USG portfolio.

MEANINGFUL MOVES

The TV character MacGyver was famous for his creative use of ordinary household items to save the day. Almost weekly, there were situations that stretched the imagination as MacGyver would somehow use things like a butter knife, gum, some cat dander, an abandoned coal mine, and ordinary tinfoil to rig up a makeshift satellite transmitter that would save the city from destruction with only seconds to spare.

In Go, there are MacGyver-like players doing the seemingly impossible with stones that were all but forgotten or whose meaning was seemingly innocuous. In Go, the ultimate moves are those that bring to life otherwise lifeless stones and effect a watershed change in lead or potential. With every stone on the board an otherwise played and sunk cost, finding value amidst the spoils is what separates the masters from the amateurs. Within every position and move—sacrificed, committed, or probed—the more you can master the gray areas, the better.

Moreover, in Go, you may have four different situations that all need addressing at once, but, as always, just one stone to play per turn. In Go's long history, there is one particular game that stands out, in which a young prodigy, named Shusaku, played a move that will forever be synonymous with the following Go rules—"Play moves with multiple meanings" and "Do more than one thing at once."

In this particular game, Shusaku was a young player who was seen as the heir apparent of the Honinbo clan, one of the four Go houses of the 1800s, which was desperately pinning its hopes on this young prodigy becoming Meijin, or master over all four Go houses. Pitted against the top challenger of the era, Gennan Inseki, who was also seeking the Meijin title from another house, Shusaku had fallen behind after a complicated opening pattern.

Because Gennan's play took advantage of the early error, Shusaku had to address a number of problematic positions across the board, as always, with only one move to play.

While it would have been nice for Shusaku to try to increase his own territory, taking more territory at this point would have let Gennan attack Shusaku's weak position and make any territory gain for Shusaku moot. And while it would have been nice to reduce Gennan's territory, again, leaving the weak position alone would have been disastrous. Protecting the weaker position first certainly was in accord with Owe Save thinking, but if Shusaku used his move to help the weaker group, Gennan would be far enough ahead in territory that Shusaku wouldn't be able to catch up. What Shusaku did play was a quintessentially MacGyverian move.

Shusaku uncovered a move that addressed his weak position on the board, reduced Gennan's territory, and helped his own. Moreover, it raised weaknesses in Gennan's positions and erased the advantage Gennan had held since Shusaku's initial error. A doctor watching the game, who did not know much about Go, noticed that when Shusaku played this move there was a direct physiological response from Gennan—his ears turned red—a sign to the doctor that Gennan was very upset. The move, the game, and Shusaku's legendary status became synonymous with this now most famous of Go moves—"the ear-reddening move."

Modern players have debates about its merits, but most agree that it is a rare move, a move so pure and simple, but effective, as to only have been played once or twice in the lifetime of the game of Go.

While ear-reddening-type moves are a once-in-a-millennium occurrence, moves that have more than one meaning are frequent among stronger players. There are any number of combinations of multiple-meaning moves, such as attacking and defending, taking territory and setting up an attack, defending and encroaching on the opponent's territory, connecting pieces while disconnecting the opponent's, and playing a move with a good follow-up, but finding these moves and having them be the right move for the game is an indicator of one's strength. In general, the more rules you can address at once, correctly, the better.

Making plays with more than one meaning is crucial when you don't know what the future will bring or what the competition can or will do. In Go, the more options and opportunities per stone, the better the player is going to be able to deal with whatever the future brings. If your moves are set on one particular objective, if that objective loses its value, the move is wasted. For this reason, you always want your stones to take on more than one meaning, if possible.

As discussed, there are a number of possible uses for a stone at one time. It can attack, defend, invade, build territory, probe, prepare, and connect, among many more possibilities. Because once you play a stone it does not move and cannot be reconsidered, you really have to sit with whatever purpose and goal this stone has at the time played.

In life, you cannot be in two places at once, but there are still opportunities to fill each move with more than one meaning. Examples are legion. On sales calls out of town, one meaning would be to visit the client, but other potential meanings could be to drum up new business, visit suppliers, or establish new partnerships. When sitting and waiting for long periods, you can work on your posture—do stretches or other beneficial exercises that do more than just have you wait around. The rule in Go is "The more meanings the better."

Advertisements are excellent examples of this. Putting up your brand and your product and talking about its benefits is a fine way to get the word out. But if you want to give people a sense of your brand's personality, pizzazz, or popularity, you are going to have to do better than a list of features, a picture of the product, and a logo. Making the ad funny, or showing the risks of not using your product, either directly or indirectly, can make those thirty seconds on the screen all the more memorable and pointed.

If you're a mass-produced beer advertiser, you almost have to be funny or cool to survive. While it's important to get your brand in front of people's faces and show people enjoying the product, that single meaning would probably be the death of an ad if that's all it did. Getting people to buy into a way of life, thinking, or associating is more important than getting a picture of the product in front of people. Most high-cost ads work multiple meanings at once, while trying to focus you, all at the same time—even if the ad itself is inclusion of meaning by omission, as are many ads in Japan that advertise a feeling or pastoral scene while supposedly selling bread or trains.

Mirrored elevator lobby doors are likewise full of meanings. The invention of the mirrored elevator lobby was sheer genius. Many of the patrons who would get upset with the long wait now have an opportunity for grooming that makes waiting for the elevator more compelling.

The Disneyland of my childhood had rides like Pirates of the Caribbean, Haunted Mansion, and It's a Small World, where you had to wait in a long line, mostly out of the building. Guests would grow weary in the sun as boredom and tension took over. Disney got smarter about waits after my peak Disney years. Instead of coiling lines around themselves umpteen times out of doors, now the line and the wait are part of the attraction. At Star Tours or Space Mountain, you enjoy the wait more, because you become part of the ride as you wait in line and watch characters and scenes from within come to life in animatronic displays. A line, in and of itself, has just one meaning. An attraction should have more than one.

Compare the two religious terms "lukewarm" from Christianity and the "Middle Way" of Buddhism. Lukewarm is in the middle when up is called for, in the middle when down is called for, and in the middle when middle is called for. Lukewarm moves in life are codependent, antagonistic relationships—pleasing everyone at all costs, underfunding worthwhile projects, or only working half-paced while dreaming about another job. The Middle Way is flowing; up when up is called for and down when down is called for. The middle part of the Middle Way is balance when called for, not counterbalancing when not called for.

In Go, it is much better to fail spectacularly, try something that's a full measure and lose, or not play in an area and learn why you lost; there's no learning in being lukewarm. A move with more than one meaning is not equidistant, equipollent, splitting the difference, or a good consensus; a move with more than one meaning means that there is full meaning to those balanced and Middle Way terms.

Many charitable and government agencies used to do this sort of thing—find a good project that needed help and give only it half as much as it truly needed. Instead of fully funding fewer worthwhile projects, they would fund many more underfunded projects. Instead of resulting in more numerous but milder successes across multiple initiatives, they would get multiple failures across most initiatives.

IGD wanted to know if it was being all things to all customers or being strategic in its choices of whom to serve and what. While gypsum was a multiple-meaning resource that could be spun into many different products, could IGD focus its diversified portfolio of products to earn better profits and deal with the competitive threats? Were there other options for making a killing in its markets? While the gypsum plant that IGD used was set up to make multiple products, should it continue to be used that way?

COMPLETELY THICK

Focusing IGD would be a difficult task, but management literature and Go knowledge seemed to speak to focus's merits. The antithesis of employing multiple-meaning moves is the Go rule "Don't try to do two things at once." In the midst of a fight, you often are forced to figure out how to defend yourself. You would like to attack the opponent and defend at the same time while not making the opponent stronger, but in reality, something has to give and you don't always have the opportunity to save two positions with one stone.

In many situations, it is better to press the opponent's strengths, making the opponent stronger where the opponent is already strong, and then attack the opponent's weaker positions. Another option is to press the opponent's weakness and escape. These are two-step Reverse Forward indirection strategies to deal with one situation. A typical beginner's move is to think one step will address the situation and the beginner will play in the middle of the two, pressing the weaker and pressing the stronger, and is completely wrong most of the time. It's the kind of thinking you do as a child when you think it is clever to skip pouring two glasses— one of orange juice and one of milk—and instead just combine the milk and orange juice in one glass. Again, such chutto hampa lukewarm moves are bad. If you play a move that does neither thing well, the opponent is not threatened and gets the opportunity to take up slack left behind. With limited resources, do as much as you can with each play.

That said, you often need to be severe in order to address the opponent. When you have made a number of investments in a territory, the opponent can invade it. The only reason that competitors typically don't do that in Go is that they will be crushed as a result of entering someone else's domain too deeply. But if you're thinking multiple meanings, you oftentimes think such severe responses are unwarranted or perhaps bad, not in line with the multiple-meaning move rules. Nothing could be further from the truth. You cannot multiple-meaning your way out of some sticky situations.

I had a manager friend who was fed up over an employee's performance. Instead of dealing directly with the employee, having the hard conversations, getting into a fight or argument— using perfectly good Go-like rules—my friend tried to champion a multiple-meaning approach to getting that employee out the door. Instead of his firing the employee, he set up a number of situations that were supposed to usher this person out. Because the situations were not clear in their intent, it was likewise not clear that the person would have to leave as a result of the situations. For years, my friend wanted this person fired, but instead of firing, there was this constant circus of performances and situations that just perpetuated the poor employee's tenure.

That may be all well and good, but unless you are committed to pulling the trigger at some point, you're bound to forever keep the situation in limbo. Indeed, that is what happened, and despite my friend's intelligence and understanding that that person needed to go, there was never the focus to do it.

Committing to something in Go is important because you need to have something with which to barter as you go through the game. If you have a number of amorphous moves out floating around, you're not going to be a credible threat to the opponent by increasing your territory. Whereas, if you take some territory instead of leaving all territory up for grabs, you have something with which to barter or threaten the opponent. Have real investments in a position or positions and you have real challenges for the opponent to face.

Of course, there is more than one way to make an investment in territory in Go. Even though the object of the game is to surround more territory than the opponent surrounds, sometimes the best way to surround territory is to not surround territory. In Go, as in life, you never know what is going to be appropriate in the future, although you need to play now. An investment in a solid, unassailable position that does not take territory now is called "thick" play. Many beginners do not understand moves that don't directly surround territory. Why? The future is too far out. Surrounding now seems more certain.

Strong players understand influence and territory are miai—taking one and giving the other to the opponent doesn't leave you at a disadvantage. It's just a matter of choice, timing, and coordination. You want to get the balance of the miai that is most consistent and focused on your overall goal, while trying to take it only when truly ripe.

It is like trying to explain savings to a child. Why not spend the money now? Why wait for the money to grow when I want that big stuffed animal now? A not-so-childish example is investing in research and development (R&D). Why invest in products that we don't know the customer will ever buy? Playing thick, your answer is that while products created may never be bought, the learning, the ideas, the exchange will have a role—that is, if R&D is coordinated with the firm's other investments.

Playing thick moves that don't take territory and playing amorphous moves that don't take any territory are two different things. Thick positions are strong in their locale, even though territory in that locale is somewhat taken. Amorphous positions are loose and not particularly strong or particularly surrounding territory. Even though neither takes territory directly, one has far-reaching impact and benefits, the other does not. The difference between thick and not thick is subtle and its effective use is an indicator of one's strength.

Part and parcel with focusing and being deliberate, and not amorphous, is coordinating around where you are focusing. For instance, if your company sponsored you for three years to get either a law degree or an MBA (including one-year MBA prep), you would pick one, right? You wouldn't take two years getting a law degree, then switch to an MBA, and get neither, would you? It is like the proverbial chicken crossing the road going two-thirds of the way across and heading back for the final third. Road kill. Poor but focused decisions are often better than changing horses midstream. The rule in Go is "Complete the pattern."

In Go, in business, in life, however, people are unable to tell the difference between switching strategies and a mixed strategy. A mixed strategy is a blend, a fusion of choices. Switching strategies is not a blend; it is throwing your car into reverse while going forward. You go neither forward nor in reverse; you strip your gears. When you're focused and moving, you already Owe that direction your life; you are not saving options at that point. You have to get to the end of the street before you can change course. Even if you know something is bad, you can make it worse by not staying the course until its natural end. Playing focused means staying coordinated, even if on a bad path to some extent, to take your medicine before trying to correct for it. Your career could progress likewise.

A job with influence—or, in Go parlance, thick—is being a police officer, judge, county commissioner, or state senator. Not necessarily big money, but you've got power. Stick with that job, focusing on the political career, and someday your influence can be converted into a high-paying lobbyist job or similarly compensated position. Coordinating on a position of influence takes time and energy, however. Most people can't switch back and forth between a more cash-oriented job and a political career, as they will not get far with either. With a focused investment in a career, you can switch once you reach the top. Successful politicians often become lobbyists and think tank leaders; successful executives and actors run for office and win. People who vacillate, sometimes power/outside, sometimes steady/inside, are not as likely to succeed. Complete the pattern and then switch. Should you need to switch, be sure to do it as infrequently as possible.

IGD wanted to be sure that if it was going to dump its current diversified strategy, it would be for good. Dumping any of its dependent customers would be a travesty if they were to get out of and then back into serving those customers. While IGD knew that it was trying to surround everything with its diversified strategy and knew that that wasn't a great way to run the business, getting out of a particular line would be costly since IGD would lose whatever customer or product set it dropped. Also, there were plenty of customers who were just reaping the benefits of their low price and were not really adding value.

GO: A GAME OF OPTIONS

Knowing when to ditch a product, exit a market, or stop production lines was not going to be an easy chore for IGD, but it would be made easier by looking at it in terms of options. Real options came into vogue in the late nineties and have since fallen a bit in popularity, but nonetheless, the models for tracking entry, exit, staged commitments, and the like are just as alive now as they were then, if not more so.

The idea behind real options evaluation came from the Black-Scholes model for valuing financial options. If you had bought a share of Yahoo! at the beginning of 2003, you might have paid $20 for it. Once you bought it, the fortune or misfortune of that $20 purchase would swing along with Yahoo!'s stock price. An option to buy Yahoo!, at that same time, might have cost $10 for a two-year option to buy Yahoo! at $15, let's say. The option gives you the right to buy, at some future specified time, a share of Yahoo! for $15 a share. If you bought the option and then immediately exercised it, you'd pay the $10 for the option and $15 for the share, or $25 dollars total. Of course, if the stock was worth $20, you would lose $5 on the transaction.

The value of the option is that you don't have to exercise the option now, but can wait up to two years to do so. Today, if you held that option and exercised it, you'd pay your $25 ($10 spent at the time of the option's purchase, plus $15 cost of the share, per the option agreement), but you would get a share worth about $40— a net gain of $15. Not bad. But, after you bought it, the share price could have also gone down. You didn't know the future, but you presumed the share price would go up or you wouldn't have bought this kind of option.

A few Nobel Prize winners found a good way to value an option based on six criteria, thereafter named the Black-Scholes model, which says that the value of the option ($10 in our Yahoo! case) is determined by a function of the stock price (in our example, $20), the price at which you'd exercise the option ($15), dividends paid (Yahoo! didn't pay any at the time), the uncertainty of the stock price (how much the stock price fluctuates up and down), how much time you have to exercise the option (two years), and the risk-free interest rate (the interest rate of a riskless security, like a T-bill, which is guaranteed). This is a great calculus for estimating how Go players have been evaluating positions for millennia.[1]

1. In Go, you do exactly this sort of calculation without the advantage of having market information. The more elaborate conceit might go something like:

The stock price in Go is the value of the territory you do or can control as a result of your play. Whether taking territory directly or influencing the amount of territory you will take based on playing thick moves, you can estimate that value as the number of points you have per a particular move.

The exercise price is the cost of converting your plays into actual territory. That

While Go has rules that fit into most of these categories, there has been no calculus in Go as there is for real options in business. Nonetheless, the rules in Go that apply fit in well with real options thinking. Some of the most important Expand principles of Go rely on the same sort of metaphor as real options methodology.

For instance, when you keep things Slack, you are also looking at it from the perspective of Expand. The Go rule "Leave options for the opponent to make mistakes; don't make things clear" is a good first example. In the midst of a fight, it is better to leave the opponent with as many opportunities to make mistakes as possi-

---

you've set up a framework for taking territory or having influence on the board doesn't mean that you actually now have done all the work to surround that territory. You need to play more stones and typically complete the end game before whatever territory is actually yours. That cost in stones you'll need to ultimately take the territory is the exercise price.

Uncertainty for Go comes in by way of how fierce the competition is, how chaotic the surrounding positions are, and how unresolved situations across the board are. The more chaotic and fractalized, the more uncertain; therefore, each new move has potentially a greater impact on resolving the game. The more restrained, quiet, and reserved the two players are, the less uncertainty, the less impact each move will have on the ultimate outcome.

The time to expiry in Go is how long an opportunity remains and what stage of the game you're in. If you're in the late beginning stage or the early middle game, each move you make will have a greater impact on the rest of the game. The longer the time to expiry of the opportunity, the greater the value of the move to the entire board. Moves in the end game have less impact and realizing the actual territory from end-game moves has a very short time to live. Just as TV sales have a time to expiry on their products ("buy in the next ten minutes to get a free . . ."—yeah, right), you need to be aware of what times to expiry are in your field.

Dividends in Go are real territory that you are missing out on because you are not actually surrounding it at this time. Since cash in hand is always more valuable than cash you might get, this is a cost to both the Go player who doesn't have the actual territory yet and the person retaining the option to buy the stock (and thereby get the dividend payment). For dividends, the analogue in Go or life is that you're not getting any younger, each move proceeds, the opportunity on the board shrinks by at least one stone. Just as going out with someone costs you the opportunity or option of going out with someone else, you're not getting any younger by not going out with anyone.

The risk-free rate is the amount of territory you could certainly surround, with each move depending on the stage of the game. Just as with real investment opportunities, the amount is significantly less than what you can build with sketching things out and then filling them in, but in the event you weren't able to make that sketched-out territory, you'd have something instead. It's the apex of Save, but hardly ever the right move until the end game.

ble. When you play moves that are option-laden, there is a lot of slack left for the opponent to hang him- or herself with.

In aikido, you want to keep the proper distance from your opponent so that you can take up slack as the opponent attacks. When the founder of aikido was facing the swordsman, he essentially removed all options for attack, and the swordsman could do nothing. The comedian leaves a joke dangling and unfinished for the audience, only to later draw on it to complete a routine. You optimize slack, but also leave the audience anticipating the final exercise of the option.

Top Go players master the art of prudent choices that don't reveal themselves till just the right moment; the quintessential now; the ultimate just-in-time strategy and tactics for the situation at hand. Knowing full well what each piece's role is in the greater scheme of things, they wait until the situation is perfectly ripe and then spring the meaning on the unsuspecting amateur when it looked for all intents and purposes as if there was nothing going on there.

With so many stones across the board, incompletely sketching out territory or exuding influence to threaten neighbors with sheer strength, the key to realizing these option investments is timing. The key to making each stone work to its maximum is to know when best to unleash each move's multipurpose meaning amidst the vagaries of stage of game, uncertainty, value to each player, and opportunity to do something with it.

In Go, you must master the timing, not invest just because there's a positive value to doing so. The value must be so positive or high as to leave no more value to waiting to see the uncertainty revealed. Pro Go players have toiled for decades to acquire this timing. Putting it to use in daily life also takes a toll.

It's the same sort of thinking that one does when investing in a new technology. I would like to buy SACDs or DVD-Audio because I like to hear the finest-quality recordings, but in which technology do I invest? Does my inclination in the past to move to Beta from Sony make me a sucker for getting into the wrong thing?

More likely what I'll do is wait for the uncertainty to play out. While I could buy in and start a collection of DVD-As or SACDs, I am probably better off waiting until one of these media becomes a standard for high-fidelity recordings.

It was the same thing when you didn't buy DVDs at the store, but bought VHS even though they sold DVDs, and you wondered, "Shouldn't I buy this on DVD?" This conversation will occur any number of times throughout one's lifetime. In mine, it's been, should I buy the eight-track, cassette tapes, VHS, Beta, should I buy 5.25-inch diskettes, 3.5-inch diskettes, Compaq, IBM, PC, or MSFT DOS, Windows or OS/2, CDs, laser disks, cell phone (numerous times), records, HDTV, and so forth. The list goes on and on ad infinitum. The issue is, do I want to act and be part of the leadership of the technology or do I wait with the old while the standard is promulgated? There's a cost in waiting and not waiting.

When you wait to see what becomes the standard, you don't make investments until the uncertainty reconciles with the value. By waiting and not investing or playing the move, you still hold the option to, unless the opponent beats you to it. The tautology, the crux of ultimate play, is "Don't play or resolve a situation until its potential value in light of uncertainty is clearly more valuable than continuing to hold it." Just as options are powerful, remember the flipside. If you're waiting to see how the board will evolve before committing to play, but your opponent can see the future more clearly, then the opponent can commit first to the winning area before you do.

Just as there are rules governing waiting, there are Go rules such as "Every good move has a good next," that are less about realizing a benefit now and more about realizing a benefit that gives you the flexibility to win the game as it changes. The more options that you can create from each move, the more successful avenues you can go down. The more meanings each option has, the more potential future scenarios you'll be able to move on and affect.

Importing this into one's operations strategy can help make downstream investments pay off. For instance, HP printers are assembled up to a point, but then customized per demand later. Each printer assembly is an option on a future one, but since it is uncertain what printer it will ultimately become, the option's not realized until the future is more resolved. Likewise, Bennetton would produce shirts of a generic type estimating the demand for shirts, but not the color and style of those shirts, and then later, once the demand for a particular color was clear, it would dye those shirts appropriately. That way, it gained the economies of scale in the production of the shirts in advance, but still was able to customize per demand.

The advice to IGD was that instead of responding to the sales order and then producing that order as soon as possible, there could be better strategic use of the raw materials as they came out of the ground.

Certain medical and food industries products required higher-grade gypsum than other products. Most of the remainder could use the higher grade but didn't require it. Instead of fulfilling orders using the higher-grade gypsum unearthed for just those products that demanded it, you would see this high-grade gypsum go into lawn gnome fodder.

Our advice to IGD was that you could make those products needing a lower-grade material wait, when medical and food products were already in the queue. That way, instead of waiting again for higher-grade material to come out of the ground, which did not happen terribly often, they would match the grade to the products, stopping others while those demands were filled.

Storing higher-grade raw material, even when there were not orders in the queue for products needing it, made sense because the shelf life of the higher-grade material lasted for some time. Because you could forecast the demand for those products needing higher-grade gypsum, you could delay production of products that could take either higher- or lower-grade raw material. When large veins of high-grade material were unearthed and once a certain inventory of forecast production of products requiring higher-grade materials were filled, you could start fulfilling orders with the higher grade for products that could go either way.

UNDERNEATH IT ALL

With so many options underlying Go play, you see only a percentage of the battles that go on in tournament matches between Go pros. With both pros knowing the potential meanings and uses for all their pieces, they have to account for many scenarios that will go unplayed. As each sees only a partial set of what the other probably sees, it's clear that the one with the perspective closer to reality is likely to be the winner.

One of the endearing qualities of Shusaku's games was his ability to read through all the complexity, see through all the fights, and then return to simple moves. Although he could reach down and fight with the best of them, his ability to find quiet but deep moves is still an inspiration to players today. The Go rule "The most terrible attack/cut is one you don't make and the opponent doesn't have an opportunity to fix, but must prepare for" is long, but intended to show the power of holding an option and threatening to use it. As when holding a trump card or a piece of information, or conducting a sting, the options become very real indeed, even if never played. With the game progressing on each turn, thousands of variations and scenarios will pass without seeing the light of the board.

The key to this sort of planning is, again, to understand the nature of planning. You cannot do your thinking after the fact. Your thinking must consider the future before the fact and enable as many good potentials for your next move as possible, taking those visions into account. As mentioned before, the rule in Go is "The key to planning is the planning, not the plan." Other rules like this are "Don't expect to reap what you sow," or a Scott McKeon favorite, "You have no right to your expectations."

As you find many good potential uses for the stone you are about to play, do not fall in love with these plans (like George Costanza). If you try to capture the wonderful plan underlying your moves, you are not playing living Go.

As IGD made changes to its production runs and storage of higher-grade material, its actions were not based on anything it saw, but on the likelihood of producing something of greater value, despite nothing currently being there—either demanded or unearthed. While this was a cool plan, there were potential revisits that might say that the marginal profit of the products needing a higher grade did not warrant the cost and inventory. The key is not to be wedded to the plan, no matter how cool, but to be wedded to the ultimate goal—which in most cases for IGD was to contribute the most profit and breakthrough opportunity back to the rest of USG.

EXIT—STAGE FRIGHT

There are a number of ways to exit or sacrifice a Go position. One is to let the opponent spend resources to kill it. The other is to force the opponent to eat your sacrifice so you can gain elsewhere. In considering an exit from a position, you want to look at the same sort of things you do in waiting to invest.

There is the cost of those spent moves that will now probably not get used. There is the relinquishing of an area to the opponent that will now be difficult to get back. There is the "complete the pattern" sense of making a number of follow-on moves to ensure its sacrifice. There are all the potentials and meanings that can still come from that position that you need to think through before ditching.

For IGD, there were all these considerations and more. If it left a particular product line, would it be able to start it back up, if needed? If it left a particular customer in the lurch, would it lose more business as a result? If it no longer was going to train new employees in how to make it, would it lose the skill set that allowed it to be able to reproduce it? There were many considerations.

Exiting from some processes and setups might mean exiting that line of business forever, while exiting other businesses now might only be as temporary as IGD wanted it to be. Just as in Go, you need to weigh when you're going to be giving something up utterly and when you aren't really giving something up. If IGD stopped producing a particular product—such as lawn-gnome mix—it might be very easy to restart producing it sometime later. Whereas, if IGD stopped producing some of its medicinal products, they wouldn't need the skilled extractor—who knows the exacting procedure for how to create this product with his hands and can train others to do it by hand—in the plant, and they might lose the skill forever. The option value depends a lot on which sort of exiting we're talking about.

One of the considerations sorely missing early in the analysis was the degree to which exiting a product line affected the product manager of that product. If all the calculations and machinations foretold the demise of a particular product line and that product line was directly managed by a single product manager whose sole role was to champion it, what did you tell the employee?

Many consultants are seen as angels of death. Employees clinging to both their products and a desire not to change things are often the first to start sounding the klaxon about how great their product is, despite the figures, despite the research, and most certainly despite the consultant. Any consultant worth his or her salt knows that this is going to be an issue and needs to factor in the human costs of making or recommending changes.

Despite not killing any one product manager's entire portfolio of products, there were voices coming to the rescue of attachments to the status quo at USG. This aversion to change is not exclusive to USG, however.

Go players who remain their whole lives at the lower amateur ranks still enjoy Go. That they miss some of the esoteric or subtle nuances doesn't mean that Go isn't enjoyable. People of all ranks enjoy Go for what it is to them. When I first started teaching Go, I couldn't understand people not wanting to improve.

Working with some of these players over the years, I now have a better perspective on why they remain at their lower levels—they don't want to change their thinking or their perspective on the game. They want to maintain the status quo. Go is comfortable now. Their lament is "If I have to start reading things out or looking at a problem for too long, I'm going to quit. It won't be fun anymore." A noble but different goal from improvement, but worthy nonetheless.

At IGD, we were approaching the situation head-on with one of the employees whose favorite products were going away. For IGD, the goal wasn't just to have fun with one's products. After trying unsuccessfully to convince us or his customers that the product should remain in production, he mentioned potentially leaving the company. Management had to decide whether this person added value or was already primed for dismissal.

If the employee was already out the door in the manager's mind, this is sort of like the Go rule "Give out the bait." The antithesis for the employee then would be "Don't take the bait." While there were people marked for termination, management would need to offer those let go a substantial severance. Letting them quit would be a much cheaper alternative.

At all times in Go, you need to look at your stones with the idea that even the most close-to-dead stones can be brought back to life in the right circumstances. The key is to keep their options alive as long as it makes sense. As an employee facing the killing of a product line, one that happens to be yours, don't assume that you're being let go because your product is. Your option value may not be tied to your product.

AJI

As with most things in Go, you want to turn things on their head to get the full perspective. Just as you want to keep your options alive, you want to extinguish options for the opponent. Of course, this is difficult to do when you aren't completing your positions. Indeed, the result of this sort of jockeying is the creation of miai—a balance between two positions, so that if you take one side, the opponent can get the other, and the two are relatively equal locally.

But when you can, you want to kill the options that are not for your side. There's a rule in Go to "eat what you can eat." It means that if the opponent has left a position open to attack and killing, you should kill it. Be savvy enough to extinguish all potential from the opponent's positions. The Japanese word for positions that don't get extinguished is "aji."

Aji is the Japanese word for taste. In Go, it refers to positions that have a meaning and portent that lingers, but is not necessarily exercisable now. Positions with aji may sit throughout the game or they may be realized, but at all times, you must account for them. Leave them alone too long and the opponent can raise their potential. Knowing when to "eat what you can eat" and extinguishing aji, creating aji for your opponent's positions and removing aji from yours, is an indicator of your strength.

Browsing the supermarket shelves during a particularly long checkout, I was skimming through one of the more popular woman's magazines. It was giving out interesting advice for its dating readers—leave your underwear behind at your date's place. This is following the Go proverb "Leave aji before leaving." In Go, before you save your stones under attack, typically by connecting them out to the center, this proverb says that you should leave some aji in the opponent's attacking positions before connecting out. This advice is similar, though I am sure there are other things you might leave (this book, a hat, a friendly note) that would accomplish the same thing without the potential for some problematic uncertainties that might result from leaving the said article.

Go beginners are fond of removing aji because they don't know where else to move. The thinking is "At least by removing aji I know the opponent will respond." The rules they are violating are "Don't play when you don't know what to do." "Play away." "Don't kill aji." "Don't fix." By fixing a position, removing its aji and options, you kill option value if you do it too soon. Force the opponent to come up with the right move or force the play so that the right move becomes clearer. "Don't resolve uncertainty before its time."

In business, trying to remove uncertainty before its time is a disastrous way to play. "Oh, I don't know, why don't we have a price war with our competitors?" Yes, this is something to do. Yes, it is something to rally behind. Yes, if you have a better cost structure you might outlive your competitor in a price war. But a price war is almost always bad. It extinguishes the potential to distinguish your services or products in another way from the competitor's. It extinguishes the opportunity to fund more R&D, and so forth. A price war for the sake of doing something is the worst kind of fear of aji. In Go, you preserve aji as long as possible. It's a form of option. When it comes to actually needing a price war, then OK, do it. But, remember, as in Go, the need is much less frequent than the actual number of silly fights or unnecessary price wars.

FOCUS EXPANSION

IGD was able to make a number of improvements by being smarter about its order of manufacturing and operations strategy. By looking at its products, customers, and services as options and by timing things differently, IGD made a number of moves, a few of which I have mentioned, that helped refocus its business and gave it options on its raw material. While IGD would have to remain ever vigilant of competitor, internal, and customer moves, it was able to make cuts strategically and focus as uncertainty was resolved.

THE LAST OF THE SEVEN

On my way through the amateur ranks, I would often think, "Wow. If I could master all these rules, I'd be set. If I could account for all these rules in every situation, that would be quite a feat and would make me a more complete player." Unfortunately, this is not the case.

As you may have suspected, these rules are the SHU and the HA of the SHU-HA-RI progression. They are the fundamentals, the antithesis to the fundamentals, but they are still missing RI to be complete. You'll never escape the amateur levels with only these preceding rules under your belt. After taking off the scaffolding of the rules presented so far, after you've put the map down, you will find that the edifice you were building, the road you were taking, does not exist. The final lesson of Go is to know that there are no rules.

If you were to prune back the 10^{170} plays and find the true solution to the game, you'd never need one rule to help you. You'd play the way that won. While it is certainly possible that this way of playing would be a nice stroll through all the rules and their trappings, it's just as likely that the moves would coalesce around something far beyond current human understanding and patterns we've explored to date. Because each of the rules so far was found, nourished, and grown in multiple environments across thousands of games, they are general shortcuts to better play, but not to exact play.

We all live in an exact environment, whatever it may be. While following the rules of general situations may prove to help us 80 percent of the time, there's the other 20 percent of the way that can still be obtained. "Sorry, there are no rules" is the rule that respects that 20 percent for every move where the other rules may not apply, and due to very idiosyncratic differences between generality and specificity, no rule possibly could have.

To find these exact moves is a tribute to spirit more than anything else. Once you've reached the higher amateur levels, you can play very well even at breakneck speed, but this is not being true to the game you're playing. Part of your success is your ability to employ these rules. Part is your attendance to whatever your goal may be. Professionals can spend hours on what seems like an obvious response they have to make because of this spirit to find the best move, and at the highest level, when trying to play kami no itte—the Hand of God. So, sorry, what we've learned so far is only going to help us so far.

CHAPTER EIGHT

———•———

SORRY

THERE ARE NO RULES

Learning the rules described in Chapters 1–7 will improve your game. They are reminders of the polar yin and yang nature of the game. But, if you think of the rules as the Way, as opposed to guides to the Way, you will never get to true Go. Rules of thumb are an outcropping of true Go, they are scaffolding. The one true move at each moment of the game does not hinge on a rule, pattern, shape, or tradition. The one true move is as unique as each game you play, each part of the nearly infinite number of possible games, which is breathed to life by your hand and the opponent's, each a potential work of art you are responsible for creating or destroying. The goal of the game is to win, the path is to find the one right move, not march lockstep with rules as if they were the Way.

No matter the rules, there is one right move for every occasion. The rules in Go are "There are no rules for the middle game," "Don't rely on simple proverbs," and so on. No matter what shape it might be, how uncoordinated it might be, how much potential it eliminates, or how overconcentrated it might be, the best moves have no bias to conform to or violate rules or known patterns. Many games suffer by keeping to the rules at the expense of the exact reality of the situation. And over the centuries, shapes and forms that used to be standards have been replaced through research and a better understanding of the positions and a spirit to recognize when a pattern, maybe even a hundreds-of-years-old one, is wrong.

The Way of Go then is a quest to find the one best move and to look beyond the rules. Sometimes violating the rules is best. Sometimes, the inefficient shape is best. Both the famous Jowa, in the infamous blood-vomiting game back in 1835, and Cho Hyun Hun, in his first world victory against Nie Wei Ping, broke with standard play and played the moves that were right for the game, not the edifice of rules.

There is no road map I can give you to win at Go, business, or life. Experience, incorporating the forms as part of SHU, learning beyond what's comfortable and set forms with HA, and developing your own technique with RI, is the only way to transcend the simple structures that are like so much scaffolding—structures that help you get there, but are not the building itself.

THE SPIRIT TO PLAY THE ONE BEST MOVE

The spirit needed to break with tradition is tough. Cho Chikun exemplifies the spirit to play the one best move. The top player in Japan in the eighties, Cho is the only professional in Japan to hold all the top titles simultaneously. This is akin to the Triple Crown of horse racing or holding all the major titles in golf. It is a unique occurrence.

Two days a week Cho graciously instructed us inseis, often showing his true strength in this informal setting. It was a Go player's dream. Some nights Cho would review insei games, some nights we would study life and death, some nights we would play speed Go tournaments (one night, I even got the chance to challenge him as White, as ridiculous as that was, as White is always the color of the stronger player). No matter the night, the spirit of Cho's attendance was to play true Go.

The most dramatic review occurred one night while Cho went through the game of one of the top female inseis (now she is one of the top female professionals in Japan). Her opponent had employed a rather typical opening structure known as the "high-Chinese opening," and Cho asked where she played next. She played a regular move to reduce the opponent's territory by not invading too deeply, but instead playing a balanced reduction move from above, a move typical of a professional game, a textbook way to reduce the opponent's area in this sort of opening. Cho was not impressed.

He shook his head and pulled at his hair. After some time, he took a stone from his bowl and flipped it onto the board. After watching Cho for months, this came as a complete shock. His board and stones, which he brought to these lessons, were priceless heirlooms that would easily fetch six figures or more if ever auctioned. Cho, who had the utmost respect for the tradition of the game, his board and stones, was now flipping stones. This was going to be a severe lesson.

Cho had little tolerance for play at her level that merely followed the current trends in professional play. Each game of Go with more than 10^{170} possible ways of play has its own character, its own nature. Each game is a potential masterpiece, a national treasure, if played with the spirit to find the one best move. Cho's respect for the game and this insei's development would not let her flip response go.

"Why here?" he asked. "Why not here?" as he flipped a stone up onto the board. All of us were speechless. "This looks good, why not here?" as he proceeded to play out the continuation from where the flipped stone landed. Indeed, he seemed to have flipped what was likely the best move. Not only did it reduce the situation in a way more in line with the game, but it showed potential she did not consider. What a good flip!

But then, he asked again "Why not here?" as he removed that continuation and flipped another stone onto the board. Again, it seemed that he had found an even better move to reduce the high-Chinese opening for this game. This continuation showed that there were a number of problems with the opponent's position and how this move addressed issues that were not covered in the others. He continued to flip stones and played out beautiful sequence after beautiful sequence from the flipped stone, explaining how each was the best possible move for the situation, wondering why this was not the best move. "Why not here?" he asked.

The point was made. Cho knew that she had the ability to play and defend each of the continuations as well. Without the spirit to play the one best move, however, almost any move may seem profound and right, especially if you have the strength and ability to defend it. The difference is that there is only *one* best approach. No two games are alike and you must respect that nature. Without the right spirit to find the *one* best move, your trajectory will always be off course in life or in Go.

SEEK WHAT THEY SOUGHT

No matter the calculus, the paradigm, or the rules, they are all probably wrong in some respects. Almost every age has thought, "We are about at the end of understanding." When we repair streams, when we award Nobel Prizes, when we talk about the best offense, defense, strategy, or formula, we are employing our best understanding of things and then glomming onto the edifice we built.

Yes, you must know the forms and their counterparts, you need to see what's there and what's not there, you must master timing from the perspective of when, how, and why not, but don't lose sight of the fact that those rules are the pointers, they are not the Way itself. Know your goal. These rules will help. Then away you Go.

APPENDIX: HOW TO PLAY GO

———•———

I derived GO'S RULES from the game itself. To master the game and to understand the descriptive rules that tell you how to play Go are beyond the scope of this Appendix.

This introduction cannot make you a Go master. It can tell you something about how Go is played, give you some inkling of why Go is both simple and difficult, and give you a sense for its aesthetic common sense.

THE EQUIPMENT

The photo is a glimpse of the Japanese Professional Go Academy in Makuhari Nishi Chiba, a suburb of Tokyo, Japan, where I trained. The academy has since closed. The games shown are at a variety of stages of either play or review. The players sitting before and amidst the boards were my usual opponents.

The boards are slightly raised from the floor so that two players sitting on the floor could play at them easily. This is the traditional style. Nowadays, table boards are used for a number of major events. The stones are lens-shaped and placed inside a bowl when not in play, placed in the lid when captured, placed on the board in play, and mashed together when a game is being reviewed and the focus of the game in review is just on one particular area.

THE GO BOARD

Go is a board game. The typical Go board is a grid of nineteen lines by nineteen lines, as is shown in Diagram 1. While beginners typically play on a 9 × 9 board or a 13 × 13 board (many of the diagrams in this Appendix are on an even smaller board), most professional matches use a 19 × 19 board. At the outset of the game, the board is empty, as is shown in Diagram 1. The bold points on the board are called star points, but have no use other than orientation in an even game.

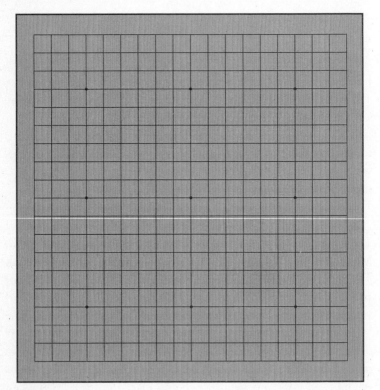

Diagram 1*

* These and other screen captures are used courtesy of David Fotland from the program Many Faces of Go 11.0.

TWO-PLAYER GAME

Go is a two-player game: One side plays Black stones, the other plays White stones. In Go, you place your stones on the intersections, as opposed to on the squares. Starting with Black, players alternate placing their stones, one at a time, on unoccupied intersections of the board.

Diagram 2

surround   stone

THE OBJECT OF THE GAME

The English word Go is borrowed from the Japanese character in Diagram 2, pronounced the same way as it is in English. The top part of the character loosely means surround, the bottom loosely means stone. The object of the game is to use one's stones to surround more unoccupied intersections than the opponent does. To surround intersections, you fence them off. Because intersections are the only playing field in Go, treat the lines like roads and surround each intersection or group of intersections so that there are no inroads to them. At the end of the game intersections exclusively surrounded by any side are points for that side.

Diagram 3 (only half of the board is shown) shows three different ways in which Black has surrounded one point. In position 1, the Black stones surround the corner point. Every intersection adjacent to the corner point is in Black's control. There is no connecting point out to the rest of the board. Likewise, Black surrounds a point on the side in position 2. In position 3, Black surrounds a point in the center of the board.

The edge of the board has a considerable role in how many stones you need in order to surround an intersection. With two Black stones, you can surround one point in the corner of the board (position 1), with two edges helping you cordon off that point. On the side it takes three stones to surround a point (position 2), and it takes four stones to surround a center point (position 3).

Using eight Black stones in Diagram 4, you can surround four points in the center (position 4), eight points on the side (position 5), and sixteen points in the corner (position 6). One of the first proverbs one learns in Go is "Corner-side-center," that is, take the corners first, then the sides, then play in the center. This way, your moves are their most efficient in relationship to what the board provides as a natural boundary. Environment matters.

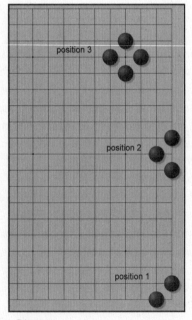

Diagram 3

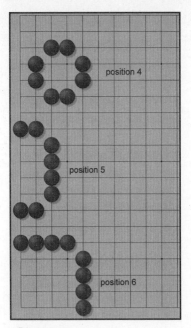

Diagram 4

ALTERNATING MOVES

Black plays first and can place a stone anywhere on the board. While it is common to find Black's first moves in a corner region, Black is free to play on any intersection. In Diagram 5, Black has played the first move on the fourth line from the top and the fourth line from the right (the 4-4 point). Once you play a stone on the board, it has to remain there. You cannot move your stones around.

Go is different from most games because it is a game of creation. Without preordained setups, each player is free to play in whatever style, way, or manner is interesting to that player. While most professional matches play corner-side-center as the order of regions, there have been very strange, wonderful, and important challenges to the status quo that really opened up theories on how best to play at the beginning of the game.

On White's turn. White can play on any of the remaining unoccupied intersections. You can only play one stone on one intersection at a time. The two sides alternate placing stones on unoccupied intersections until the end of the game.

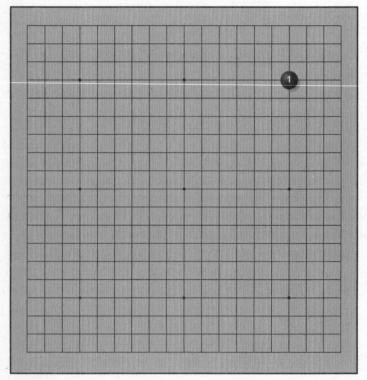

Diagram 5

Play alternates Black and White, one move per player per intersection, until there are no more ways to exclusively surround empty intersections with either player's stones. Because there are four corners, four sides, and a big center to surround, you often have battles raging across the board, potentially in each of those nine areas. But, with only one move per turn, you cannot affect every local situation optimally and you must keep the global goal in mind to stay ahead in intersections surrounded. This skill and spirit is what professionals train their whole lives to do. With no hidden moves, no chance, and nothing but an equal arsenal of plays per player, you win because your play is more attuned to GO'S RULES.

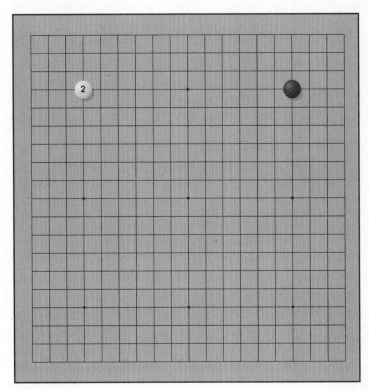

Diagram 6

PASS

Diagram 7 shows a completed game. This is the 1987 Honinbo tournament, which was sponsored by the Mainichi Shimbun, that pitted perennial champion Takemiya, playing White, against Yamashiro, playing Black.

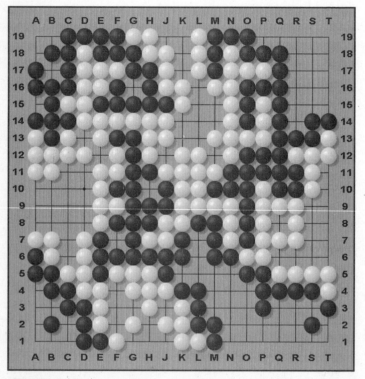

Diagram 7

At this stage of the game, both players pass, as neither player can surround any more intersections exclusively than each has already done. White stones exclusively surround the White regions and Black stones exclusively surround the Black regions. The game is over. The player with more unoccupied intersections surrounded, wins.

If you are having trouble seeing what's what here, that's normal.

It's called stone-blinded. Let's outline this game from a more abstract vantage point.

REGIONS

In Diagram 8, regions of the board have been outlined. There are two White regions and four Black regions. Black has each of the four corners and some neighboring points surrounded. White has one big sprawling group that spans from the top edge to the left edge to the bottom side and another on the right edge. This is typical of Takemiya, who plays a center-oriented strategy.

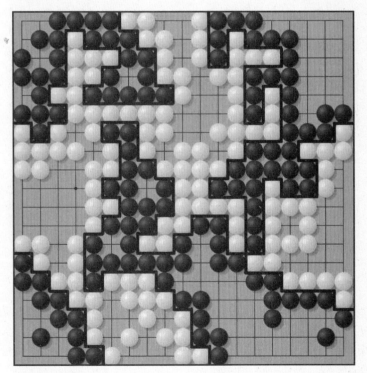

Diagram 8

There are all sorts of rules on how to score Go. The simplest way is to look at the surrounded points and count empty intersections.

SCORING

In this game, it seems as if Black has won. Black has 62 surrounded points and White has 54 surrounded points.

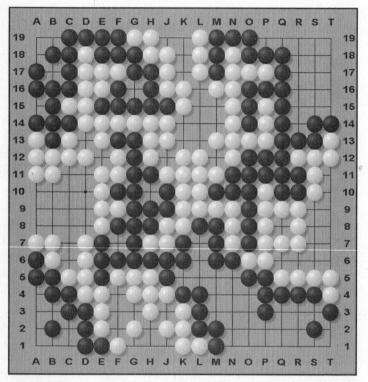

Diagram 8A

In the lower right corner, Black has 28 points surrounded. In the lower left, Black has 8 points. In the middle, Black has 2 points. In the upper right, Black has 18 points. In the upper left, Black has 6 points. In total, Black has 62 points surrounded on the board (28+8+2+18+6 = 62 points).

On the right side, White has 13 points. On the upper side and the middle, White has 14 points. On the left side, White has 18 points. On the lower side, White has 9 points. So White has 13+14+18+9 = 54 points.

It seems as if Black has won, but the stones on the board do not reflect part of the history of the game. Because Black moved first, Black received an advantage, and in modern Go, White is awarded compensation for this first-mover advantage Black has. Likewise, there are captures not reflected.

FIRST-MOVER ADVANTAGE

Modern Go recognizes that Black will win most games because of the first-mover advantage. The points awarded the second mover are called a komi. The komi includes a half-point that ties, since there are no half-points on the board to surround. Komi changes from time to time and country to country. At the time this game was played in Japan, White received only 5.5 points, versus the 6.5 White would now receive. So, to this game, add to White's total 5.5 points.

Seems as if Black still wins, 62 to 59.5. But, before going to the final tally we need to account for the stones that are not on the board—those captured by White and Black.

CAPTURE

For a group (one or more stones connected via intersections) to remain on the board, it must have one intersection adjacent to the group unoccupied by the opponent. Adjacent unoccupied intersections are called a group's "liberties." In Diagram 9, the Black stone has only one intersection, or liberty, remaining—the intersection immediately below it.

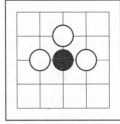
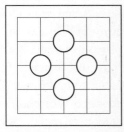

Diagram 9   Diagram 10   Diagram 11

If Diagram 9 depicts White's last move, where White had played a move immediately to the right of the Black stone, then White is said to have put that Black stone into "atari." Atari (the namesake of Atari, the video-game manufacturer) is akin to the chess word "check." You atari a stone by playing on its next-to-last liberty.

If on White's next turn, the situation in Diagram 9 remains as is, White can capture this Black stone by placing a stone on Black's remaining liberty below it, as shown in Diagram 10. When White plays on this last Black liberty, White removes the Black stone from the board, as in Diagram 11, and stores the Black stone off the board until the end of the game. At the end of the game, each side returns the captured stones of the other side, called prisoners, back into the opponent's territory, thereby reducing the other player's total territory by the number of repatriated prisoners.

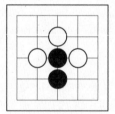

Diagram 12

Of course, Black can respond, if ataried by White, as in Diagram 9. Black can save that stone by playing a move that increases the size of Black's group by adding a stone immediately below the lone Black stone, as in Diagram 12. Now, the Black group has three liberties. If White wants to capture the two stones, White will need to play on all of the Black group's liberties, which are now three.

In this match, White had captured six Black stones and Black had captured three White stones. In Diagram 13, Black places the captured White stones into White's territory (at the points marked with a triangle). White places the captured Black stones into Black's territory (at the points marked with a square). Now, the total number of points for Black is reduced by 6, and the total number of White's points is reduced by 3.

Revising the tallies from earlier, White had 54 points on the board, 5.5 points komi, and this total is reduced by 3 for the stones that Black captured. Black had 62 points on the board, no komi, since Black moved first, and Black's total is reduced by 6 points for the stones that White captured. White's postrepatriation total is 56.5 points and Black's total is 56 points. White wins by half a point. Takemiya won by virtue of the komi and fewer captures by Black.

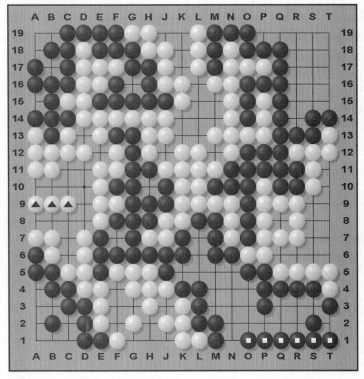

Diagram 13

NO SUICIDE

Just as the capture rule allows the opponent to remove stones with no liberties, you cannot play a stone on the board that results in a group with no liberty free unless that stone is capturing an opponent's group. For instance, in Diagram 14, Black cannot play on the point in the center of the White stones. This would be suicide, because at the end of Black's turn, there would be no liberties for the Black stone there.

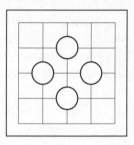

Diagram 14

In Diagram 15, White has a group with only one liberty free. In Diagram 16, Black plays on the final liberty of the White group, and in Diagram 17, Black removes the White stones. The Black stone can play on a point with no liberties as long as it is capturing the opponent, because after the capture, there will be liberties for the Black stone on the points to the right and below the Black stone.

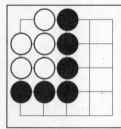

Diagram 15

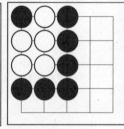

Diagram 16

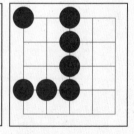

Diagram 17

KO

The "ko" rule states that you cannot immediately repeat a board position already played. There are circumstances where it is possible to repeat a position already played on the board. Diagrams 18–20 show how.

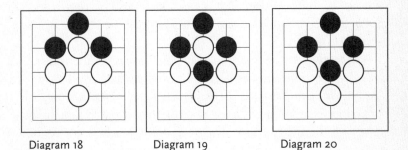

Diagram 18   Diagram 19   Diagram 20

In Diagram 18, it is Black's turn to move. Black can capture the White stone by playing a move in the center, as in Diagram 19. After Black plays in the center as in Diagram 19, Black captures the White stone and the board ends up like Diagram 20. On White's turn, after Diagram 20, it would make sense that White could then recapture the Black stone in the center now, which, after capture, would result in Diagram 18 again. To keep the game from repeating from Diagram 18 to 20 ad nauseam, the ko rule states that you cannot repeat a board position immediately. Therefore, when Black captures in Diagram 20, White cannot go back and capture Black immediately. White needs to play somewhere else on the board first. If Black does nothing about the ko situation, then White can recapture the Black stone later.

The word ko is derived from the Sanskrit word "kalpa." Kalpa has a number of colorful meanings. The time it would take for a dove, flying with a tassel of silk, to fly around the world and wear down Mount Everest, or the time it would take to empty the ocean a spoonful at a time. Whatever your poison, a kalpa was a long time, practically forever. Basically, the amount of time required to resolve a ko, if you were to play it ad nauseam.

SOME IMPLICATIONS AND METAPHORS

The Go board has provided many analogies for people in business, astrology, politics, and so on. The draw is easy to see.

The board is empty. Go is a game of creation. The board starts out empty. It is a green field, a new employee, a fresh start with every new game. It's as if you and your opponent are competing without the built-up assets, advantages, relationships, or privileges that may face you now. All that matters in each new game is how you play in this match.

Play on the intersections. You play your stones on the intersections. Intersections are like roads. There is no action off-road in Go. That is, if you have pieces diagonally from each other they are not connected and do not form a group, they are just close. If you occupy all the intersections diagonally from a stone, you do not capture it. Likewise, you do not surround intersections through diagonal placements; only moves connected by lines and intersections count. Infrastructure and environment matter.

The object of the game. Each player in turn tries to surround more points than the opponent, but the game is wide open enough for both to have their own ideas. You can shoot for influencing the future or taking opportunities now. You can play risky or safe. You can aim for peaceful negotiations with the opponent or act warlike. It's all up to you and your opponent.

One move per player. With each move, you have to think about its long-term implications. You don't get to move your stones around. And only the most nefarious players request to have their moves taken back. All your plays are sunk costs once played. You don't get to undo what you have done; you play your pieces where they lie. This raises a problem for how to deal with more than one territory, more than one weakness, and more than one strength. You can't play everywhere at once. And you would be remiss to attempt to play something in the middle thinking that half-measures all across the board will address real issues at all the local spots. As you saw at the end of the professional game above, you had better not expect to have just one main territory; expect to have many scattered ones.

Maximize the utility of each move. That said, you can see the benefits of trying to hold corner territory versus side or center territory. With every move, you try to maximize the amount of territory you will ultimately control. As you saw in Diagrams 3 and 4, corner territory requires fewer stones than side territory, and side fewer than center. The Go proverb is "corner-side-center"—corners are the first priority, sides the second, and center the last.

The capture rule. Not only do you need to be concerned with the many needs of your positions across the board, but you need to be vigilant about capture. One of the most difficult parts of the game to master is life and death. In Diagram 12, Black played one move and created three more liberties for the stone about to be captured. In Go, you can gain more liberties for a group by adding more stones. That is, there is safety in numbers. Since the attacker typically needs more stones to capture than the defender does to defend, there is a bias toward defense.

Life and death. The no-suicide rule coupled with the one-move-at-a-time rule is very important, because it can create a situation in which the opponent surrounds you but cannot capture you. In Diagram 21, White has Black surrounded, but because of the suicide rule, White cannot play in either of the two opponent points within Black's corner.

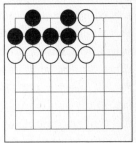

Diagram 21

Neither spot has a liberty free for an invading White stone. If White plays a move in the corner, it does not have a liberty free. Two intersections to the right, there is likewise no liberty free for a White stone.

In Go, these two separate points are called "eyes." Living configurations are those with "two eyes"—two connected but separate points. With two eyes, you are alive, no matter how surrounded you are.

Compare this with Diagram 22. Now, Black has only one eye, the point in the corner. White can play on this last liberty of the Black group because of the capture rule; that is, Black has only one intersection free and therefore White can play on it. After White plays in the corner spot, the Black stones are captured and there are plenty of liberties for the White capturing stone, as shown in Diagram 23.

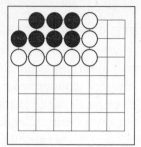

Diagram 22

The implications of this are that more stones don't necessarily help a situation. In Diagram 21, Black has fewer stones on the board, but is alive. In Diagram 22, Black has one more stone on the board, but White can kill these stones, as in Diagram 23. When you play in areas you already control, you not only lose the opportunity to play elsewhere, but lose a point of your own territory.

Stones exert influence. The other facet of Go not mentioned in the rules, but something you find out by experience, is that stones exert influence—influence to surround territory, influence to capture other stones, and influence to defend stones. They exert their influence not just to the points adjacent, but to two or three intersections away from that stone.

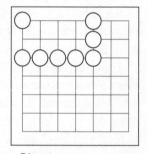

Diagram 23

Groups of two or more stones, likewise, extend their influence over even greater distances across the Go board. The notion of influence is important, because otherwise, you will rush to build territory directly rather than sketch out territory whose details can be sorted out later.

Sketched versus secured territory. In Diagram 24, Black has played Black's first eight moves to secure the upper right corner. White has played White's first eight moves sketched out over a wider area. Because each stone exerts some influence over its local area and because for one stone that range is something like two or three points extending from it, Black has played a number of moves that are overconcentrated. While Black has a very real 12 points in the upper right, White, however, has options on three-fourths of the board. If only half of them are realized, that is still .75 times 360 divided by 2, or 135 points. Black can invade White's area, but Black will be at a disadvantage in most areas of the board, save Black's corner.

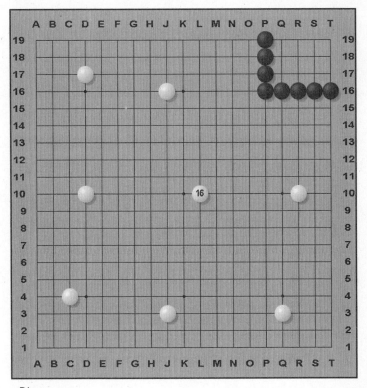

Diagram 24

Fourth line versus third line. Another interesting facet of the Go board is that territory split at the third and fourth lines from the edges get a similar results-per-move-played, as shown in Diagram 25. White has 136 points surrounded for 56 stones played on the third lines in from the edge, which works out to be 2.4 points per move. Black has 121 points surrounded for 48 played on the fourth lines in from the edge, or 2.5 points per move. While it looks as if Black has more area surrounded, White benefits from the edge, which acts as a natural border.

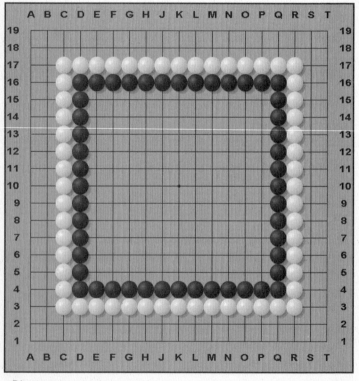

Diagram 25

Appendix: How to Play Go

GETTING AN INTUITIVE FEEL FOR GO

Go can be played at a variety of speeds. From long championship matches where each player gets ten hours each to speed matches where each player gets ten seconds a move, each type of game has a different flavor. An interesting thing about the fast games is that the level of play stays high despite the lack of time to analyze situations fully. Using mostly intuition, top players' games don't degenerate into poor play, but still retain a professional caliber. In this section, we will build your intuition of Go using elements with which you are already familiar.

"There exists, with the root of our judgments, a certain number of essential concepts which dominate all our intellectual life; these are those that the philosophers, since Aristotle, call the categories of understanding: concepts of time, space, kind, number, cause, . . ." (Emile Durkheim, *Les formes elementaires de la vie religieuse,* 1912, pp. 22–23).

You can extend your knowledge of the rules with your understanding of life's simple elements to understand strength and weakness in Go positions—the primary dichotomy important to understanding Go.

One of the first things to know and intuit about Go is that each stone has some influence on its environment. The capture rule showed how each stone played a part in capturing the opponent's stone(s). Certainly, a stone has an effect on the points adjacent to it, but it also has an effect on intersections beyond its immediate neighbors. The more stones, typically, the stronger the position.

Diagrams 26–28 show three different Black groups. Can you order them from strongest to weakest?

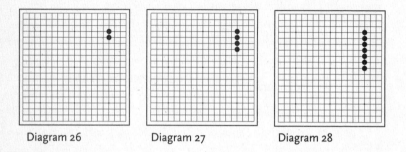

Diagram 26   Diagram 27   Diagram 28

The line of seven stones is strongest. With all other aspects removed, you can use your understanding of number to assess which group is stronger; that is, there is strength in numbers.[1]

Diagrams 29–31 take a close-up of the positions, using arrows to depict each group's influence.

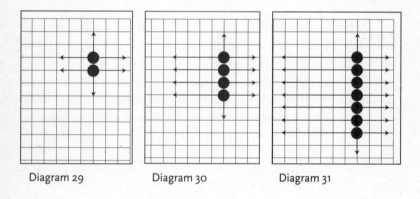

Diagram 29   Diagram 30   Diagram 31

1. Another way to determine strength is to look at the number of liberties a group has. The two-stone group has six liberties, the four-stone group has ten liberties, and the seven-stone group has sixteen liberties.

While this is not the exact way stones exert their influence on the board, it is close enough to give you a hint at how much more influence the figure on the right would have over the two other figures. Note how little influence the top and bottom stones have in relation to the stones in the middle. The strength is not like a train, but like a mountain range—these stones become a wall whose influence extends farther and farther the more stones are part of that range.

With that understanding, let's look at another set of positions in Diagrams 32–34. Try to arrange them from strongest to weakest.

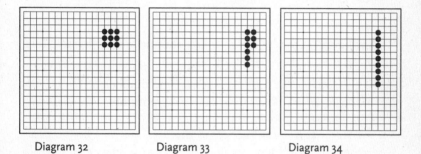

Diagram 32   Diagram 33   Diagram 34

The figure on the right is the strongest. The stones reach farther across the board than the stones in the other positions. The effect of each stone is not as redundant as in the other positions, and the number of liberties for the group is greater (twenty liberties). The figure on the left is by far the weakest of the three, with the figure in the middle in between. The stone in the middle of the shape in the figure on the left has no relevance on the board whatsoever, and if the position were at least hollow, not a big black clump, Black would be better off.

Now, differentiate the positions in Diagrams 35–37 in their influence on the entire board and their strength.

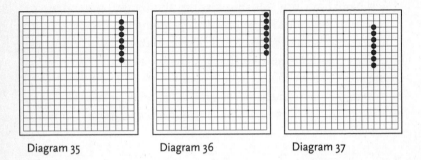

Diagram 35   Diagram 36   Diagram 37

The figure on the right is strongest and the most influential, the figure on the left the next, and the figure in the middle the weakest. The stones in the figure on the right influence the side and the rest of the board quite effectively. The stones in the figure on the left influence the rest of the board, but not as closely as those in the figure on the right, and the influence on the right side is a bit overkill. The stones in the middle certainly have some influence on the rest of the board, but their effect is greatly minimized as they are right on the first line. Also, the stones in the middle figure have no influence on any intersections to the right as there are none.

In the next set of figures, try to order the Black groups again from strongest to weakest, given their relationship to the White stones.

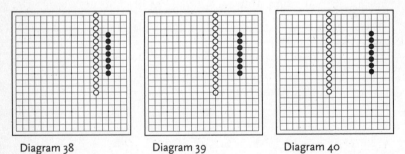

Diagram 38   Diagram 39   Diagram 40

The Black group farthest from the White line is strongest, the one closest the weakest. Using your understanding of space and distance, you can feel how White's influence dissipates as it gets farther and farther from the Black stones. If you were to portray arrows from both the White and Black positions, you would find the influence between White and Black is negated completely between the stones in the figure on the left. In the figure in the middle, there's a bit of overlap between the two, but not as much as in the figure on the left. In the figure on the right, the Black and White stones are far enough apart that the overlap in influence is not so great.

Given what you know so far, can you order the Black groups in Diagrams 41–43 from strongest to weakest?

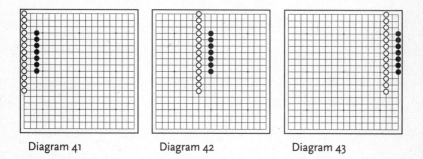

Diagram 41   Diagram 42   Diagram 43

The group on the left is the strongest, as the influence Black has on the remainder of the board affords it room on the right. The figure on the far right shows Black with only one line between it and the strong white line. You can say that the Black group on the left has the most space, the one on the right the least space. The White group gets stronger and stronger as you go from the figure on the left to the one on the right, because of White's distance from the edge and influence on the rest of the board. As a result, the Black group becomes weaker, but also suffers from its own weakness as it influences less and less of the board.

ACKNOWLEDGMENTS

———•———

I drew inspiration and understanding for this book from far and wide. The following are just some of the people who have helped and to whom I am grateful as part of this book's fifteen-year gestation.

It all started at home. My parents were unconditional supporters of my Go career and have continued to cheer me on. Two utter opposites, my father was the first to notice Go's deep connection with business and strategy-at-large and my mother gave me deeper understanding of duality and the dangers of seeing just one side of the coin. Together with my brothers, I learned how to and how not to get along and think about things from different perspectives. Thanks to my grandparents for all the years of support and love.

Since I was a not-slow large fellow, my sports career was practically assured. Ushering me into the world of sports and martial arts and its finer points were some excellent coaches, senseis, and teammates, including my father, Shang Kai, former SuperSonic John Johnson, Doug Kamm, Dwayne Hatch, Neal Buckmaster, Dennis Meade, Frank Doran, William Reed, and a bevy of Stanford Cardinal football coaches and players, to name a few who inspired and made me a better person through hustle, toil, pain, and camaraderie. Thanks are also due to the Stanford Training Room, especially Scottie, for nursing a rotator cuff fiasco. Through all these sports and more, strategy is most real when it's in your face day in and day out; there is no better proving ground for understanding competition at its fiercest.

Teachers and professors taught me the forms, but some went beyond the call of duty: Hildegard Hinds, Dave Sherbrooke, Dave Powell, Ivan Sag, John Perry, Joseph Greenberg, Barry Merkin, Dave Besanko, Roger Myerson, Leigh Thompson, Robert Duncan, Philip Kotler, and Anne Gron. My Kellogg classmates endured more than their fair share of half-baked Go metaphors. Special mentions: Scott McKeon and Jan Van Mieghem, who instilled a love of decision sciences and operations strategy; James Fox, who sponsored, promoted, and encouraged me to struggle through and to a reference work in Miluk lexicography; and Marty Stoller, who was individually responsible for more than his fair share of epiphanies.

Spiritually, I've been blessed to pray, meditate, study, fight, goof off, work, and sweat with Anne Medicine, Umnatl QwLai, Kongo Roshi Richard Langlois, and others at ZBTC, George Wasson, Tim Lobato, Michael Raymond, and other Yo-semites, Orval Lookinghorse, Jordan Singer, Steve Roos and Rooses, Reg Pullen, Sharon Parrish, Judy Rocha, Jason and Shirod Younker, Rosemary Cambra and Norma Sanchez, and those fighting the good fight for NALA, IPOLA, and the soon-to-be-moribund languages of the Americas and the world.

My career has been equally blessed, with substantial contributions coming from 360 degrees in order of appearance: Jerry Croft, Tom Wuellner, Chris Streuli, CEDCO, Barney Pell, Mark Torrance, Robert and Lena Boucher, Terence Pua, Kevin Kopanon, Walter Reed, SM in general, John Battelle, Ann Marie McGowan, Paul Caparotta, David Newhoff, Barry Soicher, Peter Beard, Jason Erdman, Allan Levy, Jennifer Kerslake, and FMF in general.

Friends not already mentioned who contributed massively to my thinking, in order of appearance: Jim and Joyce Mitchell, MT, Priscilla, Julianna, Emily, Herb Mead, the Pointers, Ilan Reuben, Jason Spievak, Wade LaGrone, Big Dogs in general, Jeff Kinsey, Sachin Mithal, Rajan Parathasarthy, and Ajay Jose.

My world of Go certainly has made a grand contribution to this work. Books from the early Ishi Press, Yutopian, Kiseido, State and Shell, Tuttle, among others, taught me how to play. Movies like *Pi*, *The Go Masters*, and *A Beautiful Mind* were great reference works in introducing Go to others. *Hikaru no Go,* a completely true perspective into the life of inseis and the life of Go players, inspires me to no end. Online sources have been interesting diversions: USGO, Senseis, Kiseido.com and KGS, IGS, Go News, Go4Go, Go, An Addictive Game, Daily Yomiuri. Charles Park, Dan Nash, WeiWei Chen, Bob, Lou Kiersky, Karen Gold (and her tremendous hospitality for wayward Go players!), Haskell Small, inseis at the academy 1990–91 (especially Kou-kun, Sasaki-kun, Chinen Kaori, Yoko Inori, Kobayashi Izumi, Kato Keiko, and Saiyamasan), Cho Chikun, Kobayashi Chizu, my English class, Tozawa sensei, my handlers, all the great games I studied—Shusaku, Go Seigen, Sakata Eio, Rin Kaiho, and Cho Chikun in particular were instrumental in my Go development.

Specifically, I would not have broken through every rank without the enormous support, teaching, and selflessness of Barney Pell, Reid Augustin, Lance Kemper, Tim Wulff, Johnny Kwei, Tommy Shwe, and my ultimate sponsorship at the Nihon Ki-In by the great Oeda Sensei and Sen Suzuki.

With his class, depth, and selflessness, Kiyoshi Sakamoto gave me new insight into the game, humanity, and strategy. To Mr. Sakamoto I am most grateful. Likewise, Hironori Kato made my non-Go life in Japan a wonderful experience, for which I am still indebted to him. Thanks, Kato-san. Hans, I will always hear "Mmmm! Just like Mom used to make!" in your voice. With every je desto herein, a tribute to you. Thanks also to dear friends Tei Meikou, Ayako Nakazawa, and Farid Ben Malek, who made dorm living more fun than it should have been. And finally, to the Sifu Hu Hsih, who took me under his wing, showed me the other rules of Go, and to whom I am forever grateful for this new worldview.

This book would have never been possible without the following individuals. Initial seeding was provided by Myron Roomkin, who saw the potential for this book and supported its initiation. Thanks to Ann Marie McGowan for her generous contacts, and to the many early pre-edited edition readers and commenters, Sachin, Rajan, Mark, Barney, Robert Boucher, Jason, Peter Beard,

Mike Lill, Jim Lund, Jim Mitchell, Jeff Kinsey, Eric Savitz, Gary Robertson, Allan Levy, Lisa Kimball, and Plexus DC, Ron Tellefson, Asha Mithal, and BA.

Despite fifteen years in the making, this book would have never been without the vision, risk-taking, and patience of Rafe Sagalyn, a true believer and an incredible agent. Rafe practically birthed this book through its massive, chaotic, and amorphous gestation. Thanks!

The other parental thank-you for this book goes to Liz Stein, Maris Kreizman, and crew at Free Press for transforming Rafe's baby into a manageable toddler. They condensed, edited, pruned, and guided as best they could with the material with which they had to work, and this book improved drastically as a result. Thanks for the patience and care in making it better. Thanks!

Thanks to the Delgados—Louis, Margarette, Justin, Lance, and Nathan—for all the help and support in so many ways, and the rest of the extended Delgado network, specifically Tom, Rose, Diane, and Guerras.

To Peyton, Cassidy, and Layne, you're all a true inspiration and joy. You're constantly teaching me, coaching me, watching me! Thanks for your love, humor, and growing wisdom.

With half the thanks already doled out, the final half comes due. Without the support, love, tension, and sanity contributed by my wife, Toni, without her passion, honesty, depth, beauty, and intelligence, neither this book nor I might be around. She saves me. She braves me. JJ and Ed were right, I married better! I thank God for you. Oh Toni!